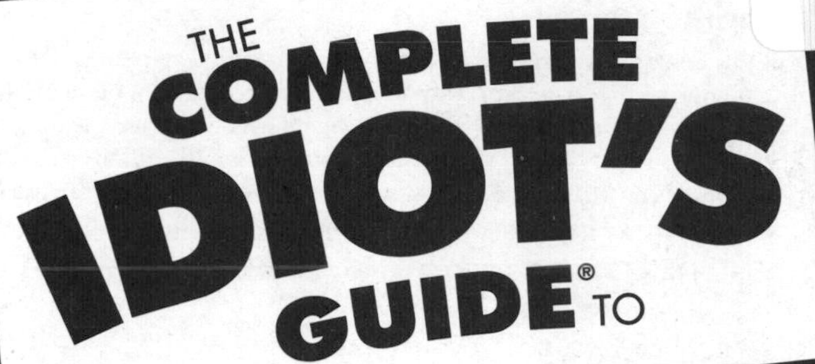

Learning Russian

by Christopher Froehlich

ALPHA

A member of Penguin Group (USA) Inc.

International Standard Book Number: 0-02-864322-4
Library of Congress Catalog Card Number: 2003113805

06 05 04 8 7 6 5 4 3

Interpretation of the printing code: The rightmost number of the first series of numbers is the year of the book's printing; the rightmost number of the second series of numbers is the number of the book's printing. For example, a printing code of 04-1 shows that the first printing occurred in 2004.

Printed in the United States of America

Publisher: *Marie Butler-Knight*
Product Manager: *Phil Kitchel*
Senior Managing Editor: *Jennifer Chisholm*
Acquisitions Editors: *Gary Goldstein and Mike Sanders*
Senior Development Editor: *Michael Thomas*
Senior Production Editor: *Billy Fields*
Copy Editor: *Keith Cline*
Illustrator: *Chris Eliopoulos*
Cover/Book Designer: *Trina Wurst*
Indexer: *Angie Bess*
Layout/Proofreading: *Angela Calvert, John Etchison, Rebecca Harmon*

Contents at a Glance

Contents

Foreword

Russia has long been a paradox for Americans. For most of the twentieth century, Russia (as the foundation of the Soviet Union) was our chief enemy, but now, twelve years after the breakup of that "evil empire" (as Ronald Reagan called it) we are learning that Russians and Americans have a great deal in common. Russians have the reputation of being gloomy, but they party harder than any other people I have ever encountered. Their literature seems forbidding—giants like Dostoevsky, Tolstoy, and Solzhenitsyn have never been accused of writing great page-turners for the beach—yet Russian humor is universally accessible. That's why American circuses are full of Russian clowns.

If you visit Russia, you are likely to be welcomed into the homes of total strangers, who will embrace you warmly when you leave. As a symbol of effusive Russian warmth, I can never forget the image of Leonid Brezhnev, head of the USSR Communist Party in the 1970s, kissing Erich Honecker (leader of East Germany) wetly on the lips! Yet an elderly Russian *bábushka* (*grandmother;* this word is the source of the English *babúshka*, meaning *scarf*) is liable to scold you on a streetcar if she feels your child is not dressed warmly enough for the Russian cold.

There are many routes to falling in love with the Russian language and culture. As a teenager in the early 1970s, I became fascinated with chess; this was that brief period when the American Bobby Fischer was breaking the Russian stranglehold on the world championship. I reasoned that since the Soviets were far and away the greatest chess players in the world, Russian chess books and magazines must also be the best. This turned out to be wrong, but I didn't realize that for a couple of years, by which time I had caught the Russian bug so hard that I made the language and culture the center of my life. My wife, on the other hand, came to love Russian via the rituals and songs of the Russian Orthodox Church. Each of my friends and colleagues has a unique reason to love Russian, and I'm sure that each reader of this book could tell a special story as well.

Some people are intimidated by Russian, especially because it uses a different alphabet. But my teaching experience has shown that it takes students no more than an hour to become comfortable with the letters. About half of them look just like English letters anyway! Tourists going to Russia with no knowledge of the alphabet learn to recognize the word *PECTOPAH*, because they are taken there at mealtimes. Once you learn the alphabet, you'll realize that this word is directly related to our *restaurant*—and it's only one of literally thousands of related words which help bridge the 6,000-mile gulf between the United States and Moscow.

How I wish I'd had a book like *The Complete Idiot's Guide to Learning Russian* in 1972! I would have made much more rapid progress in teaching myself Russian. Of course, it is ideal to learn any language with a teacher, but if your career and family do not give you the luxury of studying Russian at a university, you can learn an enormous amount from this book. It has many fine features. Above all, it offers an excellent coverage of the major grammatical patterns of Russian: everything crucial is treated, and sufficient examples are given so that you can grasp the pattern. The vocabulary is sensibly selected, including all the highest-frequency words and phrases, and there is good coverage of the important vocabulary items in especially vital subject areas for readers who visit Russia (directions, shopping, travel, etc.). Russian phrases and words are accompanied by an intuitive transliteration scheme that will help beginners learn how to pronounce words from the very outset, and keep the reader firmly on track throughout the book.

What can the interested reader do after working through this book? It is ideal preparation for business or leisure travel to Russia, where even a modest knowledge of the language can elevate your trip. (An anecdote: My wife tutored a stockbroker, who went on a very expensive escorted hunting trip to Siberia. Because he had learned enough Russian to schmooze with the non-English-speaking guides on the trip, they ensured that he got better game than the others in the group, who hadn't made this effort.) Russian videos are widely available in this country (and with DVDs, you can turn on Russian subtitles to reinforce the Russian soundtrack). Many larger cities, especially in the eastern part of the United States, have a sizeable Russian-speaking population, with cultural events for these immigrants. If there is a grocery store or deli that serves this population, try going there and looking at the inevitable bulletin board, or striking up a conversation with customers.

In the final analysis, this book can give you a good start in Russian, but you must seek out opportunities to use the language after you finish the book. A little effort in this direction will be rewarded many times over.

—George Fowler, Ph.D.
Associate Professor of Russian, Indiana University
Director, Slavica Publishers

Introduction

One of the greatest encouragements when studying Russian is knowing that the average Russian knows as much about how the language works as the average English speaker knows about English. You probably don't remember all the little rules, why we say *you are* and not *you is*, or why *to whom* is correct and *to who* is not. But you speak English the way it seems most natural to you, "correctly" or not. While memorizing long lists of grammar may teach you to grade Russian term papers, your goal of study is to communicate in Russian, and that's the goal of this book.

If grammar is not your greatest strength, have no fear. If you use this book, gesture and make facial expressions, and open your bilingual dictionary, chances are good that you will be understood. Russians not only love their language, but they truly want other people to try to learn it as well. No matter how badly you think you speak, wherever you go, you will find a willingness to understand.

Before you begin, it may be profitable for you to take a moment and think about what you want the Russian language to do for you. It might be the case that you will need to study cognates and basic vocabulary more than grammar; or the opposite could be true: You might be better served by learning some rules of grammar and recognizing root words to guess at the general meaning of sentences. Before moving forward, you should finalize, in your mind, your reasons for studying Russian. Consider the following examples:

- If art is your motivation, whether it be modern or classical, music or theater, paintings or films, your focus may not be strictly on grammar. Rather, you may want to focus on fluid pronunciation, sounding authentic, and basic comprehension. Performance may be your goal, and you may not need to spend a great deal of time on any other aspect of the language, other than to develop a basic understanding of what is happening.
- If you need to fill a prerequisite for your history major, or you want to diversify your philosophy or literature studies, your focus may not necessarily be on grammar; instead, you may want to build vocabulary specific to your area of study, and absorb as much grammar as you think necessary to help you. Learning idioms, helpful phrases, and vocabulary may be enough to fulfill your needs.
- Should you want to read original Russian novels, such as the classics by Tolstoy, Chekov, or Pushkin, or modern works, plays, histories, or other complicated texts, your focus may be more inclined toward grammar. You may want to learn the rules more carefully, so that you always know exactly *who* is doing *what* to *whom*.

- Should you want to travel to Russia—if you envision yourself strolling through Moscow, seeing the Kremlin, Red Square, Lenin's tomb, and visiting the Большóй (Big Theater), or just wandering through the city's open market, experiencing the sights and smells of the various foods—you'll want to learn some language basics to make your trip go more smoothly, along with some tidbits about Russian life and traditions to help you appreciate the culture more.

If you understand what you want to learn, you can quickly make this book work to fulfill your needs.

What You'll Find in This Book

I've arranged this book in five parts.

In **Part 1, "Russian Language Basics,"** we're off and running with an introduction to the Russian alphabet, some tips on pronunciation, and helpful guidance on Russian cognates (words that are the same in both Russian and English) and idiomatic expressions. This part provides you with the foundation upon which you can structure your learning.

Part 2, "Getting Down to Grammar," covers the basic grammatical aspects of Russian. You'll learn about Russian nouns, verbs, adjectives, and adverbs, as well as get an introduction to cases. The reality of learning any language is that you have to spend some time with grammar, so this part of the book is a must. However, I've boiled it down to the basics to make it as painless as possible.

Part 3, "Traveling Around," introduces you to a variety of Russian phrases and concepts, using a hypothetical trip to Russia as the framework around which you'll learn. We'll cover meetings and greetings, conversations, and finding your way around airports, airplanes, and hotels.

Part 4, "The Fun Stuff," extends our imaginary trip. We'll go shopping, sightseeing, and restaurant hopping. You definitely don't want to miss this part!

Traveling is fun, but sometimes the unexpected can present problems. Even the expected can sometimes turn out to be tough going! In **Part 5, "Anybody Can Handle Challenges,"** you'll learn how to surmount such everyday traveling obstacles as going to the doctor and using the telephone. For more adventuresome readers, we'll even cover phrases related to such topics as going to the bank, finding an apartment or house in Russia, and running a business.

Extras

Throughout the book I've included sidebars on various topics associated with Russia and the Russian language. Be sure to watch for the following:

Hot Topic

These sidebars give you important definitions of grammatical terms.

Evening Recap

Evening Recap sidebars provide quick grammar summaries.

Memory Serves

I've provided these sidebars to give you memory tips and tools for learning tricky aspects of the Russian language.

Внимáние

These sidebars give you critical do's and don'ts. Be sure to read them!

Культýра

These sidebars contain notes on Russian history and culture.

Acknowledgments

A great number of professionals and peers assisted me in writing this book, and I would like to acknowledge a few of them here:

Thanks to the folks at Alpha Books, including but not limited to Jacky Sach, Gary Goldstein, and Mike Sanders, for working miracles to turn my manuscript into a book.

Thanks to all of the Russian professionals with whom I have worked, Elena Bondareva, Natasha A. Sadakova, and Irina S. Schmidt, for their time and assistance proofreading this book. Additional thanks go out again to the teachers and staff of the Defense Language Institute, without whom none of this would have been possible.

Thanks also to the Russian linguists who have served beside me and aided me technically and unabashedly over the course of writing this book. Specifically, I would like to thank Jennifer Elms, Robert Caruthers, Jeremy Ireland, Craig Amundson, Tim Farrar, and Angela Gilbert, as well as those other Russian linguists with whom I have had the honor of serving.

Special thanks to the military leadership who so accommodated me as I wrote this book. Sergeant First Class Barbara Henson and First Sergeant Manuel Sanchez deserve special thanks.

Additional and final special thanks also go to my father, Steve Froehlich, who coordinated editing and submission of various chapters of this book while I was deployed or otherwise unable to do so myself.

Dedication

This book is dedicated to the teaching team staff of the Defense Language Institute that guided me to an understanding of the Russian language. Specifically, I want to mention Dr. Sarah Jospehs; and additionally, I would like this dedication to include Dr. Emmerson, Ms. Novitskaya, and the Military Language instructors whose contributions and guidance defined the team. Without them, I could not have succeeded, and it was their work more than mine that made a book like this possible.

Special Thanks to the Technical Reviewer

The Complete Idiot's Guide to Learning Russian was reviewed by an expert who double-checked the accuracy of what you'll learn here, to help us ensure that this book gives you everything you need to know about the basics of the Russian language. Special thanks are extended to Dr. Maria Pavlovszky.

Trademarks

Part 1 Russian Language Basics

A comfortable chair and a quiet corner are the only qualifications required to learn the Russian language. In the first section, you will find all the reason you need to dust off that armchair and spend a little of your time learning Russian. After introducing you to a taste of the culture and giving you some basic rules to follow, you will be well on your way to reading and speaking Russian words with the confidence of a native.

Chapter 1

The Russian Alphabet

In This Chapter

- Grab the alphabet and go
- Set your palate
- Vowel and consonant sounds that are similar or identical to English
- Learning new sounds

Congratulations, you've decided to tackle Russian! While you wait for that Congressional Medal of Honor to arrive in the mail, take a moment to think about learning a new alphabet. If that scares you, remind yourself of the poor folks studying Chinese, which has over 60,000 characters to learn, or even Arabic, which is written "backward"! Consider yourself wise for having chosen Russian, with a mere 33 letters (most of which you already know).

Although it may seem intimidating at first, you will soon learn that in some ways, Russian is easier to read, spell, and even pronounce than English. Have you ever had to decide whether it was *there, their,* or *they're?* Never again! Russian is a phonetic language. This means that, with few exceptions, what you see is what you hear.

First things first, though. You need to learn the letters of the Cyrillic alphabet. Some of the letters will be immediately recognizable to you, whereas others will be unfamiliar. When you've become comfortable pronouncing the sounds of the letters by themselves, pronouncing whole words will be a snap. You already know most of the sounds of the Russian language. In this chapter you learn a few new ones, plus you learn to match the sounds you know with the Russian alphabet.

With an Alphabet on the Mind

The Greek monks St. Cyril and St. Methodius created the first version of the Cyrillic alphabet in 962 C.E. Using the letters of the Greek alphabet, and adding new characters for the specifically Slavic sounds (those not existing in Greek), Cyril's disciples later formalized the Slavic language, which is called Old Church Slavonic. (We can't speak about the "Russian" language prior to the fourteenth century.)

> **Культу́ра**
>
> Because of their Greek origins, you may notice many similarities between Russian letters and those of your favorite Greek fraternities.

The Russian alphabet has 33 characters, introduced in the following chart. Like English, Russian features both uppercase and lowercase letters.

	Uppercase	Lowercase
1.	А	а
2.	Б	б
3.	В	в
4.	Г	г
5.	Д	д
6.	Е	е
7.	Ё	ё
8.	Ж	ж
9.	З	з
10.	И	и
11.	Й	й
12.	К	к
13.	Л	л
14.	М	м
15.	Н	н
16.	О	о
17.	П	п

	Uppercase	Lowercase
18.	Р	р
19.	С	с
20.	Т	т
21.	У	у
22.	Ф	ф
23.	Х	х
24.	Ц	ц
25.	Ч	ч
26.	Ш	ш
27.	Щ	щ
28.		ъ
29.	Ы	ы
30.		ь
31.	Э	э
32.	Ю	ю
33.	Я	я

The Letters You Already Know

The two charts that follow give you a closer look at the first 18 letters of the Cyrillic alphabet. The first chart guides you through the nine letters that are most similar to English (although some of them are, admittedly, only faintly similar), and the second chart introduces you to nine more letters that appear slightly different but represent similar vowel or consonant sounds in English. Each chart includes the Russian letter, its closest English equivalent, the pronunciation of the letter by itself, an English word that includes the target sound, and a Russian word (with its phonetic pronunciation).

Внима́ние

Note that the letter "c" is *never* pronounced hard (like the "k" sound in *cat*), as in English. It *always* represents the "s" sound (like the "s" sound in *center* or *cease*).

Russian Letter	English Equivalent	Pronunciation	English Word	Russian Word with Pronunciation
А а	a	ah	father	а́том (AH-tohm) atom
Б б	b	beh	boy	бале́т (bahl-YET) ballet

continues

continued

Russian Letter	English Equivalent	Pronunciation	English Word	Russian Word with Pronunciation
Е е	e	yeh	yet/yes	метр (m-YET-hr) meter
К к	k	kah	kit	экрáн (ehk-RAHN) screen
Л л	l	ell	lamp	лáмпа (LAHM-pah) lamp
М м	m	em	map	мáма (MAH-mah) mom
О о	o	oh	bought/go	он (OHN) he; it
С с	s	ess	see	спорт (SPOHRT) sport
Т т	t	teh	top	теáтр (tee-AHT-rh) theater

The following letters appear slightly different from their English equivalents, and produce slightly different sounds.

Russian Letter	English Equivalent	Pronunciation	English Word	Russian Word with Pronunciation
В в	v	veh	voice	волейбóл (vollay-BOHL) volleyball
Д д	d	deh	day	дóктор (DOHK-tar) doctor
З з	z	zeh	zero	зимá (zi-MAH) winter
И и	e	ee	feel/feet	ímпорт (EEM-pohrt) import
Н н	n	en	now	ресторáн (restohr-AHN) restaurant
П п	p	peh	pan	порт (POHRT) port
Ф ф	f	eff	fun	футбóл (food-BOHL) soccer
Э э	e	eh	pet/net	э́ра (EHR-ah) era
*Р р	r (rolled)	errr	—	мотóр (mah-TOHR) motor

**Note that* Р *is rolled, much like the trill of a Spanish "r." Let your tongue curve toward the roof of your mouth and vibrate against the front of your palate.*

Memory Serves

Н, Т, and Д are pronounced as in English but more defined: The tip of your tongue should rest against your upper teeth and not further back.

Who Are These Guys?

The following letters represent vowel and consonant sounds that can be imitated in English: those happy "sh" and "ch" and "ts" sounds, for which English does not have individual letters. Although this may sound intimidating, you'll soon realize that they are easy to pronounce—and you may even begin to wish that English were so simple!

Russian Letter	English Equivalent	Pronunciation	English Word	Russian Word with Pronunciation
Г г	g	geh	go/girl	грам (GRAHM) gram
Ё ё	yo	yoh	yoke	ёлка (YOHL-kah) fir tree
Ж ж	zh	zheh	measure	журна́л (zhoor-NAHL) magazine
Й й	y	(y-glide)	yes/boy/buy	музе́й (moo-ZAY) museum
У у	oo	ooh	boot/shoot	тури́ст (too-REEST) tourist
Х х	kh	khah	Bach/loch	э́хо (EHK-hoh) echo
*Ц ц	ts	tseh	cats/bits	центр (TSENTHR) downtown
Ч ч	ch	cheh	chair/chimp	чемпио́н (chempee-OHN) champion
Ш ш	sh	shah	she/rush	шок (SHOHK) shock
Щ щ	shch	shchah	mesh chain	това́рищ (tahv-AHR-eeshch) comrade
**Ы ы	iy	yery	tarry	му́зыка (MOOZ-iykah) music
Ю ю	you	yoo	unite/use	ю́мор (YOO-mohr) humor
Я я	yah	yah	yard/yacht	як (YAHK) yak
Ъъ	(hard sign)	—	object	объе́кт (ohb-YEHKT)
Ь ь	(soft sign)	—	role	роль (ROHL)

**Most English words require "er" to produce the "ehr" sound. Russian words, however, produce the same "ehr" sound, without the equivalent vowel "e." For instance,* центр *is pronounced nearly the same as the English center, without the extra vowel.*

***English has no exact sound for this vowel. Practice pronouncing it by practicing the words* could *and* fit. *Pay attention to the position of your tongue between the vowels "i" and "ou." This will help you to properly pronounce this vowel.*

Внима́ние

It is important to note that **Г/г** is never pronounced like its English "g" equivalent. It is never soft, as in *George*, but always hard, as in *gift* or *guide*.

Also note that **Й/й**, which equates to the English "y," is never a vowel, as the English "y" sometimes is. In Russian it is considered a consonant.

Remember to try to pronounce each letter correctly, every time you say it. Develop rigid habits in the beginning, and learn each sound exactly. Repeat letters over and over until you can say them confidently.

> **Внимáние**
>
> Russia, even after the breakup of the Soviet Union, is the largest country in the world. Home for more than 160 million people, it covers 11 time zones and dozens upon dozens of regional dialects.

Now You've Got It!

Congratulations! You have just finished the first hurdle in language learning—you have broken the alphabet barrier. Don't worry about the number of mistakes you make at this point; as you get used to making these new sounds, or the old sounds in new ways, you'll notice a decrease in your hesitation and improvements in fluidity. Make mistakes! Make them boldly; but keep practicing and you will discover the natural flow of the language.

The Least You Need to Know

- St. Cyril and his disciples combined letters of the Greek alphabet with new characters (for Slavic sounds) to create the early Cyrillic alphabet.
- The Russian language has 33 characters, many of which are similar to English.
- Russian is a phonetic language, which means that what you see is usually what you hear.
- Some Russian letters represent sounds such as "sh," "ch," and "ts" for which English does not have individual letters.
- Don't be afraid to make mistakes when practicing your Russian sounds.

Chapter 2

Speak Like a Russian!

In This Chapter

- Sweating the small stuff
- Voiced and voiceless consonants
- Stressed and unstressed vowels
- Hard and soft vowels and consonants

Russian is a phonetic language, which means that every syllable in every word is pronounced, and more importantly, pronounced according to the phonetic alphabet.

Although it is important to properly pronounce every word as you begin to study Russian, understand that as you become more comfortable with the language the actual difference in pronunciation is very small. Most Russians speak quickly, and the audible difference between letters is slight. As an adult learner, you can check and monitor your speech, repeating words and syllables as necessary. Perfection is not necessary—strive to approximate the sounds as nearly as possible, and you will almost always be understood.

This chapter covers several concepts important to good pronunciation, such as voiced and voiceless, stressed and unstressed, and hard and soft.

Don't let the jargon scare you—remember, each concept can be learned as a pair, and they all apply specifically to pronunciation.

Learning the Concepts

Let's take a minute to become familiar with the concepts of voiced and voiceless, stressed and unstressed, and hard and soft as they apply to consonants and vowels in Russian.

Voiced and Voiceless = Consonants

The concept of voiced and voiceless applies only to consonants. A voiced consonant is a consonant that vibrates the vocal chords. As you might guess, a voiceless consonant is a consonant that doesn't vibrate the vocal chords. We'll look at this in more detail in the section "Voiced or Voiceless? Consonants."

Stressed and Unstressed = Vowels

The concept of stress is important in Russian pronunciation. Russian words have only one accented, or stressed, syllable. This is unlike English, in which a word such as *revolution* can have a main accent (lu) and a secondary, lesser accent (rev). To speak and be understood in Russian, you need to know not only the word you want to use, but its stress as well.

Just remember that in Russian, stress applies only to vowels, not to consonants.

Hard and Soft = Vowels and Consonants

The concept of hard and soft applies to both vowels and consonants. Nearly all Russian vowels and consonants (there are exceptions) have both hard and soft forms, and these are best learned in pairs. When you learn a vowel or consonant, keep in mind that it usually comes in both a hard and soft version.

Soft vowels are usually a combination of "y" plus the corresponding hard vowel—for example, "a"/"ya." Some consonants are *always* soft (for instance, "ch," "shch," "y"). Some are *always* hard (for instance, "zh," "sh," "k," "g," "kh"). Other consonants can be either soft or hard, depending on whether they precede a hard or soft vowel. We'll get into this more later in the chapter, but for now, be aware of the need to learn vowels and consonants in pairs of hard and soft.

Voiced or Voiceless? Consonants

As mentioned previously, consonants are usually voiced or voiceless. A *voiced* consonant refers to those consonants that vibrate the vocal chords as the word is pronounced. Its corresponding *voiceless* consonant uses the same shape of the mouth to pronounce the word, but your vocal chords don't vibrate. Try pronouncing these pairs of English consonants (voiced/voiceless): "d"(*done*)/"t"(*ton*), "b"(*big*)/"p"(*pig*), "v"(*vine*)/"f'(*fine*). Did you notice the effect of each pronunciation on your vocal chords?

Think of the following voiced and voiceless consonant pairs as substitutes for each other. Remembering which consonant substitutes for another will help you later on.

Voiced	Voiceless
Б б	П п
Д д	Т т
Г г	К к
В в	Ф ф
З з	С с
Ж ж	Ш ш

Losing Your Voice

It would be nice if voiced and voiceless consonants were as predictable in the language as they are in a chart. In language there are always exceptions to rules, however, and now you'll learn a few.

First, realize that just because a consonant is a voiced consonant doesn't mean it's always *pronounced* as a voiced consonant. (Yes, it's confusing, but bear with me!) A couple of things can affect whether a voiced consonant is actually voiced in practice.

For example, the type of vowel—hard or soft—that follows a consonant can determine whether it will be voiced or voiceless in pronunciation (more on this to come).

The position of the consonant in a word can also determine whether it is voiced or voiceless when pronounced. One important rule to remember is that a consonant that would normally be voiced becomes voiceless when it occurs at the end of a word. Another way of saying this is that a consonant at the end of a word is always voiceless.

Examine the following chart of consonant pairs and observe how consonants that would normally be voiced are pronounced as voiceless when they occur at the end of words.

Voiced	Voiceless	Examples
Д д	Т т	шокола́д (шокола́т) shahk-ah-LAHT
Г г	К к	друг (друк) droohk
В в	Ф ф	гото́в (гото́ф) kgah-TOHF
З з	С с	джаз (джас) djahs
Ж ж	Ш ш	бага́ж (бага́ш) bahg-AHSH
Б б	П п	гриб (грип) greep

Paying attention to the chart, practice these words, and focus on the voice of the consonant.

1. хлеб (хлеп) khlehp
2. зыбь (зыпь) ziyhp
3. гото́вь (гото́фь) kgah-TOHF
4. рог (рок) rohk
5. обе́д (обе́т) ah-BYET
6. медь (меть) myeht
7. ёж (ёш) yosh
8. рожь (рошь) rosh
9. раз (рас) rahs
10. всё (фсё) fsyoh

Внима́ние

Consonants at the end of words are *always* voiceless!

All Together Now!

Even consonants get lonely; and Russian letters like to be agreeable when they meet. When two or more consonants are combined within a word, the rule for pronunciation is as follows: The last consonant determines whether the consonants before it are voiced or voiceless. If the last consonant is voiced, all the consonants that precede it are also voiced. If the last consonant is voiceless, the consonants that precede it are also voiceless. Study the following examples:

Exemplary Conduct: футбо́л (фудбо́л) во́дка (во́тка)

In the first example, the т and д are the consonants. Because the last one (б) is voiced, the one preceding it (т) is voiced. In the second example, the к is voiceless, so the preceding д becomes voiceless as well.

So to sum up what you've just learned about pronunciation of consonants …

1. A consonant in Russian can be either voiced or voiceless.
2. A hard or soft vowel can determine whether the consonant before it is voiced or voiceless.
3. A consonant occurring at the end of a word is always voiceless.
4. The last consonant in a consonant cluster (or when two consonants are next to each other) determines whether the consonants before it are voiced or voiceless.

Memory Serves

Remember that the rule of the last consonant applies not only to the consonants inside a word, but when two words are pronounced together.

Example: **в кни́ге** (**ф кни́ге**)—in the book

You'll learn more about hard and soft vowels in a bit. First, let's turn to the concept of stress. It's something that really needs to be, well, stressed!

Don't Get Stressed over Stress

You may have noticed that many of the Russian words you've seen have had a "*stress* mark" or small accent over one of the vowels. Russian words aren't normally written with stress marks, but the concept of stress is so important to pronunciation that they're used throughout this book. When you learn a new word in Russian, you need to learn its stress.

Unlike English, Russian words have only one stress. (Secondary stresses, common in English, appear in Russian only in compound words.) It's important to make sure you pronounce that word with the correct stress. To explain, consider the English word *travel.* Normally it's pronounced TRAvel. Think about pronouncing it with the stress on the wrong syllable. English speakers would understand traVEL (though it would sound strange). If a word were pronounced with the wrong accent in Russian, however, the difference would be much greater.

Sometimes changing the stress of a word will change its tense or grammatical value and sometimes alter its meaning entirely.

Memory Serves

Stress is the emphasis you place on one individual syllable of a word as you pronounce it.

Again, as you pronounce each word, pay close attention to the stress marks. They will guide you in learning how to speak Russian.

Try these examples, paying close attention to the stress.

Russian Word	Pronunciation	English Meaning
Африка	(AHF-freekah)	Africa
Антáрктика	(an-TARKT-eek-ah)	Antarctica
Азия	(AH-zeeyah)	Asia
Австрáлия	(ah-FSTRAHL-eeyah)	Australia
Еврóпа	(ev-ROHP-ah)	Europe
аспéкт	(asp-YEKT)	aspect
бáзис	(BAH-seec)	basis
эффéкт	(ehf-FYEKT)	effect
идéя	(eeh-DYEH-ya)	idea
интерéс	(eentehr-EHS)	interest

Внимáние

Only vowels can be stressed in a Russian word. Consonants are never stressed, although they may be exaggerated.

As mentioned earlier, stress applies only to vowels. A stressed vowel is pronounced fully, as you see in the first three charts in this chapter; however, an unstressed vowel is pronounced like a weaker version of the stressed. Unstressed vowels are just as important to note as stressed vowels. It is critical to memorize and practice the changes that vowels undergo depending on stress.

The Hard and Soft of It

Just as you can have hard and soft versions of sounds in English, you can have hard and soft versions of Russian sounds. Think about the soft and hard "g" in *George* and *gift*, respectively, or the soft and hard "c" in *city* and *cat*, respectively.

The Russian language features hard and soft vowels. The catch is that they really refer to the consonant that precedes the vowel. A hard vowel makes the consonant that precedes it hard; a soft vowel makes it soft. Let's look at these vowels more closely.

Vowels

Like English, Russian has 5 vowel sounds, which are represented by 10 letters: 5 *hard* vowels and 5 *soft* vowels. As mentioned earlier, the designations "hard" and "soft" vowels are somewhat misleading, because the hardness or softness has to do not with the vowel in question, but with the consonant that precedes it.

Hard Vowels (Vowels Indicating Hardness of the Preceding Consonant)

The five hard vowel sounds are а, э, о, ы, and у. The following chart describes the stress patterns for these vowels. Pay close attention to the patterns and remember to say each word aloud as you progress.

Vowel	Stress	English Sounds	Examples
А а	stressed unstressed	ah (arm) ah (sofa)	а́рмия, ла́мпа, ма́ло каде́т, каранда́ш, магази́н
Э э	stressed unstressed	eh (enter) no change	э́то, поэ́т, эта́ж, э́ра
О о	stressed unstressed	oh (honor) ah (sofa)	гото́в, он, окно́ объе́кт, мото́р, а́том, ю́мор
Ы ы	stressed unstressed	no exact sound ee (feet)	мы, ты, вы, мы́ло, малы́ ла́мпы
У у	stressed unstressed	ooh (boot) no change	стул, суп, у́тро, туда́

Soft Vowels (Vowels Indicating Softness of the Preceding Consonant)

The five soft vowel sounds are я, е, ё, и, and ю. Again, you must memorize the stress patterns for these vowels.

The Russian soft vowels have what is called a *y-glide.* That is, the vowel is softened by a preceding "y" as in "a"/"ya." This y-glide is always fully pronounced when the vowel is stressed, but often shortened when the vowel is in an unstressed syllable. The following chart shows you the soft vowels, in the order that they correspond to their hard vowel counterparts. Pay attention to the stress patterns of soft vowels as you pronounce each word aloud.

Memory Serves

The **y-glide** is an extended vowel, and sounds almost as if a "y" or **Й** (the Russian "y") preceded the vowel. The y-glide for **А–Я** changes the sound from "ah" to "yah" and makes the vowel soft, meaning that the vocal chords do not vibrate as much (very similar to the change in voice of consonants). A soft vowel is a vowel that has a y-glide.

Vowel	Stress	English Sounds	Examples
Я я	stressed unstressed	yah (yacht) ah (sofa)	себя́, я́сно, я́год Герма́ния, Англия, зда́ния
Е е	stressed unstressed	yeh (yet) eh (bet)	не́бо, ме́ра, поезда́, всегда́, жена́, ве́тер
Ё ё	always stressed	yoh (yoke)	ёлка, льёд, самолёт
И и	stressed	ee (feet)	кит, бить
	unstressed	no change	интере́с
Ю ю	stressed unstressed	yoo (unite) no change	ю́мор, интервью́, люблю́ юри́ст

Consonants

Russian consonants can be either hard or soft. If this seems like a repetition of what you learned with vowels, then you've already grasped the concept. Before diving into the Russian consonants, stop for a moment and think about English. Think of the English letters "d," "t," and "n." For a moment, notice the changes that English words go through based on the vowels that follow them. As examples of pairs of hard and soft, repeat these words: *due/done, tune/tin, new/net.*

> **Memory Serves**
>
> Get your tongue involved! A soft consonant is pronounced by placing the tongue closer to the roof of your mouth than with the corresponding hard consonant. The soft consonant of a word is slightly prolonged, whereas a hard consonant is sharper and briefer. Think of the difference between the "d" in *due* and the "d" in *dot*.

Consonants can be soft one of two ways. First, a soft sign Ь/ь indicates that the preceding consonant is soft. The soft sign has no pronunciation—it's just there to signal the softness of the consonant before it. Review these words aloud: лить, тюрьма́, день, де́ньги.

Second, the soft (or y-glide) vowels indicate softness. The most noticeable change occurs with the letters Л and М. Examples: нет, нёс, ряд, стиль, мать.

Memory Serves

[Ь]—the soft sign has no sound of its own. Rather, it tells you that the consonant before it is soft.

[Ъ/ъ]—the hard sign also has no sound of its own. It indicates that the preceding consonant is hard; you make a slight break in the word, immediately after the consonant that it follows.

Vowels and Consonants Together

Finally, review the following consonant and vowel pairs. Notice that each pair is pronounced alike, with almost no noticeable difference in sound.

- These combinations are pronounced alike: жо–жё (pronounced "zho").
- These combinations are always pronounced hard: цэ–це ("tseh"), цы–ци ("tseeh"), шо–шё ("shoh").
- These combinations are always soft: чо–чё ("choh"), що–щё ("shchoh").

Not all consonants come in pairs—some of them are always hard and some of them are always soft.

- ж, ц, ш are always hard.
- ч and щ are always soft.

Evening Recap

Unlike the many spelling rules for English ("i" before "e," except after "c" …), Russian has only three. Fortunately for us, no exceptions apply to these three rules. For the time being, simply memorize these rules and note how they affect pronunciation.

7-letter rule: After the letters **г**, **х**, **к**, **ч**, **ш**, **щ**, and **ж**, always write **и** and not **ы**.

5-letter rule: Never write an unstressed **о** after these 5 letters: **ч**, **ш**, **щ**, **ж**, **ц**. Always write **е** instead.

Finally: After these 8 consonants, **к**, **г**, **х**, **ч**, **ш**, **щ**, **ж** and **ц**, never write **я** or **ю**. Always write **а** or **у**.

Add Accent and Stir Vigorously

At this point, you may want to experiment with a Russian accent. As you watch Russian films and listen to Russian radio broadcasts, pay special attention to the way Russians emphasize their words. While you won't, immediately, be mistaken as Lenin's brother, you'll begin to get a feel for the flow of the language.

The Least You Need to Know

- Consonants can be either voiced or voiceless.
- When two consonants are next to each other, the second consonant determines the voicing of the first.
- Only vowels can be stressed in Russian.
- Memorize the stressed syllable as part of each word.
- A hard or soft vowel indicates the hard or soft pronunciation of the consonant that precedes it.
- Practice often!

Chapter 3

Russian Words You Already Know

In This Chapter

- Russian has borrowed words from English!
- Noun, adjective, and verb cognates
- Putting simple sentences together
- Sometimes looks can deceive: false cognates

What you didn't know, as you've been speaking English all these years, is that you've been speaking Russian, too. For the last few hundred years, as English speakers have been borrowing words from Latin, Greek, German, and French, Russian speakers have been borrowing from all of those languages and from English as well. In fact, the Russian language has borrowed so many words that nearly 25 percent of it is made up of *cognates.* Many of these words are so new to the Russian language that their pronunciation is nearly identical to the original. By the end of this chapter, you will be able to recognize what some common English cognates look like in Russian, and put together some short but reliable Russian sentences.

They Use Our Words!

So you have arrived in Moscow to meet an old friend from college. As you walk away from the plane, into the аэропóрт (airport), Masha waits for you near a small кафé (café). As you hop into a таксй (taxi) to check in to your отéль (hotel), Masha tells you about the years of living in Россйя (Russia), how she learned the language, and what the people are like. It seems that she is now a секретáрша (secretary) for a large фйрма (firm) in Москвá (Moscow).

Hot Topic

Cognates are words borrowed from English—or any other language—that share a common pronunciation and meaning. The Russian version of an English word may look strange to you at first, but as you become familiar with Russian characters you'll learn to recognize a cognate when you see it.

Культýра

During the height of the reign of the tsars, the nobility was mostly bilingual. Especially during Napoleon's empire, French was the official language of the royal, upper class in Russia. As a result, many French words that are also common to English were incorporated into the Russian language.

After settling into your room, you begin to walk down the streets of Moscow toward a ресторáн (restaurant); you pass through Red Square, catch a glimpse of the Bolshoi Theatre; and, everywhere around you, people are speaking Russian. At first, most of what you hear sounds incomprehensible, but after a few patient minutes of listening, you discover that you not only recognize many of the words that these Muscovites are speaking, but that you actually understand a little bit. Компьютер (computers), журнáл (journals, magazines), радиостáнция (radio stations), and телевйзор (television sets) are everywhere.

You'll soon discover just how much these cognates will help you learn the language. Not only do cognates share a similar pronunciation with their English brothers, their true meanings are also nearly identical. As you learn these words, you'll become familiar with the changes that the words go through in spelling, and you'll even begin to recognize patterns. After you have become familiar with the general pattern of cognates, namely the location of the stress, you will begin to build an impressive vocabulary that will enable you to communicate clearly and effectively—using words you already know!

People, Places, and Things: Noun Cognates

Perhaps the easiest cognates to recognize are the nouns, because they undergo the fewest changes from English to Russian. Use the pronunciation guide in Chapter 2 to say these words like a natural Russian. Remember to say each word slowly out loud to yourself, focusing your attention on the stress. Also use this time to review the sounds you learned from the first two chapters.

Note that the following words are divided into columns of masculine, feminine, or neuter. Chapter 6 covers gender in more detail, but for now, just recognize that Russian nouns (and adjectives, as you'll see) fall into one of these categories.

Masculine	Feminine	Neuter
дирéктор (dee-REHK-tohr) director	полúтика (nah-LEEHT-ee-ka) politics	интервью́ (eehn-tehr-VIEW) interview
парашю́т (pah-ra-SHYOOT) parachute	идéя (ee-DYAY-ya) idea	вúски (VEEH-skee) whiskey
футбóл (food-BOHL) football (soccer)	лéкция (LYEK-tsee-yah) lecture	брáво (BRAHV-ah) bravo
трáктор (TRAHK-tohr) tractor	вóдка (VOT-kah) vodka	винó (vee-NOH) vine
класс (klahs) class	Москвá (mohsk-VAH) Moscow	кафé (kah-FYEH) café
Вашингтóн (vash-ing-TOHN) Washington	террито́рия (tehr-ree-TOHR-ee-yah) territory	меню́ (mehn-YOO) menu
шоколáд (shok-oh-LAHT) chocolate	Еврóпа (yeh-VROPE-ah) Europe	кóфе (KOH-feh) coffee
материáл (mah-ter-ee-AHL) material	математика (mah-te-MAH-tee-kah) mathematics	телевúдение (tehl-eh-VEED-ehn-ee-yeh) TV broadcast
климáт (klee-MAHT) climate	пропагáнда (prah-pah-GAHN-dah) propaganda	вúдео (VEE-de-oh) video

continues

continued

Masculine	Feminine	Neuter
актёр (ahk-TYOR) actor	маши́на (mah-SHEE-nah) car	кано́э (kahn-OH-eh) canoe
план (plahn) plan	пробле́ма (prah-BLEHM-ah) problem	лото́ (lah-TOH) lottery
блок (blohk) block	астроно́мия (ahst-rahn-NOHM-ee-yah) astronomy	авто́ (ahv-TOH) car (auto)
абсу́рд (ahp-SOORHT) absurd	фле́йта (FLEYT-ah) flute	би́стро (BEEST-roh) bistro
автомоби́ль (af-tah-mah-BEEHL) automobile	биоло́гия (bee-oh-LOGE-ee-yah) biology	желе́ (jdyeh-LYEH) gelatin
америка́нец (ahm-yer-ee-KAHN-ets) American	анато́мия (ah-nah-TOME-ee-yah) anatomy	капучи́но (kahp-oo-CHEEN-ah) capuccino
англича́нин (ahng-lee-CHAHN) Englishman	систе́ма (seest-YEHM-ah) system	по́нчо (POHN-chah) poncho
анекдо́т (ahn-ehk-DOHT) anecdote	дие́та (dee-YET-ah) diet	барбекv (bahr-beh-KYOO) barbecue
бар (bahr) bar	ро́за (ROSE-ah) rose	рандеву́ (rahn-deh-VOO) rendezvous
бюрокра́т (byoo-roh-KRAHT) bureaucrat	администра́ция (ahd-meen-ees-TRAHTS-ee-ya) administration	табу́ (tah-BOO) taboo
бана́н (bah-NAHN) banana	ба́ржа (BARH-jyah) barge	бюро́ (byoo-ROH) bureau
аспири́н (ahs-pee-REEHN) aspirin	шка́ла (SHKAHL-ah) scale	аге́нтство (ah-GYEHN-stvah) agency
архите́ктор (ahr-khee-TYEHK-tohr) architect	ата́ка (ah-TAH-kah) attack	турне́ (toohr-NYEH) tournament

Masculine	Feminine	Neuter
текст (tehkst) text	балери́на (bahl-er-EEN-ah) ballerina	
аге́нт (ah-GYEHNT) agent	блу́зка (BLOOS-kah) blouse	
брюне́т (broo-NYET) brunette	па́ника (PAHN-eek-ah) panic	
аппети́т (ahn-neh-TEET) appetite	Аме́рика (ah-MEHR-eek-ah) America	
	плане́та (plah-NYET-ah) planet	
	ма́ска (MAH-skah) mask	

Now that you've had some exposure to common nouns, you can put some basic sentences together, and even carry on a small conversation with Masha—your very patient friend, Masha.

Now learn a few words that will enable you to create simple sentences. Study the following list of demonstrative pronouns:

э́то (EH-tah)	This is
э́то (EH-tah)	This is [a thing]
э́тот (EH-toht)	This thing (masculine)
э́та (EH-tah)	This thing (feminine)
э́то (EH-tah)	This thing (neuter)

Evening Recap

Russian does not distinguish between indefinite articles (*a/an*) and definite articles (*the*). The sentence "**э́то газе́та**" could either mean "this is *a* newspaper" or "this is *the* newspaper." In translating, rely on the context of the sentence to tell you whether to use *a* or *an* or *the*.

Although э́то (this is a thing) and э́тот, э́та, or э́то (this thing) are all demonstrative pronouns, it's best to think of the latter three as adjectives. Это (this is a thing) takes the place of a noun: "A book is an object. *This* is a book"; whereas э́тот, э́та, or э́то describe a noun: "*Which* book? *This* book."

Let's create some simple sentences using the demonstrative pronoun э́то, "this is."

Try to say the following sentences, speaking to yourself out loud. If you haven't made this a habit, make an effort to do so as you complete these exercises.

> **Memory Serves**
>
> The Russian verb "to be" has no present tense form, and many common sentences will not appear to have a verb at all. Remember, as you put these basic sentences together, *is* and *are* are invisible, or understood.

1. This is a car.
   Это автомоби́ль.
   EH-tah av-tah-mah-BEEHL.
2. This is a class.
   Это класс.
   EH-tah KLAHS.
3. This is whiskey.
   Это ви́ски.
   EH-tah VEEH-skee.
4. This is a menu.
   Это меню́.
   EH-tah mehn-YOO.

> **Memory Serves**
>
> Russian has no sound to exactly correspond to the English "h" or "j." When forming cognates, Russians have generally used **Г** for "h," so that *Hamlet* becomes **Га́млет**. To make a "j" sound, the two consonants **ДЖ** are generally used. *John* becomes **Джон**.

Adjective Cognates

When you want to describe something in Russian, you need to grab an adjective or two. Russian adjectives that are cognates look slightly different from their English kin. As you review the following adjectival cognates, you may notice that they differ slightly more than the nouns. Focus on pronouncing each word correctly.

As you learn in Chapter 8, because adjectives modify nouns, they must match their nouns in terms of gender. So keep in mind that the adjectives you see here can take different forms.

Russian Adjective	Meaning	Russian Adjective	Meaning
минера́льный (meen-ehr-AHL-nee)	mineral	англи́йский (ahn-GLEE-skee)	English
грандио́зный (grahn-dee-OHZ-nee)	grandiose	регуля́рный (reg-ool-YAR-nee)	regular
америка́нский (ah-myer-ee-kahn-skee)	American	не́рвный (NYERV-nee)	nervous

Russian Adjective	Meaning	Russian Adjective	Meaning
универса́льный (oo-nee-vehr-SAHL-nee)	universal	типи́чный (tee-PEECH-nee)	typical
класси́ческий (klahs-SEECH-ehs-kee)	classical	религио́зный (reh-leeg-ee-OHZ-nee)	religious
акти́вный (ahk-TEEV-nee)	active	серьёзный (sehr-YOHZ-nee)	serious
фина́льный (fee-NAHL-nee)	final	эффекти́вный (ehf-fyeh-TEEV-nee)	effective
лимо́нный (lee-MOHN-nee)	lemon	гига́нтский (gee-GAHNT-skee)	gigantic
абстра́ктный (ahp-STRAHKT-nee)	abstract	лингвисти́ческий (leeng-vees-TEECH-eh-skee)	linguistic
мо́дный (MODE-nee)	fashionable; modern; stylish	ора́нжевый (ah-RAHN-jyeh-vwee)	orange
оригина́льный (ohr-eeg-ee-NAHL-nee)	original	фиоле́товый (fee-oh-LYET-ov-wee)	violet
авиацио́нный (ahv-ee-aht-see-OHN-nee)	aviation	истори́ческий (ees-tah-REECH-eh-skee)	historical
тома́тный (tahm-AHT-nee)	tomato	элемента́рный (eh-leh-mehn-TAHR-nee)	elemental
официа́льный (ahf-eets-ee-AHL-nee)	official	популя́рный (pah-poo-LYAHR-nee)	popular
техни́ческий (tehk-NEECH-eh-skee)	technical	спорти́вный (spahr-TEEV-nee)	sport
форма́льный (fahr-MAHL-nee)	formal	тропи́ческий (trah-PEECH-eh-skee)	tropical
полити́ческий (pahl-ee-TEECH-eh-skee)	political	максима́льный (mahk-see-MAHL-nee)	maximum
		минима́льный (mee-nee-MAHL-nee)	minimal

You've already learned how to form a simple sentence. Let's add an adjective to the sentence "This is a table."

This is a table.

Это стол.

This table is big.

Этот стол – большо́й.

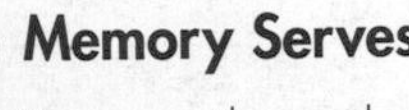

Memory Serves

Because the verb "to be" is not used in the Russian present tense, a dash is often used in written Russian to stand in for "to be." So in a sentence like "This table is big," the dash replaces *is* to make the sentence "This table – big."

You've just learned something important about word order in Russian. Word order is not as important in Russian as it is in English; you can often move adjectives and nouns around in a sentence without changing the meaning. Стул в ко́мнате. The chair is in the room (chair in room). В ко́мнате стул. In the room there is a chair (in room chair). Sometimes, by accident, the word order is identical to English.

Note also that in the first sentence, Это means "this is," or functions as a pronoun. Этот, Эта, and Это mean "this," or function as adjectives. The difference is the same in English.

Read the following simple sentences. Pay attention to the endings of each noun and adjective. Don't worry about these patterns right now—simply try to recognize that they can take different forms. The reason has to do with gender, which is fully explained in Chapter 6.

1. This is a car.

   Это автомоби́ль.

2. This car is American.

   Это автомоби́ль америка́нский.

3. This bistro is typical.

   Это би́стро типи́чное.

4. This is a tractor.

   Это тра́ктор.

Verbal Cognates

Hot Topic

Infinitive refers to a verb that has not been conjugated, or changed to "match" with a noun. English infinitives appear as "to do" or "to watch." Instead of using a preposition, like *to*, Russian infinitives almost always end in ть.

Verbal cognates go through the most change as they come into the Russian language; however, they are the easiest to learn, because the pattern for verbal cognates is simple and consistent. There are generally two types of verb cognates—verbs that end in -овать, and verbs that end in -ировать.

In the following tables, pay attention to both the stress and the ending of the verb. The verbs are in their *infinitive* forms.

The following verbs end in -ова́ть with the stress usually on the "ah" sound of the á. These are the first type of Russian verb cognates.

Russian Verbs	Pronunciation	Meaning
арестова́ть	ah-rehst-ah-VAHT	to arrest
критикова́ть	kree-teek-ah-VAHT	to criticize
организова́ть	ahr-gahn-eez-ah-VAHT	to organize
рекомендова́ть	reh-koh-mehnd-ah-VAHT	to recommend
публикова́ть	poo-bleek-ah-VAHT	to publish
интересова́ть	een-tehr-ehs-ah-VAHT	to interest
характеризова́ть	kharh-ahk-tehr-eez-ah-VAHT	to characterize
протестова́ть	prah-tehst-ah-VAHT	to protest

The following chart lists the second type of verb cognates, a much larger group. These verbs end in -и́ровать in which the и́ is usually stressed.

Russian Verbs	Pronunciation	Meaning
идеализи́ровать	ee-deh-ah-lee-ZEER-ah-vaht	to idealize
классифици́ровать	klahs-see-feet-SEER-ah-vaht	to classify
модифици́ровать	mah-dee-feet-SEER-ah-vaht	to modify
сигнализи́ровать	see-gnah-lee-ZEER-ah-vaht	to signal
демонстри́ровать	deh-mahn-stree-REER-ah-vaht	to demonstrate, show
специфици́ровать	snet-see-feet-SEER-ah-vaht	to specialize
фотографи́ровать	fah-tah-grah-FEER-ah-vaht	to photograph
эмигри́ровать	eh-meeg-REER-ah-vaht	to immigrate
плани́ровать	plah-NEER-ah-vaht	to plan
дисквалифици́ровать	dees-kvah-lee-FEER-ah-vaht	to disqualify
унифици́ровать	oon-eef-eet-SEER-ah-vaht	to unify

Not as bad as you thought, is it? Read these sentences and try to guess their meanings.

1. Он был дисквалифици́рован от футбо́ла.

   He was disqualified from football.

2. Президе́нт Аме́рики плани́рует импорти́ровать автомоби́ли из Герма́нии.

   The President of America plans to import cars from Germany.

3. Это бы́ло опублико́вано в популя́рном журна́ле.

   This was published in a popular magazine.

Внима́ние

Remember that verbs are always listed in the dictionary by their infinitive forms.

Hot Topic

False cognates are words that share a similar pronunciation (from English to Russian) but have a different meaning in Russian than they do in English.

Wolves in Sheep's Clothing

Cognates are the single greatest help to foreigners learning Russian; however, as with all good things, there are pitfalls, and these pitfalls are called *false cognates*.

A false cognate is a word that shares a similar pronunciation between two languages, but means one thing in one language and something else in the other. If a Russian asks you what you're doing and you say you're reading a *magazine*, you'd sound pretty strange to use the word магази́н, which is pronounced "mah-gah-ZEEN," but actually means *store!*

Fortunately, the list of false cognates is not overly long, but it is important to be aware of them. This list highlights some of the most important to be aware of.

English Word	Russian Word	Meaning
magazine	магази́н (mah-gah-ZEEN)	store
costume	костю́м (kahs-TYOOM)	suit
family	фами́лия (fah-MEEL-ee-yah)	surname
mark	ма́рка (MAHR-kah)	stamp
artist	арти́ст (ahr-TEEST)	actor
fabric	фа́брика (FAHB-reek-ah)	factory
cabinet	кабине́т (kah-bee-NYET)	office/study (a room)
novel	нове́лла (nah-VYEL-lah)	short story
prospect	проспе́кт (prahs-NYEKT)	avenue
accurate	аккура́тный (ahk-koo-RAHT-nee)	punctual

English Word	Russian Word	Meaning
auditorium	аудитóрия (ah-oo-dee-TOHR-ee-yah)	audience/also a classroom in university
intelligent	интеллигéнтный (een-tehl-lee-GYENT-nee)	cultured

Wow! In just three short chapters you've gone from learning the characters of the Russian alphabet to putting simple sentences together. You've also discovered that you possess a wider Russian vocabulary than you thought, thanks to cognates! In the next chapter we'll continue this pace by learning some common Russian idioms. Although idioms don't always follow the rules of grammar, they are easy to learn and are indispensable in helping you become a strong speaker of Russian.

The Least You Need to Know

- Russian contains many cognates, or words borrowed from English and other languages.
- Noun, adjective, and verb cognates can help you speak smoothly and easily in Russian, using words you already know.
- Это is a demonstrative pronoun, taking the place of a noun ("A book is an object. *This* is a book"), whereas э́тот, э́та, or э́то, also demonstrative pronouns, are best thought of as adjectives, describing a noun ("*Which* book? *This* book.").
- Word order is not as important in Russian as it is in English; you can often move words around in a sentence without changing the meaning.
- Russian has no definite articles (*a*, *an*, and *the*). In translating, rely on the context of the sentence to tell you whether to use *a* or *an*, or *the*.
- Don't let false cognates trick you into saying something you don't intend.

Chapter 4

Idioms and Other Useful Expressions

In This Chapter

- Idiomatic expressions
- Expressions of time, location, direction, and weather
- Expressions you can use to get your opinion across
- Say it right with Russian sayings

So you're back in Moscow, and Masha has insisted that you stay at her place instead of at a hotel; and as the evening passes, you relax in the living room to watch television with her parents. You notice a couple of American actresses in an advertisement on television. Her parents don't seem to recognize them, so you think about ways to ask them in Russian if they know them. You may know that знать means "to know," and жéнщины means *women;* so you ask them "Знáете ли вы жéнщин?" Masha's father's face goes pale; he coughs and excuses himself from the room. Masha explains to you later that you had used a Russian *idiom* that means "to be intimate with many women"!

Although an accidental mistake would not normally have such embarrassing consequences, it's important to know what idioms are and how to use them.

I Feel Like Idioms Tonight

Idioms are phrases or sayings that can't be understood by translating them word by word; they must be understood as a whole. For example, to wish someone good fortune in Russian, you would say, "не пуха́ не пера́," which literally means "no fluff, no feathers." In response, the Russian would say "к чёрту," which means "to the devil." This exchange may sound bizarre to an English speaker, but it is a common part of the Russian language.

Hot Topic

Idioms are expressions or phrases peculiar to a language; their meanings cannot be determined through a word-by-word translation, but have fixed meanings that have to be understood as a whole. If you say something is "music to your ears," you're using an English idiom.

Idiomatic expressions are an excellent way for a new learner to dive into the everyday, practical use of a language. Idioms say a lot with a little. They are ready-made and waiting for you to use; all you have to do is memorize them. You don't have to understand their underlying complexity to use them with authority and to sound like a native speaker.

As you listen to Russian dialog or read Russian magazines and come across phrases that appear strange after you have translated them, don't jump to conclusions—what you are hearing or reading may be an idiomatic expression.

Idioms are cultural expressions, because they rely on cultural history, famous plays or novels, phrases coined by great leaders, and the Russian people themselves. Many idioms or phrases date back hundreds of years; they do not rely on the meanings of the individual words, but on a rich cultural context.

Here are some Russian idioms that neatly correspond to their English equivalents.

Russian Idiom	Pronunciation	English Idiom
ра́нняя пта́шка	RAHN-ya-ya PTAH-shkah	an early bird
я́сно как день	YAC-nah kahk dehn	clear as day
на како́й коне́ц?	nah kah-KOY kahn-YETS	to what end?
волк в ове́чьей шку́ре	vohlk vah-VYECH-yay SHKOOR-yeh	a wolf in sheep's clothing

Riddle Me This

Idiomatic expressions enable you to state simply and effectively how you feel, what you want, and how you want to do something. They'll also help you order coffee or make hotel reservations. Moreover, properly using and understanding idioms will make your speech more fluid—and even sound native—and are well worth your time to memorize.

The following chart provides some common Russian idioms that you may find useful in day-to-day speech.

Russian Idiom	Pronunciation	English Meaning
гляде́ть из чужи́х рук	glyah-DYET eez choo-ZHEEHK roohk	to depend on someone else for support ("to look from strangers' hands")
не по́мнить себя́ от	nee POHM-neet she-BYAH oht	to be beside oneself with … ("not to remember-self from")
но́ги подломи́лись	NOH-geeGEE pahd-lah-MEEL-eehs	to become very tired ("the legs were folding under")
гоня́ть ло́дыря	gah-NYAT LOHD-iyr-yah	to idle away one's time
во всю ива́новскую	vah-VSYOO ee-VAHN-ahv-skoo-yoo	with all one's might
не на во́лос	nee nah VOHL-ahs	not the least bit

Taking Off

After Masha explains to her father what you meant to say, all is forgiven, and you decide to take a journey across the country. While you are still thinking about which cities you most want to see, Masha asks you how you want to travel. You want to fly out of Moscow to Vladivostok, take the train back across the country, stopping to drive through the countryside both by car and by horseback, only to come back into Moscow by boat. In trying to put all of this into words, you realize that you need to use some new expressions. Follow the chart for examples.

Russian Phrase	Pronunciation	Meaning
на самолёте	nah sahm-ah-LYOH-tyeh	by plane
на по́езде	nah POH-yehz-dyeh	by train
на маши́не	nah mah-SHEEN-yeh	by car
на такси́	nah tahk-SEE	by taxi

continues

continued

Russian Phrase	Pronunciation	Meaning
на авто́бусе	nah ahv-TOH-boohs-yeh	by bus
на тролле́йбусе	nah trahl-LAY-boohs-yeh	by trolley
на метро́	nah meh-TROH	by subway
на мотоци́кле	nah mah-tah-TSEEK-lyeh	by motorcycle
на теплохо́де	nah the-pleh-HOHD-yeh	by boat
на лы́жах	nah LEEZH-ahk	by skis
на ло́шади	nah LOHSH-chah-dee	by horse
на велосипе́де	nah vee-lah-cah-PEHD-yeh	by bicycle
пешко́м	peh-SHKOHM	on foot

Now that you have studied the list, let's see if you can choose the right phrases for the following sentences. (See Appendix B for answers.)

Exercise 4.1

1. Тури́сты лета́ют в Ме́ксико-Си́ти из Нью-Йо́рка ________________.

   Tourists travel from New York to Mexico City (by plane).

2. Лю́ди е́здят на рабо́ту ________________ в Атла́нте.

   People go to work in Atlanta (by bus).

3. Пое́здка в Евро́пу ________________ 3 ме́сяца.

   The journey to Europe (by boat) is 3 months long.

4. Мы хо́дим ________________ к ба́бушке.

   We walk (by foot) to Grandmother's house.

5. Я пое́ду к врачу́ ________________ за́втра.

   I will drive (by car) to the doctor's office tomorrow.

6. Они́ ката́лись со спу́ска горы́. ________________.

   They went down the side of the mountain by (on skis).

Sometimes it's useful not only to know how you're getting somewhere, but where that somewhere is. Here's a helpful list to give you a sense of location and direction.

Russian Phrase	Pronunciation	Meaning
за угло́м	zah-oog-LOHM	around the corner
пря́мо	PREYAH-mah	straight ahead
сле́ва	SLEH-vah	to the left (location)
спра́ва	SPRAH-vah	to the right (location)
нале́во	nah-LEH-vah	to the left (movement toward)
напра́во	nah-PRAH-vah	to the right (movement toward)
ря́дом с	RYAH-dahms	next to
впереди́	fpeh-reh-DEE	in front of
вдоль	fdohl	alongside
под	pohd	beneath
над	nahd	above
где?	gdyeh	where (location)?
куда́?	koo-DAH	where (movement toward)?
вот тут	voht toot	right here
вон там	vohn tahm	over there
здесь	sdyes	here

Memory Serves

Russian has two different ways of expressing place, depending on whether motion is involved. For location of static items—a book on a shelf, say—you would use **где** to say "Where is the book?" However, for movement or motion in a direction—as in "We are going to the theater"—you would use **куда́** to ask "Where are we going?" Verbs of motion are discussed further in Chapter 9, but for now be aware that Russian has two different ways of expressing and asking for location versus direction.

Masha asks you some questions about your cross-country trip. Try to use the correct word in the sentences that follow. (See Appendix B for answers.)

Exercise 4.2

1. Доро́га идёт ______________________________ бе́рега.

   The road goes (alongside) the shoreline.

2. Где нахо́дится магази́н? Он ______________________________.

   Where is the store located? It's (around the corner).

3. Кафе́ ______________________________ с метро́.

   The café is (next to) the subway.

4. Я вас ви́дел вчера́. ______________________________ вы шли?

   I saw you yesterday. (Where) were you going?

5. Ника́к не мог найти́ мою́ ру́чку. ______________________________ она́?

   I can't find my pen. (Where) is it?

Now It's Time To ...

English speakers use time expressions such as "after a while," "soon," and "in a moment" every day. But what do these expressions really mean? How soon will you take out the trash when you say "Give me a minute"? The meanings of these phrases aren't precise; they don't indicate a specific amount of time. While "at 5" or "10 till 7" offer more specific ways to express time, these can be imprecise as well.

Time expressions in Russian are similar to English in this respect, offering varying degrees of exactness. The following chart gives you a few to get started.

Russian Phrase	Pronunciation	Meaning
уви́димся	oo-VEED-eem-syah	see you soon
до за́втра	doh-ZAH-ftrah	until tomorrow
во́время	VOH-vreh-myah	on time
пока́	pah-KAH	see you later
в конце́	fkahn-TSEH	at the end of
до свида́ния	dahs-vee-DAHN-yeh	goodbye
ра́ньше	RAHN-shyeh	earlier
ра́но	RAHN-oh	early
вре́мя от вре́мени	VREHM-yah oht VREHM-eh-nee	from time to time
ка́ждый день	KAHZH-dee dehn	every day

Russian Phrase	Pronunciation	Meaning
по́зже	POHZ-zhyeh	later
по́здно	POHZ-nah	late
тому́ наза́д	tah-moo-nah-ZAHD	ago
ско́ро	SKOH-rah	soon
неме́дленно	neh-MEHD-leh-noh	immediately
до́брое у́тро	DOH-bruhe OOT-rah	good morning
до́брый день	DOH-brey dehn	good afternoon
до́брый ве́чер	DOH-brey VEH-chehr	good evening
здра́вствуйте	ZDRAS-voo-tyeh	hello
приве́т	PREEH-vyet	hello (informal)
у́тром	OOT-rahm	in the morning
днём	dnyohm	in the afternoon
ве́чером	VEHCH-eh-rahm	in the evening
сейча́с	see-CHAHS	now
сего́дня	seh-VOHD-nyah	today
вчера́	fcheh-RAH	yesterday
за́втра	ZAHF-trah	tomorrow

Now that you've wrestled Father Time to the ground, how would you use the expressions listed above in the following situations? (See Appendix B for answers.)

Exericse 4.3

1. Your spouse leaves for a weekend retreat in the mountains, and you say (see you soon): ____________________
2. After you have dropped the kids off at school, you tell them (see you later): ____________________
3. Your late afternoon meeting began at 3:30, but you arrive (late) at 3:45: ____________________
4. You hope that you find that winning lottery ticket (soon): ____________________
5. The concert started at 8 P.M. and you arrived exactly at 8 P.M. You were (on time): ____________________
6. You check the status of your stocks (every day): ____________________

What Are Your Thoughts On …

So the power went out during the night, your alarm clock failed to wake you up by more than half an hour, and, having fought morning traffic, you arrive late to work. After your boss finishes his unpleasant commentary on your lateness, you hear a co-worker comment on the unsurprising defeat of your favorite baseball team. Suddenly, you find that you have very strong opinions on nearly every conversation in the workplace: from politics to sports, from the current weather conditions in the Baltic republics to the population density of penguins in the Arctic. You are ready to assert yourself with confidence using the appropriate Russian phrases for expressing your opinions.

Russian Phrase	Pronunciation	Meaning
да	Dah	yes
нет	Nyet	no
мóжет быть	MOHZH-yet bweet	maybe
я тóже так дýмаю	ya TOHZH-yeh tahk DOO-mah-yoo	I feel similarly
конéчно	kah-NYEH-shnah	certainly
мне всё равнó	mnyeh fsyoh rahv-NOH	it's all the same to me
я не знáю	ya nee ZNAH-yoo	I don't know
мéжду прóчим	MEZH-doo PROH-cheem	by the way
к счáстью	KSHAHST-yoo	fortunately
вы прав́ы	vwee prah-VEE	you are right
э́то не прáвильно	EH-tah nee PRAH-veel-nah	that is wrong
спаси́бо вам	spah-SEE-bah vahm	thank you
нé за что	NEH-zah-shtah	not a problem
помóему	pah-MOH-yeh-moo	in my opinion
лáдно	LAHD-nah	okay
э́то возмóжно	EH-tah vahz-MOZH-nah	it's possible
не дýмаю	nee DOO-mah-yoo	I don't think so

After you have thoroughly expressed yourself in English, one of your co-workers, who happens to speak a little Russian, pulls you aside to talk about last weekend. How would you answer his questions in the following examples?

1. Вам понрáвился фильм?

   Did you like the movie?

2. Вы отремонти́ровали мою́ маши́ну? Спаси́бо большо́е.

   You fixed my car? Thanks a lot.

3. Ду́маете, что бу́дет дождь сего́дня днём?

   Do you think it will rain this afternoon?

4. Где вы хоти́те обе́дать сего́дня?

   Where do you want to eat lunch today?

How Does This Make You Feel?

Sometimes to describe an emotional or physical state, the English speaker will automatically choose an idiom, like "I have a splitting headache" or "He has a weak stomach." The same is true of Russian. To express many such feelings, you need to use the first person pronoun *I*, or я. (я is actually *I* in the dative case мне, a process that is explained in full in Chapter 7.) Pay close attention to these expressions—understanding their meanings now will make later chapters easier.

Внима́ние

If you were to directly translate "I am cold" into Russian using a standard dictionary, you would probably arrive at "**я холо́дный**"; however, if you were to say this to a Russian, they might think you meant something like "I am dead." Instead, you need to use the idiomatic expression "**мне хо́лодно**," which translated literally means "to me it is cold."

Russian Phrase	Pronunciation	Meaning
ему́(ей) … лет	yeh-MOO (yeay) lyet	he/she is … years old
я бою́сь, что	yah bah-YOOS shtoh	I'm afraid that …
серди́ться на кого́-то за что́-то	ser-DEET-syah nah kah-VOH-tah zah SHTOH-tah	to be angry at someone for something
беспоко́иться за кого́-то/что́-то	behs-spah-KOY-eet-syah zah kah-VOH-to/SHTOH-tah	to be worried about someone/something
я го́лоден(-на)	yah GOHL-ah-dehn	I am hungry
я рад(-а)	yah rahd(-ah)	I am happy
мне жа́рко	mnyeh ZHAR-kah	I am hot
мне хо́лодно	mnyeh HOHL-ahd-nah	I am cold
я уста́л(-а)	yah oo-STAHL(-ah)	I am tired

continues

continued

Russian Phrase	Pronunciation	Meaning
у меня́ серьёзнаяболь	oo-mehn-YAH ser-YOHZ-nah-yah bohl	I have a serious ache
полюби́ть друг дру́га	pah-loo-BEET droogk DROOG-kah	to come to love each other
мне ну́жно	mnyeh NOOZH-nah	I need …
мне ка́жется, что	mnyeh KAHZH-yeht-syah shtoh	it seems to me …
похо́ж(-а) на …	pah-HOZH(-ah) nah	to resemble …

Using the preceding chart, put your expressions to use. (See Appendix B for answers.)

Exercise 4.4

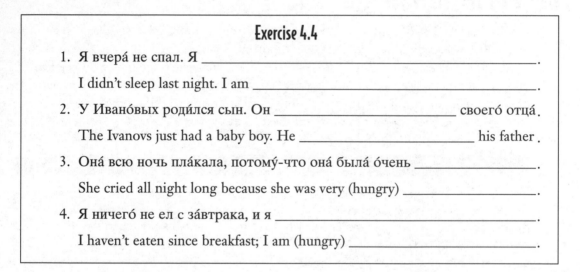

1. Я вчера́ не спал. Я ____________.

   I didn't sleep last night. I am ____________.

2. У Ивано́вых роди́лся сын. Он ____________ своего́ отца́.

   The Ivanovs just had a baby boy. He ____________ his father.

3. Она́ всю ночь пла́кала, потому́-что она́ была́ о́чень ____________.

   She cried all night long because she was very (hungry) ____________.

4. Я ничего́ не ел с за́втрака, и я ____________.

   I haven't eaten since breakfast; I am (hungry) ____________.

Now You've Got It!

Idioms are everywhere, in every part of the language. Understanding how to use them is a critical part of the process of communication, and is a matter of repetition and practice. Remember that the idioms you learn are rooted in nearly a thousand years of history and culture, and they allow you to easily share in the richness of Russian speech.

The Least You Need to Know

- Every language has idioms that are specific to that language.
- Idiomatic expressions help make your speech personable and real.
- Certain expressions are especially useful when you want to express location or direction.
- When translating popular sayings, don't translate them into Russian word for word.
- Remember that to convey the meaning you intend, you need to learn the appropriate Russian idiom.

Part 2 Getting Down to Grammar

Now that you have started the process of reading and pronouncing words written in Russian, it's time to add some structure to your speech. While grammar may not be what you had in mind, you will find that a familiarity with a few basic rules and definitions will increase your ability to speak, and to say anything within the limits of your imagination. When you have made some of these foreign concepts a bit more native, you will find the Russian language to be fluid and easy-going.

Chapter 5

Nouns and Gender

In This Chapter

- All about nouns
- How to determine the gender of nouns
- Noun endings and what they mean
- Exceptional exceptions
- Forming plurals to indicate gender
- More exceptions

A *noun* is a word that names a person, animal, event, place, thing, or idea. A noun can be something physical, like *tree* or *dog* or *sailor;* or a quality or abstract idea like *kindness* or *fun* or *knowledge.* In both English and Russian, proper nouns that name specific people or places begin with a capital letter: Moscow and George Washington are proper nouns. Common nouns do not begin with a capital letter and name any generic person, place, or thing: *doctor*, *yard*, and *love* are common nouns.

All Russian nouns come in one of three types: masculine, feminine, or neuter. In this chapter, we'll look at these three types of nouns as they occur in the nominative case. (Don't worry; we'll talk about cases in Chapters 6 and 7. I know … you can't wait!)

Determining Gender

Not only do Russian nouns name all the stuff we have in the world, but they also have sex while doing it. Sorry to disappoint you, but in this case sex refers to the gender of words in Russian. Every noun has a gender (masculine, feminine, or neuter) and number (singular or plural); and every adjective or verb must agree with, or complement, the gender of the Russian noun. The gender of every noun is fixed—that is, it does not change.

Hot Topic

Nouns name a person, place, animal, thing, or idea. Nouns can be common or proper, and every noun in Russian has gender. The gender of nouns can either be masculine, feminine, or neuter. In addition to gender, nouns have number (either singular or plural) and case (nominative, accusative, prepositional, genitive, dative, or instrumental). Case defines the role or function of a noun in a sentence, which we'll discuss more in Chapter 6.

Memory Serves

Keep in mind that nouns that refer to males, their professions, or their nationalities are generally masculine nouns. Nouns that refer to females, their nationalities, or their professions are generally feminine. Most abstract nouns, or nouns that refer to an idea or state of being (happiness, sadness, life), are usually feminine.

Although some biology may help you from time to time—"boy" is a masculine noun in Russian, too—this will not always work. Grammatical gender is random and unchangeable. A noun is always feminine or always masculine or always neuter. The rules for gender must be memorized; however, the process is relatively simple. When it comes to nouns, the last letter or letters determines the gender of the word.

You will find roughly the same number of feminine nouns in Russian as you will masculine; and after you learn the following rules, which govern gender, you will be able to instantly recognize whether nouns are masculine, feminine, or neuter.

Masculine

Most masculine nouns end in a consonant, such as -т or -л; but there are other possibilities for the ending of a masculine noun, such as -ь and -й. Study the following chart. Keep in mind that we are only discussing singular nouns, and that Russian has no indefinite articles (no *a*, *an*, or *the*).

Masculine Endings	Examples	Pronunciation	English Meaning
consonant	студéнт	stoo-DYEHNT	student
	стол	stohl	table
	стул	stool	chair
	человéк	cheh-lah-VYEK	person
-ь	учи́тель	oo-CHEET-ehl	teacher
	дождь	DOHSHD	rain
	гóспиталь	GOHS-pee-tahl	hospital
-й	музéй	moo-ZAY	museum
	край	kry	edge
	чай	chae	tea

To get an idea of how gender makes your life in Russian slightly different than it is in English, watch the endings of the nouns and adjectives in the following sentences.

1. Этот мужчи́на—краси́вый.

   This man is handsome.

   "-ый" is the Russian, masculine adjectival ending for this masculine noun. Remember, мужчина is masculine, even though it ends with an 'a.'

2. Этот стул—большóй.

   This chair is big.

3. Высóкий мужчи́на—ýмный.

   The tall man is smart.

Feminine

Feminine nouns usually end in -a, but there are three other possibilities for the ending of a feminine noun: -я, -ия, and -ь. The following chart provides some examples.

Feminine Endings	Examples	Pronunciation	English Meaning
-a	рýчка	ROOCH-kah	pen
	газéта	gah-ZYEH-tah	newspaper
	дорóга	dah-ROHG-ah	road
	кни́га	KNEEH-gah	book

continues

continued

Feminine Endings	Examples	Pronunciation	English Meaning
-я	неде́ля	neh-DEHL-yah	week
	семья́	sehm-YAH	family
	дере́вня	deh-REHV-nyah	village
	земля́	zehm-LYAH	earth
-ия*	Росси́я	rahs-SEE-yah	Russia
	деклара́ция	deh-klah-RAHT-see-yah	declaration
	Англия	AHG-lee-yah	England
-ь	дверь	dvehr	door
	любо́вь	lyoo-BOHF	love
	мя́гкость**	MYAHK-ohst	softness

**Nearly all country names in Russian end in* -ия. *If you're uncertain how to translate a country name into Russian,* -ия *is a safe bet.*

***Nearly all Russian nouns ending in* -ость *are feminine, and they usually indicate an abstract idea or quality.*

Внима́ние

The ending -ь can indicate either a feminine or masculine gender; these are the only nouns whose gender cannot be immediately determined, and their gender must be memorized. It is helpful to note that many abstract nouns (**ра́дость**, *joy,* **жизнь**, *life,* and so on) end with a -ь and are feminine.

Compare the same adjectives that were used in the first exercise in this chapter to how they appear here; they're used here to describe some feminine nouns.

1. Эта де́вушка—краси́вая.

   This girl is pretty.

2. Эта ка́рта—большáя.

   This map is big.

3. Высо́кая же́нщина—у́мная.

   The tall woman is smart.

Neuter

Most neuter nouns end in -o, but they can also take several other endings: -e, -ие, and -[м]я. Although the number of masculine and feminine nouns in the Russian language is approximately equal, there are a far smaller number of neuter nouns.

Neuter Endings	Example	Pronunciation	English Meaning
-o	окно́	ahk-NOH	window
	ме́сто	MYEH-stah	place

Neuter Endings	Example	Pronunciation	English Meaning
	у́тро	OOT-rah	morning
	лицо́	leet-SOH	face
-е	по́ле	POHL-yeh	field
-ие	чте́ние	chteh-EHN-ee-yeh	reading
	зда́ние	ZDAHN-ee-yeh	building
	сообще́ние	soh-oh-PSHCHEN-ee-yeh	report
-[м]я*	и́мя	EEM-yah	name (first)
	пла́мя	PLAHM-yah	flame
	вре́мя	VREHM-yah	time

**This group of neuter nouns has ten words that require special attention—we will return to them toward the end of this chapter.*

Boys and Girls

Whereas English speakers are gradually replacing nouns like *waiter* and *waitress* with non-gender-specific words, like *server*, Russians use gender indicators to refer to each according to their biological gender. For example, if a woman is a teacher, the noun for teacher will reflect the fact that she is a woman. Some professions do not change, such as до́ктор (*physician, doctor*), which can refer to either a man or a woman; дире́ктор (*director*), администра́тор (*administrator*), and президе́нт (*president*) are some others. To make professions, nationalities, or other proper nouns feminine is rather easy: simply adding a -ка or -ница to the end of a word will suffice. The following list shows you some common professions and nationalities.

Masculine Noun	Pronununciation	Feminine Noun	Pronununciation	English Meaning
учи́тель	oo-CHEET-ehl	учи́тельница	oo-CHEET-ehl-neet-sah	teacher
шко́льник	SHKOHL-neek	шко́льница	SHKOHL-neet-sah	schoolboy/-girl
америка́нец	ah-mehr-ee-KAH-nyets	америка́нка	ah-mehr-ee-KAHN-kah	an American
англича́нин	ahn-glee-CHAN-ehn	англича́нка	ahn-glee-CHAN-kah	Englishman/-woman
францу́з	frahn-TSOOS	францу́женка	frahn-TSOOZ-zhehn-kah	Frenchman/-woman
актёр	ahk-TYOHR	актри́са	ahk-TREE-sah	actor/actress
официа́нт	ah-feet-see-AHNT	официа́нтка	ah-feet-see-AHNT-kah	waiter/waitress

Gender Exceptions

Learning gender rules is a painstaking, laborious process. To speak confidently, and correctly, it is essential that you know all the rules, and even the exceptions. Unfortunately a few Russian nouns cross-dress, or appear to be feminine by their endings, but grammatically are masculine. Fortunately, the list is short and relatively easy to commit to memory.

Russian Word	Pronunciation	English Meaning
па́па	PAH-pah	dad
дя́дя	DYAH-dyah	uncle
де́душка	DYEH-doosh-kah	grandfather
мужчи́на	moozh-CHEEN-ah	man
ю́ноша	YOON-ah-shah	youth, young person

Hot Topic

Case endings are the last letter (or letters) of a noun that determines its grammatical relationship to the sentence. Whereas English uses word order, Russian identifies the purpose, gender, and quantity of the noun (one or more than one), all through the ending of the word.

Внима́ние

You must remember their singular form when forming plurals. Moreover, when forming plurals from professions, occupations, or nationalities, remember to form the plural from the masculine noun, and not the feminine. To say *teachers*, you would want to say **учителя́**, not **учи́тельницы**, which would imply a group of female teachers.

Plural Nouns

While one fish is fine, two fish are still fish, and three fish means that you need to invest in a bigger aquarium. One shoe is better than none; however, better still is a pair of shoes. English uses "s," in general, to show the idea of more than one, and Russian works similarly. To make nouns plural in Russian, you only need to add Ы or И. As you might have already anticipated, Russian has some exceptions to this rule. If you begin to think of the gender of nouns as your first exposure to *case endings*, which we'll get into in Chapter 6, you may find the idea of gender and quantity more accessible.

The nouns in the following tables are formed by removing the vowel, Ь or Й (for the singular version), and replacing it with Ы or И (to make the noun plural). Remember that the guidelines for the alphabet that you learned in Chapter 2 still apply here. Soft consonants must be followed by soft vowels, hard consonants by hard vowels.

Masculine Plurals

This chart shows you how to form the plurals of standard masculine nouns. Nouns ending in a consonant (remember your spelling rules from the end of Chapter 2!) will add -ы to the end of the noun to become plural.

Russian Noun Singular	Pronunciation	Russian Noun Plural	Pronunciation	English Meaning
мéсяц	MYEH-syahts	мéсяцы	MYEH-syat-see	month(s)
инженéр	een-zhen-EER	инженéры	een-zhen-EER-ee	engineer(s)
докумéнт	dah-koo-MYENT	докумéнты	dah-koo-MYENT-ee	document(s)
журнáл	zhoor-NAHL	журнáлы	zhoor-NAHL-ee	magazine(s)
стол*	stohl	столы́	stoh-LEE	table(s)

**Note the change of stress for this masculine noun. Further examples of this pattern are discussed in the next few sections.*

The nouns in the following chart employ И to make them plural. The 7-letter rule you learned in Chapter 2 is the rule to follow: Remember, after г, к, х, ж, ч, ш, and щ, the plural noun takes И and not Ы. When ь or й is the last letter of the word, drop the ь or й and add И. Watch the progression of endings very closely.

Russian Noun Singular	Pronunciation	Russian Noun Plural	Pronunciation	English Meaning
музéй	moo-ZYAY	музéи	moo-ZYEH-ee	museum(s)
ключ	klooch	ключи́	kloo-CHEE	key(s)
гарáж	gah-RASH	гаражи́	gah-raZHEE	garage(s)
учеéбник	oo-CHEHB-neek	учéбники	oo-CHEHB-nee-kee	textbook(s)
дождь	dohshd	дожди́	dah-ZHDEE	rain(s)
карандáш	kah-rahn-DAHSH	карандаши́	kah-rahn-dah-SHEE	pencil(s)
зверь	zvehr	звéри	ZVEHR-ee	beast(s)

Feminine Plurals

So far, you have learned both of the plural forms for masculine nouns. To form the plural of feminine nouns differs only slightly from the previous charts. Because all feminine nouns have endings (А, Я, ь), those endings must be dropped off, or replaced by the И or Ы, the same vowel as for masculine nouns. The same spelling rules apply for feminine nouns, so make sure you know which letters are always hard. For feminine nouns, it is sometimes easiest to remember that A goes to Ы, and Я and ь go to И.

Внима́ние

When speaking, the difference between the way И and Ы are pronounced is often so slight that it becomes difficult to tell what the ending is. This makes it easier when speaking, because you can make the same sound for plurals; however, it's important to know the grammatical difference between the two similar sounds.

Russian Noun Singular	Pronunciation	Russian Noun Plural	Pronunciation	English Meaning
неде́ля	nyeh-DEHL-yah	неде́ли	nyeh-DEHL-ee	week(s)
ста́нция	STAHN-tsee-yah	ста́нции	STAHN-tsee-ee	station(s)
маши́на	mah-SHEEN-ah	маши́ны	mah-SHEEN-ee	car(s)
у́лица	OOL-leet-sah	у́лицы	OO-leet-see	street(s)
голова́*	gah-lah-VAH	го́ловы	GOH-lah-vwee	head(s)
рука́*	roo-KAH	ру́ки	ROOHK-ee	hand(s)
гора́*	gah-RAH	го́ры	GOHR-ee	mountain(s)
стена́	styeh-NAH	сте́ны	STYEN-ee	wall(s)

**Note the change in stress from the singular to plural forms of these words. In several Russian notes, the stress does not remain fixed between case and* number*—it is extremely important to learn the changes in stress as they occur. These changes will always be noted.*

Neuter Plurals

Neuter nouns take either A or Я to form their plurals, depending on the ending of the noun. Remember that regular neuter nouns end in -о, -е, -ие and -[м]я. Take a look at the following two charts of hard and soft nouns.

Hot Topic

Number refers to the quantity of a noun. A noun is said to be singular if it represents a single unit (one chair, one man), and plural if it represents more than one (chairs, men). The number of a noun is simply its quantity: singular or plural.

Russian Noun Singular	Pronunciation	Russian Noun Plural	Pronunciation	English Meaning
окно́*	ahk-NOH	о́кна	OHK-nah	window(s)
ме́сто*	MYEH-stah	места́	myeh-STAH	place(s)
вино́*	vee-NOH	ви́на	VEE-nah	wine(s)
зе́ркало*	ZEHR-kah-lah	зе́ркала́	ZEHR-kah-LAH	mirror(s)
мы́ло	MEEH-lah	мы́ла	MEEH-lah	soap(s)
ма́сло	MAHS-lah	ма́сла́	MAHS-lah	oil(s)
ведро́*	vehd-ROH	вёдра	VYOHD-rah	bucket(s)
письмо́*	peeh-SMOH	пи́сьма	PEEH-smah	letter(s)
сло́во*	SLOH-vah	слова́	slah-VAH	word(s)

**Most neuter nouns ending in -o undergo a change in the location of stress from singular to plural. You'll need to learn this pattern.*

The following chart lists the much more common neuter nouns—the soft neuter. These nouns end in either е or ие and take я to form their plurals. Some of the same stress issues that you have already seen reappear in this list.

Russian Noun Singular	Pronunciation	Russian Noun Plural	Pronunciation	English Meaning
мо́ре*	MOHR-yeh	моря́	mahr-YAH	sea(s)
зда́ние	ZDAHN-ee-yeh	зда́ния	ZDAHN-ee-yah	building(s)
по́ле*	POHL-yeh	поля́	pahl-YAH	field(s)
собра́ние	sah-BRAH-nee-yeh	собра́ния	sah-BRAH-nee-yah	meeting(s)
реше́ние	peh-SHEN-ee-yeh	реше́ния	peh-SHEN-ee-yah	decision(s)
назва́ние	nah-ZVAHN-ee-yeh	назва́ния	nah-ZVAHN-ee-yah	name(s)

**Most neuter nouns ending in -e undergo a change in the location of stress from singular to plural. You'll need to learn this pattern.*

Exceptions

The nouns you have learned so far follow the Russian rules for forming plurals to the letter; however, some common exceptions apply to these rules, which must be memorized. These are all masculine nouns, many of them borrowed from English, which require A or Я to form the plural. Pay careful attention to the stress, because it changes syllables inside these words.

Russian Noun Singular	Pronunciation	Russian Noun Plural	Pronunciation	English Meaning
дом	dohm	домá	dah-MAH	house(s)
глаз	glahs	глазá	glah-ZAH	eye(s)
сорт	sort	сортá	sahr-TAH	sort(s)
дóктор	DOHK-tahr	докторá	dahk-tahr-AH	doctor(s)
нóмер	NOH-mehr	номерá	nah-meh-RAH	number(s)
вéчер	VEH-chehr	вечерá	veh-cheh-RAH	evening(s)
учи́тель	oo-CHEET-ehl	учителя́	oo-cheet-ehl-YAH	teacher(s)
гóрод	GOH-raht	городá	gah-rah-DAH	city(-ies)
пóезд	POH-yezd	поездá	pah-yez-DAH	train(s)
гóлос	GOH-lahs	голосá	gah-lahs-AH	voice(s)

**This list of nouns is very short; there are perhaps a dozen more such nouns in the Russian language. As an odd coincidence, they are often some of the most frequently used words, and must be committed to memory.*

The following nouns change drastically from singular to plural: think *child* to *children* in English. There's nothing to be done but to memorize the list.

Russian Noun Singular	Pronunciation	Russian Noun Plural	Pronunciation	English Meaning
ребёнок	reh-BYOH-nahk	дéти	DYAY-tee	child/children
человéк	cheh-lah-VYEHK	лю́ди	LYOO-dee	person/people

These masculine nouns take the ending -ья to form their plurals. Carefully review these nouns, because they affect the way these nouns act in different cases.

Russian Noun Singular	Pronunciation	Russian Noun Plural	Pronunciation	English Meaning
брат	braht	брáтья	BRAHT-yah	brother(s)
друг	drook	друзья́	drooz-YAH	friend(s)
сын	siyn	сыновья́	seehn-ah-VYAH	son(s)
лист	leest	ли́стья	LEEST-yah	leaf(-ves)
стул	stool	сту́лья	STOOL-yah	chair(s)
перó	peh-ROH	пéрья	PEHR-yah	feather(s)
муж	moosh	мужья́	moozh-YAH	husband(s)
отéц*	ah-TYETS	отцы́	ah-TSEE	father(s)

Russian Noun Singular	Pronunciation	Russian Noun Plural	Pronunciation	English Meaning
па́лец*	PAHL-yets	па́льцы	PAHL-tsee	finger(s)
кусо́к*	koo-SOHK	куски́	koo-SKEE	piece(s)
ковёр*	kah-VYOHR	ковры́	kah-VREE	rug(s)

**These nouns experience a vowel reduction—the e or o disappears from the words altogether in the plural form.*

Feminine and neuter nouns have very few irregulars; but, like some of the other nouns, you will need to use them frequently.

Russian Noun Singular	Pronunciation	Russian Noun Plural	Pronunciation	English Meaning
дочь	dohch	до́чери	DOHCH-eh-ree	daughter(s)
мать	maht	ма́тери	MAHT-eh-ree	mother(s)
и́мя	EEM-yah	имена́	ee-meh-NAH	name(s)
вре́мя	VREHM-yah	времена́	vreh-meh-NAH	time(s)
пла́мя	PLAHM-yah	пламена́	plah-meh-NAH	flame(s)
де́рево	DEHR-eh-vah	деревья́	der-YEHV-yah	tree(s)
коле́но	kah-LEHN-ah	коле́ни	kah-LYEH-nee	knee(s)
плечо́	pleh-CHOH	пле́чи	PLYEH-chee	shoulder(s)
у́хо	OOK-hah	у́ши	oo-SHEE	ear(s)
я́блоко	YAHB-lah-kah	я́блоки	YAB-lah-kee	apple(s)
жена́	zheh-NAH	жёны	ZHYO-nee	wife(-ves)
сестра́	sehs-TRAH	сёстры	SYOH-stree	sister(s)

The following neuter nouns never change form. Yes, that's right—these guys are indeclinable, or they always look the same no matter how many of them there are, or how they work in a sentence. Look over this list of words (many of them are cognates), and remember, they always stay the same.

Noun	Meaning	Noun	Meaning
бюро́ byoo-ROH	bureau	ко́фе KOHF-yeh	coffee
ви́ски VEE-skee	whiskey	пальто́ pahl-TOH	overcoat

continues

continued

Noun	Meaning	Noun	Meaning
кинó kee-NOH	movie theatre	пиани́но pee-ah-NEEN-oh	piano
кафé kah-FYEH	café	рáдио RAHD-ee-oh	radio
метрó meh-TROH	metro, subway	такси́ tahk-SEE	taxi

There is no getting around the three genders of Russian nouns. If you want to speak Russian, you have to learn your genders. Learning gender is helpful in more ways than one, though. If you begin to think of the gender of nouns as your first exposure to case endings, you'll have a significant head start on the next chapter, in which we deal with the six cases of Russian.

The Least You Need to Know

- Every noun has a gender (masculine, feminine, or neuter) and number (singular or plural); and every adjective or verb must agree with, or complement, the gender of the Russian noun.
- To properly understand Russian nouns, you need to know how to recognize gender.
- Many exceptions apply to the rules of forming plurals; but they usually follow specific patterns. The plural forms of exceptions should always be memorized.
- Stress can shift between the singular and plural form of a noun. This stress shift should always be memorized.
- Most masculine nouns end in a consonant, such as -т or -л; but there are other possibilities for the ending of a masculine noun, such as -ь and -й.
- Feminine nouns usually end in -a, but there are three other possibilities for the ending of a feminine noun: -я, -ия, and -ь.
- Most neuter nouns end in -o, but they can also take several other endings: -e, -ие, and -[м]я.
- A few Russian nouns appear to be feminine by their endings, but grammatically are masculine, and they must be memorized.

Chapter 6

Cases, Part 1

In This Chapter

- Cases in Russian
- The nominative case
- The accusative case
- The prepositional case

While studying grammar rules may seem as appealing as watching C-SPAN all weekend, it's quite necessary when learning a new language. Idioms and cognates will take you only so far; eventually you have to learn the grammar basics that enable you to converse freely with native speakers.

Luckily, you don't have to become a grammar expert to speak a language, and that includes Russian. Look at all the nouns you learned in Chapter 5. As you'll recall from that chapter's introduction, you learned them in the nominative case. So already, you know a bunch of nouns in their nominative case form.

In this chapter, you will expand on what you already know about nouns, and form sentences with them. But first, let's answer a question: What do we mean by nominative case? What the heck do we mean by *case*, anyway?

Colliding with Cases

All languages have their peculiarities. When it comes to case, English is a peculiar language. English is one of the few languages that doesn't rely on case, although at one time, with Old English, it did. We still get a glimmer of it here and there with pronouns. Think about *I* and *me*, *they* and *them*, or *we* and *us*. The only difference between the words in these pairs is the way they're used in a sentence. Otherwise, they mean the same thing.

Doing Your Case Work

Case has to do with the forms that nouns, pronouns, and adjectives take to represent their grammatical relation to other words in a sentence. In Russian and other languages, case manifests itself as different word endings that let you know how a word in any sentence is used grammatically. Case helps clarify what you mean and helps prevent any misunderstanding on the part of the listener.

In English, we rely on word order for grammatical sense. If I say "John punched Bill," you know who threw the punch and who got the black eye. If I switch the position of the nouns and say "Bill punched John," you get a different puncher and a different punchee. However, as we learned in Chapter 3, word order is more flexible in Russian; you can often vary the word order of a sentence without changing the overall meaning. In Russian, you could switch the placement of Bill and John in the sentence, and the puncher and punchee would remain the same, because of case endings.

Hot Topic

Cases are the forms nouns, adjectives, and pronouns take to represent their grammatical function in a sentence. In this chapter and the next, we focus on nouns and pronouns, and in Chapter 8 we focus on adjectives.

After studying the following sections, you will understand why the use of cases makes it impossible to confuse the meaning of a sentence.

The Six Cases

Russian has six cases with which to show the grammatical relationship between words: nominative, accusative, prepositional, genitive, dative, and instrumental. Let's look briefly at each:

- The *nominative* case marks the subject, or the doer of the action or the predicate.

  "The boy is sleeping."

In this sentence, the word *boy*, being the subject and doing the action, would be in nominative case form.

- The *accusative* case marks the direct object, or the object of the action.

  "The boy is reading a book."

  The word *boy* in this sentence would take the nominative case form, whereas the book, being the direct object, would take the accusative case.

- The *prepositional* (or locative) case shows the location, or where the action takes place.

  "The boy is in bed."

  The word *boy* in this sentence takes the nominative case form, whereas *bed* takes the prepositional.

- The *genitive* case shows possession—as in "the boy's dog" or "the dog of the boy."

  "The boy's dog (the dog of the boy) is in the house."

  The word *boy* in this sentence takes the genitive case form. (*House* would take prepositional.)

- The *dative* case shows the indirect object, or the receiver of the action.

  "The boy is giving a bone to the dog."

  The word *boy* in this sentence takes the nominative case, *bone* takes the accusative case, and *dog* takes the dative case.

- The *instrumental* case shows the "instrument" (or means) of the action, or how the action is done.

  "The collar was made by hand."

  The word *collar* takes the nominative case, and *hand* takes the instrumental case.

Obviously, an intensive study of case is beyond the scope of this book. Instead, in this chapter and the next I'll show you how they work with respect to nouns and give you the best introduction and overview of them possible.

Внима́ние

Although you don't need to become a grammar expert to learn Russian, to study cases, you do need to refresh yourself on grammar. If you aren't comfortable with terms like prepositional phrase, you'll need to do some reviewing.

Remember, nouns and adjectives will still need to agree in gender as well as case. What this means is that for any noun, pronoun, or adjective, there are 6 (cases) times 3 (genders) for 18 possible forms. (In this chapter and the next we'll focus on nouns, and in Chapter 8 we'll look at adjectives.)

Take this chapter and the next at your own pace. Case might be a different concept to you, but you can't learn Russian without it. And in the long run, learning it will make your goal of speaking Russian easier.

Starting with the Nominal: Nominative

Nouns in the nominative case act as subjects, or the doers of action (or predicates). To form even the most basic sentences—noun + verb, as in "John ran"—the nominative case is necessary.

You remember how to pick the subject out of a sentence, right? You find the verb, then ask who or what is connected with the verb. In the sentence "Steve saw Myra," the verb is *saw*, and if you ask who or what saw, the answer is *Steve*. So Steve is the subject, or doer of the action, and would take the nominative case in a Russian translation of this sentence.

> **Hot Topic**
>
> **Declension** is a way to describe all the possible forms, or case endings, a word can take in any of the cases. When you have learned all the possible case endings (the last few letters of the word), you have then learned how to "decline" that word.

Remember that gender affects the *declension* of nouns and the changes they undergo in each case, every step of the way. As you study the declensions in this chapter, focus on learning the patterns of case endings, and consider making some flash cards for yourself to help you chart your progress.

A declension table is a chart that lists the possible case endings for nouns in an easy-to-read fashion. Here is a declension table for the nominative case.

Nominative Case Endings

Masculine	Feminine	Neuter	Plural
-consonant	-А/-Я	-О/-Е	-Ы/-И А/-Я
-Й/-Ь	-Ь/-ИЯ	-ИЕ	-И/-Я

Study the following charts for an overview of how the nominative case functions for masculine, feminine, and neuter nouns.

Nominative Case: Masculine

Nominative Singular	Example	English Meaning
кабинéт (office)	Кабинéт большóй.	The office is big.
стол (table)	Стол мáленький.	The table is small.
чай (tea)	Чай горя́чий.	The tea is hot.
дождь (rain)	Дождь си́льный.	The rain is strong.
дя́дя* (Uncle)	Дя́дя Вáня	*Uncle Vanya* (Chekov)
пáпа* (Father)	Пáпа ещё молодóй.	Father is still young.

**Remember that certain masculine nouns such as* дя́дя *and* пáпа *appear to be feminine by their endings; however, they must always be modified by masculine adjectives and pronouns.*

Nominative Case: Feminine

Nominative Singular	Example	English Meaning
кни́га (book)	Кни́га большáя.	The book is big.
недéля (week)	Недéля дли́нная.	The week is long.
Росси́я (Russia)	Росси́я-странá.	Russia is a country.
дверь (door)	Дверь откры́та.	The door is open.

Nominative Case: Neuter

Nominative Singular	Example	English Meaning
мéсто (place)	Это моё мéсто.	This is my place.
пóле (field)	Где пóле?	Where is the field?
здáние (building)	Ви́дишь э́то здáние?	Do you see that building?
врéмя (time)	Врéмя летéло.	Time flew.

Nominative Case: Plural

Nominative Singular	Nominative Plural	Example	English Meaning
стол (table)	столы́ (tables)	Столы́ здесь.	The tables are here.
недéля (week)	недéли (weeks)	Эти недéли бы́ли хорóшие.	These weeks were good.

continues

Nominative Case: Plural (continued)

Nominative Singular	Nominative Plural	Example	English Meaning
ме́сто (place)	места́ (places)	Эти места́ свобо́дные?	Are these places free?
по́ле (field)	поля́ (fields)	Поля́ зелёные.	The fields are green.
вре́мя (time)	времена́ (times)	Времена́ тяжёлые.	Times are hard.

What you want to remember about the nominative case is that it's the case to use for the simplest sentences you want to put together. Obviously, it is extremely beneficial to focus on this case at some length. You don't want to leave home without it!

Bring Forth the Accused—Accusative

When you change *who* to *whom*, or *we* to *us*, you are using the accusative case. The accusative marks the direct object in a sentence, or tells you to *whom* or to *what* the action is being done.

Do you remember how to find the direct object in a sentence? Look at the following:

> The boy is reading a book.

In this sentence, *boy* is the subject modified by reading. To find the direct object, ask what the boy is reading. The answer is a book, so *book* is the direct object and would take the accusative case in a Russian translation of this sentence.

The accusative case throws you one extra little curve that the other cases don't: the distinction between animate and inanimate masculine nouns. *Inanimate nouns* refer to items that are not animate, or alive. Paper, food, and clothes are inanimate nouns, as would be *book* in the preceding example. Animate nouns are nouns that define animate, or living, people or animals. This distinction applies only to masculine nouns in the singular; feminine nouns are neither animate nor inanimate in the singular. Names, professions, nationalities, animals, and positions are considered to have an "animate" quality.

If all of this seems complicated, remember this: Inanimate masculine nouns (nouns that are not people or animals) and neuter nouns remain the same in both Nominative and Accusative.

Here is a declension table for the accusative case.

Accusative Case Endings

	Masculine	Feminine	Neuter	Plural
Inanimate	-consonant	-У/-Ю	-О/-Е	-Ы/-И
	-Й/-Ь	-Ь/-ИЮ	-ИЕ	-А/-Я
Animate	-А/-Я	——	——	——

The following charts show the declensions of nouns in the accusative case. Pay attention to animate and inanimate masculine nouns, and remember the gender changes that you studied in Chapter 5.

Hot Topic

Inanimate nouns refer to items that are not animate, or alive. Paper, food, and clothes are inanimate nouns. Animate nouns are nouns that define animate, or living, people or animals. This distinction applies only to masculine nouns; feminine nouns are neither animate nor inanimate. Names, professions, nationalities, animals, and positions are considered to have an "animate" quality.

Accusative Case: Inanimate Masculine

Nominative Singular	Accusative Singular	Example	English Meaning
кабинéт (office)	кабинéт (office)	Он лю́бит свой кабинéт.	He loves his office.
стол (table)	стол (table)	Он брóсил стол из окнá.	He threw the table out of the window.
чай (tea)	чай (tea)	Я кладý сáхар в чай.	I put sugar in tea.
дождь (rain)	дождь (rain)	Онá ненави́дит дождь.	She hates rain.

Accusative Case: Animate Masculine

Nominative Singular	Accusative Singular	Example	English Meaning
человéк (person)	человéка (person)	Когдá вы ви́дели человéка?	When did you see the person?
студнéт (student)	Студéнта (student)	Ты знáешь студéнта?	Do you know the student?

continues

Accusative Case: Animate Masculine (continued)

Nominative Singular	Accusative Singular	Example	English Meaning
учи́тель (teacher)	учи́теля (teacher)	Я люблю́ моего́ учи́теля.	I like my teacher.
геро́й (hero)	геро́я (hero)	Арестова́ли геро́я.	They arrested the hero.
дя́дя* (uncle)	дя́дю (uncle)	Я люблю́ дя́дю.	I love my uncle.
па́па* (father)	па́пу (father)	Я зна́ю твоего́ па́пу.	I know your father.

**These animate, masculine nouns are declined as feminine nouns, because they have feminine endings. Remember that the adjectives that modify them must be masculine.*

Accusative Case: Feminine

Nominative Singular	Accusative Singular	Example	English Meaning
кни́га (book)	кни́гу (book)	Мы прочита́ли э́ту кни́гу.	We read this book.
неде́ля (week)	неде́лю (week)	ехали туда́ на неде́лю.*	They went there for a week.
Росси́я (Russia)	Росси́ю (Russia)	Я хочу́ пое́хать в Росси́ю.	I want to go to Russia.
дверь (door)	дверь (door)	Откро́йте дверь!	Open the door!

**To indicate the duration of an event or action, the accusative case is often used.*

Accusative Case: Neuter

Nominative Singular	Accusative Singular	Example	English Meaning
ме́сто (place)	ме́сто (place)	Он сел на моё ме́сто.*	He sat in my place.
по́ле (field)	по́ле (field)	Она шла в по́ле.*	She was walking to the field.
зда́ние (building)	зда́ние (building)	Я ра́ньше ви́дел э́то зда́ние.	I have seen this building before.
вре́мя (time)	вре́мя (time)	Невозмо́жно смотре́ть вре́мя.	It is not possible to watch time.

**The accusative case can be used with certain prepositions—*на *(on),* в *(in),* над *(above),* под *(under),* за *(behind), and so on—to indicate motion, or the direction of movement.*

Remember, inanimate masculine nouns and neuter nouns remain the same in both nominative and accusative.

What's in a Phrase?—Prepositional

As you might have noticed, certain prepositions can accompany each case in Russian; both motion (or the destination of a certain motion) and time expressions employ the most common Russian prepositions: B and HA.

But although other Russian cases can use prepositions, the prepositional case is the only case that *requires* the use of a preposition to work. To indicate the position or location of something, either B or HA is used; but to speak or think about someone or something, the preposition O is used.

Here is a declension table for the prepositional case.

Prepositional Case Endings

	Masculine	Feminine	Neuter	Plural
Prepositional	-Е/-У	-Е	-Е	-АХ
	-Е/-И	-И/-ИИ	-ИИ	-ЯХ

Study the following charts to see how prepositional case is used. The prepositional case has only two primary endings: E or И. Feminine and masculine nouns often have the same endings in their prepositional form.

Prepositional Case: Masculine

Nominative Singular	Prepositional Singular	Example	English Meaning
кабине́т (office)	кабине́те (office)	Он в кабине́те сейча́с.	He's in the office right now.
стол (table)	столе́ (table)	Кни́га лежи́т на столе́.	The book is on the table.
чай (tea)	ча́е (tea)	Что ты ду́маешь об э́том ча́е?	What do you think about tea?
дождь (rain)	дожде́ (rain)	Ра́зве, вода́ в дожде́?	Really! There's water in rain?
дя́дя (uncle)	дя́де (uncle)	Па́па всегда́ говори́т о на́шем дя́де.	Dad always talks about our uncle.
па́па (Dad)	па́пе (Dad)	Но дя́дя ре́дко говори́т о па́пе.	But Uncle seldom speaks about Dad.

Prepositional Case: Feminine

Nominative Singular	Prepositional Singular	Example	English Meaning
кни́га (book)	кни́ге (book)	Что бы́ло напи́сано в э́той кни́ге?	What was written in this book?
неде́ля (week)	неде́ле (week)	Я не рабо́таю на э́той неде́ле.	I am not working this week.
Росси́я (Russia)	Росси́и (Russia)	Мно́го люде́й живёт в Росси́и.	Many people live in Russia.
дверь (door)	две́ри (door)	Муха́ сейчас на две́ри.	The fly is now on the door.
мать* (Mom)	ма́тери (Mom)	Дочь ду́мает о ма́тери.	The daughter thinks about her mom.
дочь* (daughter)	до́чери (daughter)	Мать ду́мает о до́чери.	The mother thinks about her daughter.

**These two feminine nouns are unique to the language; they are the smallest group of exceptions, but follow a predictable pattern.*

Prepositional Case: Neuter

Nominative Singular	Prepositional Singular	Example	English Meaning
ме́сто (place)	ме́сте (place)	Наконе́ц, всё на своём ме́сте.	Finally, everything is in its place.
по́ле (field)	по́ле (field)	Трава́ растёт в по́ле.	Grass grows on the field.
зда́ние (building)	зда́нии (building)	У них но́вая ме́бель в э́том зда́нии.	They have new furniture in this building.
вре́мя* (time)	вре́мени (time)	О вре́мени нельзя́ ду́мать.	One should not think about time.

**Russian has approximately a dozen of these neuter nouns (refer to Chapter 5), which are declined almost identically. These include* и́мя *(name),* пле́мя *(tribe),* пла́мя *(flame),* вре́мя *(time), and a few others.*

Prepositional Case: Plural

Prepositional Singular	Prepositional Plural	Example	English Meaning
ме́сте (place)	места́х (places)	Все сидя́т на своих места́х.	Everyone is sitting in their own places.
по́ле (field)	поля́х (fields)	Есть дере́вья в поля́х.	There are trees in the fields.
кни́ге (book)	кни́гах (books)	Мно́го глав в э́тих кни́гах.	There are many chapters in these books.
дом (house)	дома́х (houses)	Лю́ди живу́т в тех дома́х.	People live in those houses.

A few single-syllable masculine nouns have some exceptions. When using the prepositions -в or -НА, they experience a stress shift and take У in their prepositional form. When using the preposition -О, these nouns take the standard endings Е or И.

Exceptions

Nominate Singular	Prepositional Singular	English Meaning	Nominate Singular	Prepositional Singular	English Meaning
порт (pohrt)	в порту́ (fpahr-TOO)	port	пол (pohl)	на полу́ (nah-pah-LOO)	floor
год (gohd)	в году́ (fgah-DOO)	year	снег (snehg)	в снегу́ (fsneh-GOO)	snow
лес (less)	в лесу́ (fles-SOO)	forest	у́гол (OOG-ehl)	на/в углу́ (nah-oog-LOO)	corner
шкаф (shkahf)	в шкафу́ (fshkah-FOO)	cupboard	лёд (lyoht)	на льду́ (hahl-DOO)	ice
сад (sahd)	в саду́ (fsah-DOO)	garden	бе́рег (BEHR-ehg)	на берегу́ (nah-behr-eh-GOO)	shore
ряд (ryahd)	в ряду́ (hahr-ya-DOO)	row	мост (mohst)	на мосту́ (nah-mah-STOO)	bridge
край (kry)	на краю́ (hahk-rah-YOO)	edge	Крым (KREEM)	в Крыму́ (fkree-MOO)	Crimea

Breathe Deeply and Exhale

You have now accomplished half of your goal in getting familiar with cases. As you take a break before Chapter 7, let's recap what we just covered: Nominative case provides the *who;* accusative case gives us the *whom;* and prepositional case delivers the *where.* As a summary, here is a declension table for the first three cases.

Case Endings for Nominative, Accusative, Prepositional

Case	Masculine	Feminine	Neuter	Plural	
Nominative	-consonant	-А/-Я	-О/-Е	-Ы/-И	-А/-Я
	-Й/-Ь	-Ь/-ИЯ	-ИЕ	-И/-Я	
Accusative (inanimate)	-consonant	-У/-Ю	-О/-Е	-Ы/-И	
	-Й/-Ь	-Ь/-ИЮ	-ИЕ	-А/-Я	
Accusative (animate)	-А/-Я	——	——	——	
Prepositional	-Е/-У	-Е	-Е	-АХ	
	-Е/-И	-И/-ИИ	-ИИ	-ЯХ	

Now let's up the ante and go to Chapter 7 to learn the last three cases: genitive, dative, and instrumental.

The Least You Need to Know

- To determine the purpose, or function, of a Russian noun, look to its case ending, which can be nominative, accusative, prepositional, genitive, dative, or instrumental.
- Nouns are declined, or the endings of nouns change, in order to change their case, or grammatical function, in a sentence. Each of the six cases has a different declension pattern.
- The *nominative* case marks the subject, or the doer of the action or the predicate.
- The accusative marks the direct object in a sentence, or tells you to *whom* or to *what* the action is being done.
- The prepositional case is the only case that *requires* the use of a preposition.
- Using some grammar flash cards will help you quickly refer to the declension patterns of Russian cases. Until you become comfortable with using all of the cases, refer back to this chapter to refresh your memory.

Chapter 7

Cases, Part 2

In This Chapter

- The genitive case
- The dative case
- The instrumental case
- A brief introduction to pronouns and case

In Chapter 6, I talked a little about how cases function in Russian, and why you need to become familiar with them. Then we looked at the nominative case, the accusative case, and the prepositional case. In this chapter, we'll look at the final three cases—genitive, dative, and instrumental—to complete your overview of the six. We'll start out with the toughest of the three, the genitive case. But I promise you, it's all downhill from there!

It's Mine, All Mine!—Genitive

In English, we usually express possession by saying "the man's briefcase" or "the girl's book bag." Using the apostrophe, to indicate which item belongs to *whom*, works in English; however, Russians think of possession as "the briefcase of the man" or "the book bag of the girl." Remembering how to rephrase these simple expressions in English will help you translate them into Russian using the genitive case.

Here is a declension table for the genitive case.

Genitive Case Endings

	Masculine	Feminine	Neuter	Plural
	-А	-Ы	-А	——
	-Я	-И	-Я	——

Possession is only one function of the genitive case: The majority of prepositions in Russian require genitive, and genitive also indicates absence, or negation. Don't worry about these secondary uses. For the time being, simply study the following charts to learn the declension patterns and observe the examples.

Genitive Case: Masculine

Nominative Singular	Genitive Singular	Example	English Meaning
оте́ц* (father)	отца́ (father)	Это газе́та моего́ отца́.	This is my father's newspaper. (This is the newspaper of my father.)
стол (table)	стола́ (table)	Здесь нет стола́.	There isn't a table here.
чай (tea)	ча́я (tea)	Это составна́я часть хоро́шего ча́я.	This is the ingredient of good tea.
дождь (rain)	дождя́ (rain)	Ду́маю, что дождя́ не бу́дет сего́дня.	I don't think that there will be rain today.
дя́дя (uncle)	дя́ди (uncle)	Это часы́ моего́ дя́ди.	This is my uncle's watch. (This is the watch of my uncle.)
па́па (Dad)	па́пы (Dad)	Па́пы нет. Он рабо́тает.	Dad isn't here. He's working.

**Do you remember the nominative plural form of* Оте́ц? Оте́ц *has what is called a "fleeting E." In all other forms of this word, the E disappears and the stress shifts to the last syllable.*

Genitive Case: Feminine

Nominative Singular	Genitive Singular	Example	English Meaning
кни́га (book)	кни́ги (book)	Пе́рвая часть э́той кни́ги хоро́шая.	The first part of this book is good.
неде́ля (week)	неде́ли (week)	Он жил там о́коло неде́ли.	He lived there about a week.

Nominative Singular	Genitive Singular	Example	English Meaning
Росси́я (Russia)	Росси́и (Russia)	Ни Росси́и ни Кита́я нет на э́той ка́рте.	Neither Russia nor China is on this map.
дверь (door)	две́ри (door)	Нет две́ри в э́той ко́мнате.	There isn't a door in this room.
мать* (mother)	ма́тери (mother)	Сын э́той ма́тери пло́хо ведёт себя́.	The son of this mother behaves badly.
дочь* (daugher)	до́чери (daughter)	Она́ но́сит оде́жду свое́й до́чери.	She wears her daughter's clothes.

**Notice that the genitive forms of the last two words above are identical to their prepositional forms.*

Genitive Case: Neuter

Nominative Singular	Genitive Singular	Example	English Meaning
ме́сто (place)	ме́ста (place)	Нет ни одного́ свобо́дного ме́ста.*	There isn't one available place.
по́ле (field)	по́ля (field)	Здесь край по́ля.	Here is the edge of the field.
зда́ние (building)	зда́ния (building)	Окна зда́ния но́вые.	The windows of the building are new.
вре́мя (time)	вре́мени (time)	У меня́ нет вре́мени.*	I don't have time.

**To indicate absence, or negation, use the genitive case.*

I Have a Date With—Dative

So you've settled the preliminaries of this year's April Fools' joke. You know what you will be doing, and where; but the question remains: to whom? Dative case proudly arrives to save the day! With the dative case, you will be able to determine the indirect object, or the person or thing that receives the action in a sentence.

Like all the cases in Russian, dative has some prepositions that accompany it; but, more importantly, dative case allows you to create critical impersonal sentences, such as "It is difficult for me to do that," or "I am cold." (Remember your phrases from Chapter 5? Some of them used dative case to say such things as "I'm hot" or "I'm not interested.")

Here is a declension table for the dative case.

Dative Case Endings

	Masculine	Feminine	Neuter	Plural
	-У	-Е	-У	-АМ
	-Ю	-И	-Ю	-ЯМ

Study the following charts to see how the dative case functions.

Dative Case: Masculine

Nominative Singular	Dative Singular	Example	English Meaning
оте́ц (father)	отцу́ (father)	Хоро́ший сын звони́т отцу́ ка́ждый день.	The good son calls his father every day.
учи́тель (teacher)	учи́телю (teacher)	Студе́нт ме́дленно шёл к учи́телю.	The student was slowly walking to the teacher.
телефо́н (phone)	телефо́ну (phone)	Позвони́ мне по телефо́ну!	Call me on the phone!
Серге́й (Sergey)	Серге́ю (Sergey)	Де́вушка дала́ Серге́ю пода́рок.	The girl gave a gift to Sergey.
дя́дя (uncle)	дя́де (uncle)	Мы е́здим к дя́де ка́ждый год.*	We go to our uncle's house every year.
па́па (Father)	па́пе (Father)	Па́пе хо́лодно в э́той ко́мнате.	Father is cold in this room.

**To indicate that you are going to someone's place, you need to use the preposition к with the person's name or profession.*

Dative Case: Feminine

Nominative Singular	Dative Singular	Example	English Meaning
Ле́на (Lena)	Ле́не (Lena)	Он давно́ чита́л Ле́не вслух по ноча́м.	He read to Lena aloud at night a long time ago.
ма́ма (Mom)	ма́ме (Mom)	Ма́ме бы́ло тру́дно ве́рить в э́ту но́вость.	It was hard for Mom to believe this news.
ло́шадь (horse)	ло́шади (horse)	Ма́льчик дал ло́шади морко́вь.	The boy gave the horse a carrot.

Nominative Singular	Dative Singular	Example	English Meaning
дверь (door)	две́ри (door)	Студе́нт подошёл к две́ри и взгляну́л на часы́.	The student approached the door and looked at his watch.
мать* (mother)	ма́тери (mother)	Дочь пошла́ к ма́тери.	The daughter went to her mother's house.**
дочь* (daughter)	до́чери (daughter)	До́чери нра́вятся цветы́.	The daughter likes flowers.

**Note that the dative forms of these two words are identical to their prepositional and genitive forms.*

***This can mean both "The daughter went to her mother's house" and "The daughter went to her mother."*

Dative Case: Neuter

Nominative Singular	Dative Singular	Example	English Meaning
окно́ (window)	окну́ (window)	Он подошёл к откры́тому окну́.	He approached the open window.
по́ле (field)	по́лю (field)	Мы хо́дим пешко́м на рабо́ту по по́лю.*	We walk on foot to work through this field.
зда́ние (building)	зда́нию (building)	Нельзя́ подходи́ть к э́тому зда́нию без про́пуска.	It is not possible to go up to this building without a pass.
и́мя (name)	и́мени (name)	Па́па зовёт сы́на по и́мени.	The father calls his son by first name.

**When trying to indicate that you are moving through something, it is possible to use the preposition ПО and the dative case.*

Dative Case: Plural

Dative Singular	Dative Plural	Example	English Meaning
ло́шади (horse)	лошадя́м (horses)	Она́ даёт са́хар свои́м лошадя́м.	She gives her horses some sugar.
отцу́ (father)	отца́м (fathers)	Всем отца́м нужны́ свои́ де́ти.	All fathers need their children.
учи́телю (teacher)	учи́телям (teachers)	Они́ говоря́т учи́телям.	They are telling teachers.
по́лю (field)	поля́м (fields)	Мы хо́дим по поля́м.	We are walking in the fields.

Play That—Instrumental

No one wants to work alone. We study Russian *with* books; we speak *with* friends; we eat *with* forks and knives; and we do it all *with* pleasure. The instrumental case enables all of that to happen without a hitch. Almost every time you grab that *with*, you are using the instrumental case.

The instrumental case primarily describes how the action is done: *with* what instrument, *with* what person, or *with* what method. The preposition C (which literally means *with*) goes hand in hand with instrumental; however, an important distinction should be made. When indicating the means *by* which you do something—to eat with a fork, to write with a pen—the preposition C is not used. Instead, when you are adding additional information—to go with friends, to work with difficulty—the preposition C is usually used.

Here is a declension table for the instrumental case.

Instrumental Case Endings

	Masculine	Feminine	Neuter	Plural
	-ОМ	-ОЙ	-ОМ	-АМИ
	-ЕМ	-ЕЙ/-ЬЮ	-ЕМ	-ЯМИ

Study the following charts to see how the instrumental case functions.

Instrumental Case: Masculine

Nominative Singular	Instrumental Singular	Example	English Meaning
труд (difficulty)	трудóм (difficulty)	Я с трудóм закóнчил э́ту рабóту.	I finished the work with difficulty.
карандáш (pencil)	карандашóм (pencil)	Учи́тель сказáл, чтóбы мы писáли карандашóм.	The teacher said we should write with a pencil.
отéц (father)	отцóм (father)	Онá встрéтилась с отцóм вчерá.	She met her father yesterday.
гарáж (garage)	гаражóм (garage)	Они́ пострóили свой дом с гаражóм.*	They built a home with a garage.
дя́дя* (uncle)	дя́дей (uncle)	Он стал дя́дей, когдá у егó брáта роди́лся сын.	He became an uncle when his brother had a son.

**In this case, they did not use a garage to build a house; rather, they built a house, which had a garage. In this instance, C is required.*

Instrumental Case: Feminine

Nominative Singular	Instrumental Singular	Example	English Meaning
ру́чка (pen)	ру́чкой (pen)	Мой брат всегда́ пи́шет ру́чкой.	My brother always writes with a pen.
Ле́на (Lena)	Ле́ной (Lena)	Мы встре́тились с Ле́ной на углу́.	We met Lena on the corner.
тётя (aunt)	тётей (aunt)	Я ходи́л в магази́н с тётей.	I went to the store with my aunt.
ло́шадь (horse)	ло́шадью (horse)	Что нам де́лать с больно́й ло́шадью?	What are we to do with a sick horse?
мать (mother)	ма́терью (mother)	Она́ ста́ла ма́терью сего́дня у́тром.*	She became a mother this morning.
дочь (daughter)	до́черью (daughter)	Приходи́ с до́черью, что́бы я с ней познако́мился.	Come over with your daughter so that I can meet her.

**The instrumental case may also be used to indicate a position or profession that someone has become.*

Instrumental Case: Neuter

Nominative Singular	Instrumental Singular	Example	English Meaning
молоко́ (milk)	молоко́м (milk)	Вот стака́н с молоко́м.	Here is a glass with milk.
пече́нье (cookie)	пече́ньем (cookie)	Хоти́те чай с пече́ньем?	Do you want tea with a cookie?
зда́ние (building)	зда́нием (building)	Ря́дом с э́тим зда́нием магази́н.	There is a store next to this building.
письмо́ (letter)	письмо́м (letter)	Нашли́ банди́та с э́тим письмо́м.	They found the bandit with this letter.

Instrumental Case: Plural

Instrumental Singular	Instrumental Plural	Example	English Meaning
ру́чкой (pen)	ру́чками (pens)	Не пиши́те ру́чками!	Don't write with pens!
дру́гом (friend)	друзья́ми (friends)	Встре́титесь ли вы с друзья́ми?	Are you meeting with friends?

continues

Instrumental Case: Plural (continued)

Instrumental Singular	Instrumental Plural	Example	English Meaning
карандашо́м (pencil)	карандаша́ми (pencils)	Мы пи́шем каранда́шами.	We write with pencils.
челове́ком (people)	людьми́ (people)	Он говори́т с ра́зными людьми́.	He talks with different people.

These following phrases in the instrumental case have become like adverbs, or time expressions. They will be incorporated into future chapters, but it will help you to remember that they are formed from the instrumental.

Phrases Formed from the Instrumental Case

Nominative Singular	Instrumental Singular	English Meaning	Nominative Singular	Instrumental Singular	English Meaning
зима́	зимо́й	In winter	у́тро	у́тром	in the morning
весна́	весно́й	In spring	ве́чер	ве́чером	in the evening
о́сень	о́сенью	In fall	день	днём	in the afternoon
ле́то	ле́том	In summer	ночь	но́чью	at night

The Air Is Fresher in Russia!

You may be wondering at this point, "Where are the plurals for the accusative and genitive cases?" Rest your soul, fearless pioneer; these plurals will emerge in Chapter 11. A few minor tasks remain to be finished before the end: Let's recap the three cases you have just learned. Genitive indicates possession, the property *of whom;* dative points out the indirect object, to *whom* the action happens; and instrumental provides the means, *with* what or whom the action happens. Review the following declension table for a quick review of the last three cases.

Case Endings for Genitive, Dative, Instrumental

Case	Masculine	Feminine	Neuter	Plural
Genitive	-А	-Ы	-А	——
	-Я	-И	-Я	——

Case	Masculine	Feminine	Neuter	Plural
Dative	-У	-Е	-У	-АМ
	-Ю	-И	-Ю	-ЯМ
Instrumental	-ОМ	-ОЙ	-ОМ	-АМИ
	-ЕМ	-ЕЙ/-ЬЮ	-ЕМ	-ЯМИ

Remember these few helpful tips: In every case but nominative, both masculine and neuter nouns take the same case endings. The masculine endings for animate nouns in the accusative case are the same as their endings in the genitive case.

Call In the Replacements!

So, you now have all your nouns in a row. You will be glad to know that nouns don't always bear the brunt of the work; instead, pronouns are called in from the benches to take over the game. Personal pronouns are used to take the place of nouns.

Pronouns, like adjectives, must match the noun that they intend to replace in gender, case, and number. It's important to know how a noun is being used in a sentence, in order to correctly exchange it for the appropriate pronoun. But why are pronouns necessary? Consider the following dialog, for a moment, and think about how awkward it sounds:

> Mike and Janet invited us for dinner at Mike and Janet's place tonight. What time would you like to go to Mike and Janet's house? Should we wait for Mike and Janet to call us, or should we call Mike and Janet?

The average person would say, instead:

> Mike and Janet invited us to their place. What time do you want to go there? Should we wait for them to call, or should we call them?

Russians streamline their speech in the same manner; pronouns are used to replace nouns that are cumbersome to continue repeating. Russian personal pronouns are declined according to the same rules as nouns.

Case	I	You	He	She	It	We	You	They
Nominative	я	ты	он	она́	оно́	мы	вы	они́
Accusative*	меня́	тебя́	его́	её	его́	нас	вас	их
Prepositional	мне	тебе́	нём	ней	нём	нас	вас	них

continues

continued

Case	I	You	He	She	It	We	You	They
Genitive*	меня́	тебя́	его́	её	его́	нас	вас	их
Dative	мне	тебе́	ему́	ей	ему́	нам	вам	им
Instrumental	мной	тобо́й	им	ей	им	на́ми	ва́ми	и́ми

**Note that the genitive and accusative forms of these personal pronouns are the same. With the exception of the nominative form, he and it are identical. This reduces your memory work quite a bit.*

Let's Wrap It Up

To show off your new skills, practice replacing the nouns in the following few sentences with their appropriate pronouns. (See Appendix B for answers.) Remember to pay attention to gender, case, and number. Whereas English speakers replace most nouns with *it*, Russian requires that the gender match—even though the translated meaning may be *it*.

Exercise 7.1

Example: Ба́бушка покупа́ет проду́кты в магази́не. (The grandmother is buying goods in the grocery store.)

Answer: Она́ покупа́ет проду́кты в магази́не. (She is buying goods in the grocery store.)

1. Друг ви́дел студе́нта в ко́мнате. (A friend saw a student in the room.)
2. Ма́льчик встре́тился с де́вочкой во дворе́. (The boy met with the girl in the yard.)
3. Жена́ что́-то сказа́ла му́жу. (The wife said something to her husband.)
4. в моём ча́е есть молоко́ ! (There is milk in my tea!)

The Least You Need to Know

- Possession is only one function of the genitive case: The majority of prepositions in Russian require genitive, and genitive also indicates absence, or negation.
- With dative case, you will be able to determine the indirect object, or the person or thing that receives the action in a sentence.
- Almost every time you use *with*, you are using the instrumental case.
- The use of personal pronouns will make your speech more natural sounding, and even easier. The gender, number, and case of the personal pronouns that you use must match the nouns that they replace.

Chapter 8

Adjectives and Adverbs

In This Chapter

- Modifying nouns with adjectives
- The adjectives you need
- Adverbs from adjectives
- Impersonal sentences

You've bought a fancy new sports car, and before you even return home with your new toy, you've already made plans to call all your friends and family to make them a little jealous. You dial the number for a colleague from work, and proceed to wax eloquent about the car: "It's bright red and so fast; the design is sleek and sexy—it's a beautiful car." Before you know it, you glance at your watch and realize that you've been talking for 20 minutes; and, what's more, you've been using nothing but a stream of adjectives to describe your new car.

In the last two chapters, you learned how to change nouns to match case. In this chapter, you'll learn how to make those same changes, or declensions, to adjectives in order to "match" adjectives with nouns. Along the way, you'll learn how to form adverbs from those adjectives.

How Adjectives Work

Adjectives are the superheroes of description; they make your conversations smooth and colorful. You don't want to tell your friends that you bought "a car"; you want to tell them you bought "a very expensive, fire-engine red, Italian sports car." Adjectives make these descriptions possible by modifying, or describing, nouns. In fact, you should think of adjectives and nouns as a single unit in Russian. They always match in form and function; that is, adjectives always agree with the nouns they modify in gender, number, and case.

> **Hot Topic**
>
> **Adjectives** are words that describe nouns. An adjective tells something about the noun by answering the question "what kind?" Russian adjectives agree in gender, number, and case with the nouns they modify.

Let's take a look at how adjectives work in Russian. Watch for matching of the ending of the noun and the adjective in gender, case, number and how the underlined adjectival endings are different. At this point you should just notice that they all change. How it happens will come later.

Nominative: Это нóвая маши́на.
EH-tah NOH-vah-yah mah-SHEE-nah.
This is a new car.

Accusative: Я купи́л нóвую маши́ну.
Yah koo-PEEL NOH-voo-yoo mah-SHEE-noo.
I bought a new car.

Prepositional: Я сижу́ в нóвой маши́не.
Yah see-ZHOO VNOH-voy mah-SHEE-nyeh.
I am sitting in a new car.

In beginning to work with and understand adjectives, you should think of adjectives in two parts: the stem and the ending. For example, the adjective Нóвый can be divided in half. The stem, НОВ-, never changes; the ending, -ЫЙ, changes to match the noun it modifies. Declining adjectives is a process of choosing the correct ending to combine with the stem.

A Return to the Nominative

In Chapter 5, you learned how to identify the gender of nouns by their endings in the nominative case. You know that, in general, nouns ending in consonants are masculine; nouns ending in -A or -Я are feminine; and nouns ending in -O and -E are neuter. Adjectives in the nominative case closely follow this pattern.

Here are the declension patterns for adjectives modifying nouns in the nominative case.

Declension Patterns for Adjectives Modifying Nouns in the Nominative Case

Masculine	Feminine	Neuter	Plural	English
нóвый NOH-vwee	нóвая NOH-vah-yah	нóвое NOH-vah-yeh	нóвые NOH-vwee-yeh	new
хорóший hah-ROH-shee	хорóшая hah-ROH-shah-yah	хорóшее hah-ROH-shyeh-yeh	хорóшие hah-ROH-shee-yeh	good
плохóй plah-HOY	плохáя plah-HAH-yah	плохóе plah-HOH-yeh	плохúе plah-HEE-yeh	bad

You may remember some spelling rules that were introduced in Chapter 2. They are especially important to remember now, when you must choose the correct ending for your adjectives. The important notes to remember are the following:

- The stressed ending for masculine adjectives is -ОЙ.
  Это большóй дом. (This is a big house.)
  EH-tah bal-SHOY dohm.

  Это плохóй ромáн. (This is a bad novel.)
  EH-tah plah-HOY pah-MAN.

- After the letters Ж, Ч, Ш, and Щ, if the ending is unstressed, neuter adjectives take the ending -EE, (not -OE).

  Stressed: Здáние—большóе. (The building is big.)
  ZDAH-nee-yeh—bal-SHOH-yeh.

  Unstressed: Утро—хорóшее. (The morning is good.)
  OOH-trah—hah-ROH-shyeh-yeh.

- The vowel -Ы is never written after the letters Г, К, Х, Ж, Ч, Ш, or Щ. The vowel -И is always used in its place.

  Это мáленький гóрод. (This is a small city.)
  EH-tah MAH-len-kee GOR-aht.

Эти стра́ны—больши́е. (These countries are big.)

EH-tee STRAH-nee—bal-SHEE-yeh.

An Evening with the Accusative

As you may recall from Chapter 6, the accusative case in Russian is slightly unusual, because it deals with masculine nouns in two groups: animate nouns (people or animals) and inanimate nouns (things or objects). Remember, this division occurs only for masculine nouns in the singular.

There's no way around it: The accusative case is no fun. Juggling nouns in your brain to determine whether it's masculine or feminine, a person or thing, isn't the most enjoyable way to spend a Saturday night. To reduce confusion, let's discuss adjectives in the accusative case into two parts: animate and inanimate.

The Inanimate

You can't believe your good fortune; it's almost like winning at the roulette table twice, on the same number. Adjectives that modify inanimate masculine and all neuter nouns take the very same accusative endings as the nominative case. The only new ending to learn is the feminine adjectival ending for the accusative.

If you think of adjectives in relation to the nouns they modify, you will find accusative endings extremely simple indeed, because they match exactly. To recap, here are the inanimate masculine and neuter endings (which you already know from the nominative case).

Inanimate Masculine and Neuter Endings

Masculine	English	Neuter	English
но́вый рома́н	new novel	но́вое зда́ние	new building
хоро́ший рома́н	good novel	хоро́шее зда́ние	good building
плохо́й рома́н	bad novel	плохо́е зда́ние	bad building

Feminine nouns in the accusative case take the endings -У or -Ю. To match with these nouns, adjectives in the accusative case that modify feminine nouns take the endings -УЮ or -ЮЮ. As an additional bonus, the plural forms for *all* inanimate adjectives are the same as in the nominative case (-ЫЕ or -ИЕ). Take a look at the adjectival endings in the next chart.

Adjectival Endings for Feminine Nouns in the Accusative Case

Feminine	English	Plural	English
но́вую маши́ну	new car	но́вые часы́	new watch
хоро́шую маши́ну	good car	хоро́шие часы́	good watch
плоху́ю маши́ну	bad car	плохи́е часы́	bad watch

The Animate

If the noun you want to modify is both masculine and animate—that is, a person or animal—its endings will be slightly different. You know that masculine nouns in the accusative take the endings -А or -Я, but the adjectives that modify these nouns take the endings -ОГО or -ЕГО. The following statements compare the nominative and accusative endings.

A Comparison of Nominative and Accusative Endings (Masculine Animate Nouns)

Nominative	English	Accusative	English
Он хоро́ший челове́к.	He is a good person.	Я зна́ю хоро́шего челове́ка.	I know the good person.
Это до́брый врач.	This is a kind doctor.	Я ви́жу до́брого врача́.	I see the kind doctor.

Внима́ние

In a few places in the Russian language—most importantly with the adjectival endings **-ОГО** and **-ЕГО**—the letter **Г** is pronounced as a **В** ("vah"). This pronunciation peculiarity also occurs with the pronoun **Его́** (yeh-VOH) (him), and the word **Сего́дня** (seh-VOH-dnyah) (today). Pay close attention to your pronunciation guides throughout the book to properly pronounce your adjectival endings.

As you learn your accusative endings, be aware that the endings you see for the masculine, animate adjectives are the very same endings for the masculine and neuter adjectives in the genitive case.

In the Mood for Genitive

After you have mastered the endings of the accusative case, you will find the genitive case to be an exercise in the ordinary. In fact, these three facts should brighten your day considerably:

- Masculine and neuter adjectives (and nouns) share the same endings in the genitive, prepositional, dative, and instrumental cases. That's one less ending that you need to learn!
- The endings that you learned for masculine, animate adjectives (and nouns) in the accusative case are the very same endings for masculine and neuter nouns in the genitive case.
- Adjectives modifying feminine nouns in the genitive case take the very same endings in the prepositional, dative, and instrumental cases.

In just a few minutes, you'll see how easy the learning process has become.

Adjectives in the Genitive Case

Masculine/Neuter	Feminine	Plural
но́вого NOH-vah-vah	но́вой NOH-voy	но́вых NOH-vweekh
хоро́шего hah-ROH-sheh-vah	хоро́шей hah-ROH-shey	хоро́ших hah-ROH-sheekh
плохо́го plah-XOH-vah.	плохо́й plah-XOY	плохи́х plah-KHEEKh

You should note that not only do masculine, animate nouns and adjectives share the same endings in the genitive singular, the genitive plural does as well. You will learn the genitive plural of nouns in Chapter 11.

Here are some examples of the genitive in use.

The Genitive Case in Action

Nominative	English	Genitive	English
Это но́вый рома́н.	This is a new novel.	Это а́втор но́вого рома́на.	This is the author of the new novel.
Это но́вая кни́га.	This is a new book.	Это глава́ но́вой кни́ги.	This is a chapter of the new book.

Memory Serves

The genitive case endings for all masculine and neuter adjectives (-**ОГО** or -**ЕГО**) and nouns (-**А** or -**Я**) are the same endings for masculine, animate adjectives (-**ОГО** or -**ЕГО**) and nouns (-**А** or -**Я**) in the accusative case.

Declension 101

You've called all your family and friends, and now you have made it halfway through the phone book. You've boasted to everyone about your new car, the size of its engine, its speed, its color, and the price tag. Now try to put your enthusiasm to work in the following exercise by filling in the blanks with the correct adjectival endings (see Appendix B for answers).

But first, here's the breakdown of the endings you've learned so far.

A Breakdown of the Endings You've Learned So Far

Case	Masculine	Feminine	Neuter	Plural
Nominative	-ЫЙ/-ИЙ	-АЯ/-ЯЯ	-ОЕ/-ЕЕ	-ЫЕ/-ИЕ
Accusative (inanimate)	-ЫЙ/-ИЙ	-УЮ/-ЮЮ	-ОЕ/-ЕЕ	-ЫЕ/-ИЕ
Accusative (animate)	-ОГО/-ЕГО	———	———	-ЫХ/-ИХ
Genitive	-ОГО/-ЕГО	-ОЙ/-ЕЙ	-ОГО/-ЕГО	-ЫХ/-ИХ

Exercise 8.1

Example: Они́ (new) но́в________________ друзья́.

Answer: Они́ но́вые друзья́.

1. Это дом но́в ________________ сосе́да (neighbor).
2. Это (big) больш ________________ кни́га.
3. Он пацие́нт (patient) хоро́ш ________________ врача́.
4. Я чита́ю (read) хоро́ш ________________ книги.
5. Она́ купи́ла (bought) но́в ________________ маши́ну.

Getting It Together

You're halfway there. With a little practice, you'll find the next three case endings for prepositional, dative, and instrumental a breeze. All the exceptions and irregularities of Russian adjectives lie behind you—you will see in the chart that follows that the remaining cases are blissfully predictable.

Prepositional, Dative, and Instrumental Case Endings for Adjectives

Case	Masculine/Neuter	Feminine	Plural
Prepositional	-ОМ/-ЕМ	-ОЙ/-ЕЙ	-ЫХ/-ИХ
Dative	-ОМУ/-ЕМУ	-ОЙ/-ЕЙ	-ЫМ/-ИМ
Instrumental	-ЫМ/-ИМ	-ОЙ/-ЕЙ	-ЫМИ/-ИМИ

Внима́ние

You will notice that the endings for adjectives in the dative plural (-ЫМ/-ИМ) are the same endings for masculine adjectives in the instrumental singular (-ЫМ/-ИМ); you should pay close attention to the nouns they modify in order to determine the case. The dative plural of nouns is -АМ/-ЯМ, whereas the masculine and neuter, instrumental singular noun takes the endings -ОМ/-ЕМ.

A Preposition for You

Learning the case endings for adjectives and nouns may seem like a good idea, in theory; but you need to know how the cases work in everyday speech. The following sentences help you focus on what the prepositional case does, and why it is important.

Prepositional Case Endings for Adjectives

Nominative	English	Prepositional	English
Это большо́е зда́ние.	This is a big building.	Я рабо́таю в большо́м зда́нии.	I work in the big building.
Это краси́вая шля́па.	This is a pretty hat.	Она́ в краси́вой шля́пе сего́дня.	She is in a pretty hat today.
Это но́вый парк.	This is a new park.	Мы гуля́ем в но́вом па́рке.	We stroll in the new park.

If the Case Calls for Dative

Indirect objects take the dative case in Russian. Here are some examples of adjectives at work.

Dative Case Endings for Adjectives

Nominative	English	Dative	English
Он наш но́вый учи́тель.	He is our new teacher.	Он говори́т но́вому учи́телю.	He is talking to the new teacher.
Она́—хоро́шая ба́бушка.	She is a good grandmother.	Дочь написа́ла хоро́шей ба́бушке.	The daughter wrote to the good grandmother.

Lay Out the Instrumental

Do you feel comfortable with your progress so far? You'll find the instrumental case as easy going as the rest. You'll find no surprises in the following phrases.

Instrumental Case Endings for Adjectives

Nominative	English	Instrumental	English
Они́ бли́зкие друзья́.	They are close friends.	Они́ встреча́ются с бли́зкими друзья́ми.	They meet with close friends.
Это кра́сная ру́чка.	This is a red pen.	Я пишу́ кра́сной ру́чкой.	I write with a red pen.
Это хоро́ший челове́к.	This is a good person.	Легко́ рабо́тать с хоро́шим челове́ком.	It is easy to work with a good person.

Adverbs

You know adjectives have a very simple purpose—they modify nouns. The question you may be asking yourself—What modifies adjectives?—has a simple answer: *adverbs*. Adverbs also modify other adverbs, verbs, and prepositional phrases. Anything an adjective can't handle by itself, an adverb modifies with ease.

Adverb and Mix

As your final conversation winds to a close, you can't think of any other way to describe your new car. Not wanting to let those long-distance minutes go to waste, you reach into your pocket of expressions and throw out some impersonal sentences, or brief statements of fact. "It's easy to drive." "It's simple to operate." "It handles well." Impersonal sentences use the subject *it* in English, but in Russian they require only a properly formed adverb.

Hot Topic

Adverbs are words that modify adjectives, other adverbs, verbs, and prepositional phrases. Adverbs answer the question "**Как?**" (kahk) (how?).

Get ready to clap your hands for joy—adverbs in Russian don't decline. They take only one form, every time you use them. Think for a moment about how you form adverbs in English: The adjective *interesting* becomes an adverb by adding "-ly" to form *interestingly*. From *easy* to *easily*, it's a simple matter of swapping the endings. The same is true for Russian. Locate the adjective интере́сный (een-teh-RES-nee) (*interesting*). Take the ending -ЫЙ, and replace it with -О. That's it. Интере́сно (*interestingly*) is your newly formed adverb.

The following chart lists some of the most common adjectives and their adverb partners. Take special note of the stress, because it sometimes changes from adverb to adjective. Please note that not all adjectives can change into adverbs.

Commonly Used Adjectives and Adverbs

Adjective	English	Adverb	English
плохо́й plah-HOY	bad, poor	пло́хо PLOH-hah	badly, poorly
краси́вый krah-SEE-vwee	beautiful	краси́во krah-SEE-vah	beautifully
чёрный CHYOR-nee	black	чЕрно́ cher-noh	—
си́ний SEE-nee	blue	—	—
дешёвый deh-SHYOH-vwee	cheap	дёшево DYOH-shyeh-vah	cheaply
бли́зкий BLEES-kee	close	бли́зко BLEES-kah	closely

Adjective	English	Adverb	English
холóдный hah-LOHD-nee	cold	хóлодно HOL-ahd-nah	coldly
тёмный TYOHM-nee	dark	темнó tehm-NOH	darkly
дорогóй dah-rah-GOY	dear, expensive	дóрого DOHR-ah-gah	dearly, expensively
трýдный TROOD-nee	difficult	трýдно trod-NOH	difficultly
тяжёлый tyah-ZHYOH-lee	difficult, heavy	тяжелó tyah-zheh-LOH	difficultly, heavily
лёгкий LYOH-kee	easy, light	легкó leg-KOH	easily, lightly
знакóмый znah-KOH-mee	familiar	знакóмо znah-KOH-mah	—
далёкий dahl-YOH-kee	far	далекó dah-leh-KOH	far away
свобóдный svah-BOH-dnee	free	свобóдно svah-BOH-dnah	freely
хорóший hah-ROH-shee	good	хорошó hah-rah-SHOH	good, well
зелёный zehl-YOH-nee	green	зелЕнó zehleh-NOH	—
здорóвый zdah-ROH-vwee	healthy, strong, big	здóрово ZDOH-rah-vah	well
высóкий vwee-COH-kee	high	высóко vwee-SOHsah-kah	highly
жáркий ZHAR-kee	hot	жáрко ZHAR-kah	hotly
интерéсный een-teh-RES-nee	interesting	интерéсно een-the-RES-noh	interestingly
свéтлый SVEH-tlee	light	светлó sveht-LOH	lightly
нúзкий NEES-kee	low	нúзко NEES-kah	lowly
нýжный NOOZH-nee	necessary	нýжно NOOZH-nah	necessarily

continues

Commonly Used Adjectives and Adverbs (continued)

Adjective	English	Adverb	English
ста́рый STAH-ree	old	ста́ро́ STAH-roh	—
гото́вый gah-TOH-vwee	ready	гото́во go-TOH-voh	—
кра́сный KRAS-nee	red	кра́сно́ KRAS-noh	—
кру́глый KROOG-lee	round	кру́гло KROOG-loh	—
серьёзный sehr-YOH-znee	serious	серьёзно sehr-YOH-znah	seriously
просто́й prah-STOY	simple	про́сто PROH-stah	simply
сла́дкий SLAHT-kee	sweet	сла́дко SLAHT-kah	sweetly
тёплый TYOH-plee	warm	тепло́ tehp-LOH	warmly
бе́лый BYEH-lee	white	бе́ло́ be-LOH	—

Memory Serves

All English sentences normally have a subject, even if it is strictly informal and doesn't refer to a specific person or thing. *It's* often fills the role of the subject in English. Many Russian sentences have no subjects, strictly speaking. In such sentences, no verb is used for *is*. Adverbs (ending in **-o**) are regularly translated into English as adjectives in sentences with the informal *it*.

Здесь прия́тно. It is pleasant here. (Literally: Here pleasant.)

Рабо́тать там легко́. It is easy to work there. (Literally: To work there easy.)

На ули́це хо́лодно. It is cold outside. (Literally: On street cold.)

Could You Be Less Personal?

One of the significant differences between English and Russian is the use of adjectives. English speakers say, "I'm cold," or even, "It's cold today." However, to say those same sentences in Russian requires an adverb. Do you remember your idioms from Chapter 4? They come into play here, when you use adjectives to act as the subjects of your impersonal sentences.

If you want to talk about yourself (or someone else), specifically about how you are feeling, you need to use an adverb and the dative case. For example:

Мне хóлодно. Вам жáрко?

Mnyeh HOL-ahd-nah. Vahm ZHAR-kah?

I am cold. Are you hot?

If you want to use a prepositional phrase, such as "in the room," that phrase needs to be modified by an adverb in Russian. For example:

В кóмнате теплó. На ýлице грязно.

FKOH-mnah-tyeh tehp-LOH. Nah-OOL-eets-yeh GRYAH-znah.

It's warm in the room. It's dirty in the street.

Finally, you can use adverbs with the infinitive forms of verbs. You'll learn the specifics of verb use next chapter, but without any knowledge of verbs at all, adverbs make it possible to use them.

Учи́ть рýсский язы́к легкó.

OOH-cheet ROOS-kee YAH-zeek leg-KOH.

It's easy to learn Russian.

Хорошó рабóтать на сóлнце.

Hah-rah-SHOH rah-BOH-taht nah-SOLN-tsyeh.

It's good to work in the sun.

How Do You Deliver?

You may have exhausted the ears of your friends and family, but don't let that stop you from expressing yourself. Take your excess energy and reinforce what you've learned by filling in the blanks of the following exercise with the correct adjective or adverb.

Exercise 8.2

Example: Он ______________________ (strong) челове́к.

Answer: Он си́льный челове́к.

He is a strong man.

1. Пла́вать ле́том ______________________ (it is good).

   It is good to swim in the summer.

2. На у́лице ______________________ (it is hot).

   It is hot outside.

3. Эта маши́на— ______________________ (old).

   This car is old.

4. Я зна́ю (know) ______________________ (serious) ма́льчика.

   I know a serious boy.

5. Они́ ______________________ (good) лю́ди.

   They are good people.

6. Она́ купи́ла ______________________ (white) хлеб.

   She bought white bread.

7. Он врач ______________________ (big) больни́цы.

   He is a doctor in a big hospital.

The Least You Need to Know

- Adjectives in Russian can be divided into two parts: the stem and the ending. The ending must be changed to match the noun it modifies.
- Adjectives in Russian must agree with the nouns they modify in gender, number, and case.
- Adverbs can be easily formed from adjectives by replacing the adjective ending with -O.
- Impersonal sentences often employ adverbs as the subjects. In these sentences, adverbs are translated into English as adjectives.

Chapter 9

All About Russian Verbs

In This Chapter

- Two types of verb conjugation
- Putting common verbs to use
- Using negated pronouns
- Asking questions

Nouns and adjectives are like dollar bills—but verbs are the investment brokers that take your words and make your language rich and profitable. In this chapter, you learn how to use verbs of different types to put your language skills in motion.

In the Name of the Verb

If someone asked you to describe your day, you could almost respond without thinking. You woke up; you ate breakfast and skimmed the newspaper. You went to work and talked with co-workers; then you took the afternoon off and relaxed.

Whether your day was something like that or radically different, you need verbs to express activity. Verbs indicate actions, motion, or states of being. As a native English-speaker, you instinctively know how to change verbs to suit the occasion. Today you *write;* yesterday you *wrote;* tomorrow it will be *written.* Matching your verb with the right tense can be as simple as changing the ending: I look, or I looked. You may also need an internal change: We do, or we did. Russian verbs experience the same phenomenon, but the *conjugation* patterns are far more predictable.

> **Hot Topic**
>
> **Conjugation** is the change that verbs undergo to show who or what is performing the action. Conjugation also indicates tense—whether something is happening now, will happen later, or has already happened.

There are two types of Russian verbs: E type and И type, also known as first-conjugation and second-conjugation verbs. They each follow the same pattern of endings, with only slight differences in the preceding vowels. For now we'll focus on the present-tense forms of first and second-conjugation verbs. Verbs in the past and future tense are explained later in the book.

E-Type (First-Conjugation) Verbs

In Chapter 4, you learned some verb cognates in their infinitive, or unconjugated, form. You may not have thought about it, but English verbs also conjugate, though they undergo only a few changes in the process. Observe the conjugation of the English verb "to do."

Conjugation of the English Verb "to do"

Person	Singular	Plural
First	I do	We do
Second	You do	You do
Third	He/she/it does	They do

To draw the appropriate comparison, keep in mind the change of the verb "to do," from "you do" to "he does." Russian verbs change form to match first, second, and third person, both singular and plural.

As you approach first-conjugation verbs, here is the paradigm you should know. Make yourself a note card and commit these endings to memory. The process: Drop the infinitive ending -ТЬ from the stem and add the appropriate ending.

Russian First-Conjugation Verb Endings

Person	Singular	Ending	Plural	Ending
First	Я	-У/-Ю	МЫ	-ЕМ/-ЁМ
Second	ТЫ	-ЕШЬ/-ЁШЬ	ВЫ	-ЕТЕ/-ЁТЕ
Third	ОН/ОНА/ОНО	-ЕТ/-ЁТ	ОНИ	-УТ/-ЮТ

Now let's do the verb "to do" again, this time in Russian. Locate the stem and the process becomes simple—remove the infinitive ending -ТЬ from the stem, and add your endings to the stem.

Hot Topic

E-type verbs, or first-conjugation verbs, have a predictable pattern of endings. They retain the vowel -**А** and add the appropriate endings. Within a first-conjugation verb, the endings and vowels -**У** or -**Ю** and -**Е** or -**Ё** are always consistent.

Conjugation of an E-Type Verb: де́лать ("to do")

Person	Singular	English	Plural	English
First	я де́лаю DEH-lah-yoo	I do	мы де́лаем DEH-lah-yem	We do
Second	ты де́лаешь DEH-lah-yesh	You do (familiar)	вы де́лаете DEH-lah-yet-yeh	You do (formal)
Third	он/она́/оно́ де́лает DEH-lah-yet	He/she/it does	они́ де́лают DEH-lah-yoot	They do

The new endings you see on these verbs will remain consistent throughout your entire conjugation experience; the only difference you will observe is a variation in the vowels that are used in the process. An important note to remember, however, is that first-conjugation verbs whose stems end in -АТЬ add the vowel Е (hence the name "E-type") in the ТЫ, ОН, ОНА, ОНО, МЫ, and ВЫ conjugations.

Rogue Verbs

Within first-conjugation verbs, a few rogue verbs have been allowed to wander the streets. Conjugating the verbs requires some inside knowledge (if in doubt, your bilingual dictionary will help), because their patterns are inconsistent. To expose these verbs for who they are, here are two of the most common exceptions.

Conjugation of an E-Type Verb: брать ("to take")

Person	Singular	English	Plural	English
First	я берý beh-ROO	I take	мы берём behr-YOHM	We take
Second	ты берёшь behr-YOHSH	You take (familiar)	вы берёте behr-YOHT-yeh	You take (formal)
Third	он/онá/онó берёт behr-YOHT	He/she/it takes	онú берýт beh-ROOT	They take

Conjugation of an E-Type Verb: давáть ("to give")

Person	Singular	English	Plural	English
First	я даю́ dah-YOO	I give	мы даём dah-YOHM	We give
Second	ты даёшь dah-YOHSH	You give (familiar)	вы даёте dah-YOHT-yeh	You give (formal)
Third	он/онá/онó даёт dah-YOHT	He/she/it gives	онú даю́т dah-YOOT	They give

Don't let the unusual pair of "to give" and "to take" scare you. They are the exceptions, and by no means the rule.

To the Chalkboard!

Did your algebra teacher ever call you to the chalkboard to explain to the class the one and only equation you hadn't heard? Fear not. This is nothing like that. After you feel comfortable with the verbs you know so far, try to complete the following sentences with the correct form of the verb. Remember, the subject and verb must be in agreement.

Exercise 9.1

Example: (брать) Он ____________ берёт ____________ кни́гу.

1. (рабо́тать) Он ____________ в музе́е.
2. (открыва́ть) Они́ ____________ магази́н в во́семь часо́в.
3. (закрыва́ть) Я ____________ дверь.
4. (начина́ть) Мы ____________ учи́ться.
5. (изуча́ть) Она́ ____________ ру́сский язы́к.
6. (игра́ть) Вы ____________ на гита́ре.
7. (ду́мать) Что ты ____________ обэ́том?

The following chart lists some of the most commonly used first-conjugation verbs. Read through the chart a few times and practice conjugating the verbs.

Commonly Used First-Conjugation Verbs

Russian	Pronunciation	English
спра́шивать	sprah-SHEE-vaht	to ask, question
меня́ть	men-YAHT	to change, exchange
закрыва́ть	zah-kree-VAHT	to close
де́лать	DEH-laht	to do, make
конча́ть	kohn-CHAHT	to end
объясня́ть	ahb-yah-SNYAHT	to explain
дава́ть	dah-VAHT	to give
ве́шать	VEH-shat	to hang
за́втракать	zahf-trah-KAHT	to have breakfast
у́жинать	OOH-zhee-naht	to have dinner
обе́дать	ahb-YED-aht	to have lunch
помога́ть	pah-mah-GAHT	to help
слу́шать	SLOO-shat	to listen
жить	zheet	to live
встреча́ть	fstreh-CHAT	to meet
открыва́ть	aht-kree-VAHT	to open

continues

Commonly Used First-Conjugation Verbs (continued)

Russian	Pronunciation	English
игрáть	eeg-RAHT	to play
читáть	chee-TAHT	to read
покáзывать	pah-KAH-zee-vaht	to show
начинáть	nah-chee-NAHT	to start, begin
изучáть	eeh-zoo-CHAHT	to study, learn
брать	braht	to take
дýмать	DOO-maht	to think
понимáть	pah-nee-MAHT	to understand
ждать	zhdaht	to wait
желáть	zheh-LAHT	to wish, hope
рабóтать	rah-BOH-that	to work

Memory Serves

As in English, a subject (noun or pronoun) can be followed by two verbs in Russian. The first verb conjugates to match the subject, and the second verb follows in its infinite form. For instance: "I want to understand" becomes "**Я хочý понимáть.**"

What Strong Verbs You Have!

Unlike nouns, which indicate their gender or case by their vowel endings, you can't always identify verbs by the vowels of their stem. It's true, most verbs that end with -АТЬ are first-conjugation verbs; however, other vowels can appear. The only way to recognize the difference between first- and second-conjugation verbs is to memorize them. The first, second, and third person singular and plural endings that you learned for first-conjugation verbs are nearly identical for second-conjugation verbs, but you will see a difference in vowel endings (first vowel of the ending), namely И instead of Е (hence the name, И-type conjugation).

И-Type (Second-Conjugation) Verbs

In beginning to conjugate И-type, or second-conjugation, verbs, you need to think of vowels as part of the infinitive ending of the verb. Most И-type verbs end with -ИТЬ; you should think of this as the ending, which needs to be removed. Some И-type verbs add a consonant in the first person singular conjugation, as you will see in the following charts. Let's begin by observing the conjugation of a classic И-type verb, "to teach."

Conjugation of an И-Type Verb: учи́ть ("to teach")

Person	Singular	English	Plural	English
First	я учу́ oo-CHOO	I teach	мы у́чим OO-cheem	We teach
Second	ты у́чишь OO-cheesh	You teach (familiar)	вы у́чите OO-cheet-yeh	You teach (formal)
Third	он/она́/оно́ у́чит OO-cheet	He/she/it teaches	они́ у́чат OO-chaht	They teach

You have probably noticed that the final endings in both E-type and И-type verbs are almost always identical—that is У/Ю, ШЬ, Т, М, and ТЕ. In all persons except the first singular and third plural, the first conjugation has the vowel -Е (or -Ё), and the second conjugation has the vowel -И. For the third person plural, first-conjugation verbs have the ending -УТ/-ЮТ and second-conjugation has the ending -АТ/-ЯТ.

Commit the following endings to memory.

Russian Second-Conjugation Verb Endings

Person	Singular	Ending	Plural	Ending
First	Я	-У/-Ю	МЫ	-ИМ
Second	ТЫ	-ИШЬ	ВЫ	-ИТЕ
Third	ОН/ОНА/ОНО	-ИТ	ОНИ	-АТ/-ЯТ

Let's take a look at another important verb, люби́ть ("to like, love"). Notice the additional consonant л in the first person singular.

Conjugation of an И-Type Verb: любить ("to like, love")

Person	Singular	English	Plural	English
First	я люблю́ loo-BLOO	I like	мы лю́бим LOO-beem	We like
Second	ты лю́бишь LOO-beesh	You like (familiar)	вы лю́бите LOO-beet-yeh	You like (formal)
Third	он/она́/оно́ лю́бит LOO-beet	He/she/it likes	они́ лю́бят LOO-byat	They like

Not all И-type verbs end with the infinitive ending -ИТЬ. The importance of including this part of the ending can readily be seen with the conjugation of the verb сиде́ть (see-DYET) ("to sit"). Note its conjugation pattern in the following chart.

Conjugation of an И-Type Verb: сидеть ("to sit, be sitting")

Person	Singular	Ending	Plural	Ending
First	я сижу́ see-ZHOO	I sit	мы сиди́м see-DEEM	We sit
Second	ты сиди́шь see-DEESH	You sit (familiar)	вы сиди́те see-DEET-yeh	You sit (formal)
Third	он/она́/оно́ сиди́т see-DEET	He/she/it sits	они́ сидя́т see-DYAHT	They sit

Verb Encounters

Many И-type verbs incur *consonant mutation* or change in the first person singular. For the purposes of this exercise, you will not use the first person singular. As before, complete the blanks using correctly conjugated verbs. Pay close attention to your subject, specifically its gender and number.

Внима́ние

A handful of Russian verbs have different infinitive endings than **-ТЬ**. Be aware that verbs like **идти́** (eed-TEE) ("to walk"), **мочь** (mohch) ("to be able"), and **нести́** (nes-TEE) ("to carry") are irregular infinitives. The number of these verbs is limited to about a dozen, and you will learn most of them throughout this book.

Exercise 9.2

Example: (сиде́ть) Мы сиди́м в маши́не.

1. (гото́вить to prepare) Мой брат ________________ дома́шнюю рабо́ту.
2. (находи́ть to find) Доктора́ __________ но́вую информа́цию ка́ждый день.
3. (слы́шать to hear) Мы ________________________________ му́зыку.
4. (корми́ть to feed) Хоро́шая мать ______________________ свои́х дете́й.
5. (лови́ть to catch) Вы хорошо́ ______________________________ ры́бу.
6. (шути́ть to joke) Он всегда́ ________________________________.
7. (стоя́ть to stand) Почему́ ты ________________________ так бли́зко?
8. (ве́рить to believe) Мои́ друзья́ не ______________________ мне.
9. (вы́глядеть to look) Ни́на хорошо́ ______________________ сего́дня.
10. (броди́ть to stroll) Ива́н всегда́ ____________________ по у́лицам оди́н.

Hot Topic

Consonant mutations occur in many И-type verbs in the first person singular. That is, the final consonant of the root verb changes in the first person, or adds another consonant before the ending. This change occurs only in the first person singular.

The following chart lists several of the most common И-type verbs. If the verbs experience a consonant mutation (in the first person singular), that change is noted in parentheses. A dash (-) indicates that a consonant is added; otherwise, the final consonant is replaced. Pay attention to the changes as you continue to practice conjugating your verbs as you learn them.

Commonly Used Second-Conjugation Verbs

Russian	Pronunciation	Meaning
люби́ть(-л)	loo-BEET	to like, love
сиде́ть(ж)	see-DYET	to sit, be sitting
учи́ть	oo-CHEET	to teach

continues

Commonly Used Second-Conjugation Verbs (continued)

Russian	Pronunciation	Meaning
кури́ть	koo-REET	to smoke
плати́ть(ч)	plah-TEET	to pay
говори́ть	gah-vah-REET	to speak
ви́деть(ж)	VEE-det	to see
ве́рить	VEH-reet	to believe
звони́ть	zvah-NEET	to call (by phone)
благодари́ть	blah-gah-dah-REET	to thank
беспоко́ить	bes-pah-KOH-eet	to worry, upset
броди́ть(ж)	brah-DEET	to wander, stroll
входи́ть(ж)	fhah-DEET	to enter
вы́глядеть	VWEE-glyah-dyet	to look, appear
выходи́ть(ж)	vwee-hah-DEET	to exit
стоя́ть	stah-YAHT	to stand, be standing
стро́ить	STROH-eet	to build
чи́стить(щ)	CHEE-steet	to clean
шути́ть(щ)	shoo-TEET	to joke
гото́вить(-л)	gah-TOH-veet	to prepare, cook
горе́ть	gahr-YET	to burn, be on fire
дари́ть	dah-REET	to give a present
дели́ть	deh-LEET	to divide
дружи́ть	droo-ZHEET	to befriend
знако́мить(-л)	znah-KOH-meet	to introduce
зна́чить	ZNAH-cheet	to mean, signify
корми́ть(-л)	kahr-MEET	to feed
крича́ть	kree-CHAHT	to scream
лови́ть(-л)	lah-VEET	to catch
находи́ть(ж)	nah-hah-DEET	to find
слы́шать	SLEE-shaht	to hear
по́мнить	POHM-neet	to remember
проводи́ть(ж)	prah-vah-DEET	to spend (time)
проси́ть(ш)	prah-SEET	to ask, request
служи́ть	sloo-ZHEET	to serve
смотре́ть	smah-TRET	to watch
спать(-л)	spaht	to sleep
ста́вить(-л)	STAH-veet	to stand, place something

It's a Question of Question

Asking questions provides you with critical information and allows you to benefit from the knowledge of others. Right now, you'll want to focus on questions with "yes" or "no" answers to keep matters simple. As you learn more words and idioms throughout the book, you will be able to ask for opinions and feedback, but let's take it easy and practice using the verbs that you have learned.

Forming questions in Russian is unusually simple. In fact, you don't need to know anything more than the necessary verb. You simply use the intonation of your voice to change any statement into a question. For example:

> Ва́ши де́ти лю́бят смотре́ть телеви́зор.
> VAH-shee DEH-tee LOOB-yaht smoh-TREHT teh-leh-VEE-zar.
> Your children like to watch television.
>
> Ва́ши де́ти лю́бят смотре́ть телеви́зор?
> VAH-shee DEH-tee LOOB-yaht smoh-TREHT teh-leh-VEE-zar?
> Do your children like to watch television?

English speakers sometimes include the word *do* to form questions; however, this auxiliary word does not exist in Russian. To change the statement into a question, you need only to raise your voice at the end of the sentence. Think about how you would ask the question in English, and use the same rising inflection with the Russian question.

Was That Your Question?

Another simple way to form questions is to use negation, or in English, the word *not*. "You don't watch television?" or "Didn't you just say that …?" are common examples. You can ask questions negatively—that is, with the particle не (nyeh) (*not*), by using не (nyeh) before the verb.

> Ва́ши де́ти не смо́трят телеви́зор?
> VAH-shee DEH-tee neh SMOH-tryaht teh-leh-VEE-zar?
> Your children don't watch television?

The Survey Says …

Answering questions is as simple as asking them. You can use the words Да (dah) (*yes*) and Нет (nyet) (*no*) to respond to most questions. For example:

Вы говори́те по-ру́сски? Vwee gah-vah-REET-yeh pah-ROOS-kee? Do you speak Russian?	Да, я говорю́ по-ру́сски. Dah, yah gah-vahr-YOO pah-ROOS-kee. Yes, I speak Russian.
Ты не говори́шь по-ру́сски? Tee neh gah-vah-REESH pah-ROOS-kee? Do you not speak Russian?	Нет, я не говорю́ по-ру́сски. Nyet, yah neh gah-vahr-YOO pah-ROOS-kee. No, I don't speak Russian.

You can vary the forms of your negative questions and answers using the words *never*, *nothing*, and *no one*. Russian has another unusual feature: the double negative. If you use the negated pronoun нет, you must also use the particle не with the verb. To begin, here are the six interrogative pronouns with their negative counterparts.

Interrogative Pronouns

Pronoun	English	Negative Pronoun	English
кто? ktoh?	who?	никто́ nee-KTOH	no one
кого́ kah-VOH?	whom?	никого́ nee-kah-VOH	no one
что? shtoh?	what?	ничего́ nee-cheh-VOH	nothing
когда́? kahg-DAH?	when?	никогда́ nee-kahg-DAH	never
где? gdyeh?	where?	нигде́ nee-gdyeh	nowhere
куда́? koo-DAH?	to where?	никуда́ nee-koo-DAH	nowhere

Observe the following examples:

Он рабо́тает. He works.
Ohn rah-BOH-tah-yet.

Он не рабо́тает. He does not work.
Ohn neh rah-BOH-tah-yet.

Он никогда́ не рабо́тает. He never works.
Ohn nee-kahg-DAH neh rah-BOH-tah-yet.

Он говори́т. He speaks.
Ohn gah-vah-REET.

Он не говори́т. He does not speak.
Ohn neh gah-vah-REET.

Он ничего́ не говори́т. He isn't saying anything.
Ohn nee-cheh-VOH neh gah-vah-REET.

What's on Your Mind?

Using what you have learned about verb conjugation and double negation, respond to the following questions. Don't forget to use the particle не before your verb!

Exercise 9.3

Example: Что вы зна́ете?

Answer: Я ничего́ не зна́ю.

1. Кого́ вы ви́дите? ______________________________.
2. Когда́ ты рабо́таешь? ______________________________.
3. Что вы де́лаете? ______________________________.
4. Кто э́то зна́ет? ______________________________.
5. Где вы слу́жите? ______________________________.

The Least You Need to Know

- Russian has two types of verbs: first-conjugation (E-type) and second-conjugation (И-type) verbs.
- E-type verbs, with a few exceptions, follow a regular pattern of conjugation.
- И-type verbs often undergo consonant mutations to the stem verb, and use the vowels A and Я in third person plural.
- Forming questions in Russian is as simple as raising your voice to inflect the end of the sentence.

- Double negation in Russian requires that negative pronouns such as никтó (*no one*), никогó (*no one* accusative), ничегó (*nothing*), никогдá (*never*) and нигдé (*nowhere*) use the particle не.

Part 3 Traveling Around

After you immerse yourself in the basics of Russian grammar, you will be able to converse on a broad range of subjects with the help of the right phrases and vocabulary. In this section, you will learn how to leap across the cultural bridge—both physically (by plane, train, or automobile) and through conversation. You will expand your vocabulary, increase the fluidity of your speech, and acquire some important conversational skills.

Chapter 10

Meetings and Greetings

In This Chapter

- Hello, there!
- Polite and familiar forms of address
- Professions
- Getting information: question words

In the last few chapters, you learned how to create and organize simple sentences, using verbs and nouns in their appropriate cases, and how to ask yes-no questions. Throughout this chapter, we will be taking the same concepts that you have already learned and using them to create short conversations.

You've decided to brave the skies; and, as you stare out the window of the plane, you notice that the person sitting next to you mumbles something in Russian as the plane begins to ascend. Here is your opportunity to test some of your newly acquired skills.

Have We Met Before?

No matter how well you learn the words and grammar of the Russian language, the real test arrives when you begin a conversation with another person speaking Russian. Reading Pushkin in the original is an admirable goal, but you need to master the basic "hellos" and "goodbyes" of conversation to begin communicating effectively in Russian. Believe it or not, Russians engage in the same small talk that Americans engage in every day. "Hi, how are you?" "Where do you live?" "What do you do for a living?" All translate almost exactly into Russian. The following conversation openers will help to get you started.

Культу́ра

When most Americans ask the question "How are you doing?" the expected response is a brief "fine" or "pretty good." Russians, however, pay close attention to the answer. If you answer "so-so," they will often ask what troubles you. Be aware that your answer to this basic question could begin a lengthy conversation. When in doubt, say **Хорошо́** (hah-rah-SHOH) (*good*).

Forms of Address

There are two forms of address in Russian—the *polite you* form (the Вы form) and the *familiar you* form (the Ты form). The form of address you choose when beginning a conversation is determined by your relationship to the person with whom you are talking. Using the familiar form of hello здра́вствуй (ZDRAH-fst-vwee) with someone you don't know very well is considered to be extremely rude. In fact, unless you are speaking with family or close friends, you will almost always want to address people as Вы (pronounced "vwee"), using the appropriate conjugation of verb to match. It is worth noting that many younger Russians have begun to use the familiar Ты (pronounced "twee") with more and more frequency.

The Вы Forms of Address (the Polite Forms)

The following chart provides some conversation openers in the polite form.

Polite Openers

Russian	Pronunciation	English Meaning
Здра́вствуйте!	ZDRAH-fstwee-tyeh	Hello!
До́брый день(ве́чер)!	DOH-bree DEHN (VEH-chehr)	Good afternoon (evening)
Господи́н	gah-spah-DEEN	Mr. (Sir)
Госпожа́	gah-spah-ZHAH	Ms. (Ma'am)

Russian	Pronunciation	English Meaning
Меня́ зову́т …	men-YAH zah-VOOT…	My name is …
Как вас зову́т?	kahk vahs zah-VOOT	What is your name?
Как вы пожива́ете?	kahk vwee pah-zhee-VAH-yet-yeh	How are you doing?
Спаси́бо, хорошо́.	spah-SEE-bah, hah-rah-SHOH	Thank you, well.
Спаси́бо, не пло́хо.	spah-SEE-bah, neh PLOH-kah	Thank you, not bad.
Спаси́бо, так себе́.	spah-SEE-bah, tahk seh-BYEH	Thank you, so-so.

The Ты Forms of Address (the Familiar Forms)

Your comrade on the plane immediately takes a liking to you; and, after only a few minutes of conversation says, "Пожалуйста, говори со мной на ты." You have made quite an impression and can now begin to speak with him on familiar terms using the Ты forms of address. The following phrases will help you make the switch.

Familiar Openers

Russian	Pronunciation	English Meaning
Здра́вствуй!	ZDRAHfst-vwee	Hello!
Приве́т!	pree-VYET	Hi!
Меня́ зову́т …	men-YAH zah-VOOT…	My name is …
Как тебя́ зову́т?	kahk the-BYAH zah-VOOT	What's your name?
Как ты пожива́ешь?	kahk twee pah-zhee-VAH-yesh	How are you?
Как дела́?	kahk deh-LAH	How are things?
Я не могу́ пожа́ловаться.	yah neh mah-GOO pah-ZHAL-ah-vaht-syah	I can't complain.
Ну, ла́дно.	noo, LAD-nah	Okay.
В чём де́ло?	fchyohm DEH-lah	What's up?
Ничего́ осо́бенного.	nee-chyeh-VOH ah-SOH-beh-nah-vah	Nothing much.

Getting Nosy

You thought you had begun an everyday conversation with your new Russian friend, but within five minutes you find yourself telling him about your pets back home, the peculiar eating habits of your boss at work, and your thoughts on the latest trade embargos. As you converse with him, you notice that he has an unusual accent that

Hot Topic

Приве́т is informal for *hello* all across Russia. More often than not, however, you will want to use the familiar **Здра́вствуй** and formal **Здра́вствуйте** to indicate *hello*.

you can't quite place, and he uses certain gestures and hand movements you've never seen before.

Sooner or later, you will want to ask him where he lives or what country he's from. Not only that, but as a polite Russian, he'll probably ask you the same question. To properly ask and respond, you should familiarize yourself with the verb Жить ("to live"). The following table shows you its conjugation.

The Verb ЖИТЬ ("to live")

Person	Singular	English Meaning	Plural	English Meaning
First	я живу́ zhee-VOO	I live	мы живём zhee-VYOHM	We live
Second	ты живёшь zhee-VYOHSH	You live (familiar)	вы живёте zhee-VYOH-tyeh	You live (formal)
Third	он/она́ живёт zhee-VYOHT	He/she lives	они живу́т zhee-VOOT	They live

Он живёт в Аме́рике. Они́ живу́т в Бо́стоне.
Ohn zhee-VYOHT vah-MYEH-reek-yeh. ah-NEE zhee-VOOT fBOAH-sto-nyeh.
He lives in America. They live in Boston.

Let's begin forming some questions. To ask where someone lives, use the question word Где (*where*).

Formal use:
Где вы живёте?
Gdyeh vwee zhee-VYOH-tyeh?
Where do you live?

Informal use:
Где ты живёшь?
Gdyeh twee zhee-VYOHSH?
Where do you live?

Response:
Я живу́ в …
Yah zhee-VOO v …
I live in …

Keep in mind that most countries end with the vowel ending -ИЯ, and are feminine. Especially important to remember at this point is the difference between Соединённые Шта́ты and Аме́рика. Just as "United States of America" is plural in English (*States*), it remains plural in Russian. *America* used by itself is a singular, feminine noun.

Remember to express location, where you live, using the preposition В followed by the prepositional case. To refresh your memory, refer to Chapters 6 and 7 for the declension of nouns in their cases.

You can question people less directly by asking them what city or country they are from. Use the preposition ИЗ + the genitive case to form your answers. For example:

> Отку́да вы? Я из Нью-Йо́рка.
> aht-KOO-dah vwee? YAH eez new-YOR-kah.
> Where are you from? I am from New York.

> Отку́да ты? Я из Аме́рики.
> aht-KOO-dah twee? YAH eez ah-MYEH-ree-kee.
> Where are you from? I am from America.

Perhaps you want to be even less specific. You can say that you live around, or near, a city or town by using the preposition ОКОЛО + the genitive case. For example:

> Я живу́ о́коло Бо́стона. Этот го́род о́коло Бо́стона.
> YAH zhee-VOO OH-kah-lah BOH-sto-nah. EH-tat GOH-rahd OH-kah-lah BOH-sto-nah.
> I live near Boston. This city is close to Boston.

Внима́ние

Addressing someone as **Ты** can be considered extremely rude, unless you have known the person for a long time. Using the polite, or formal, form **Вы** is always a safe approach. Remember, the older generation often addresses younger people using **Ты**, but they expect to receive responses in the **Вы** form.

And Who Might You Be?

After you have discussed home and country, your comrade in flying will probably begin to ask you about work. You want to grin and proudly talk about your big promotion last month; but first, you need to learn the verb Рабо́тать ("to work") and refresh your memory of the instrumental case (see Chapter 7). Let's start off with the conjugation table for Рабо́тать.

The Verb Рабóтать ("to work")

Person	Singular	English Meaning	Plural	English Meaning
First	я рабóтаю rah-BOH-tah-yoo.	I work	мы рабóтаем rah-BOH-tah-yem.	We work
Second	ты рабóтаешь rah-BOH-tah-yesh.	You (familiar) work	вы рабóтаете rah-BOH-tah-yet-yeh.	You (formal) work
Third	он/онá/онó рабóтает rah-BOH-tah-YOOT.	He/she/it works	они́ рабóтают rah-BOH-tah-yet.	They work

Я рабóтаю инженéром. Онá рабóтает врачóм.

YAH rah-BOH-tah-yoo een-zheh-NEHR-ahm. ah-NAH rah-BOH-tah-yet vrah-CHOHM.

I am an engineer. She is a doctor.

(Literally: I work as an engineer. She works as a doctor.)

Stating someone's position in Russian is as simple as in English. To say, "He's the boss," Russians will say, "Он начáльник." The following table of words will help you state positions quickly and simply.

Stating Positions

я …	он …	онá …
YAH …	OHN …	ah-NAH …
I am …	He is …	She is …

Titles and Positions

Russian	Pronunciation	English
начáльник	nah-CHAL-neek	boss
руководи́тель	poo-kah-vah-DEE-tel	supervisor
главá	glah-VAH	head
управля́ющий	oo-prav-LYAH-yoo-shee	manager
помóщник	pah-MOSCH-neek	assistant
штат	shtat	staff

Russian	Pronunciation	English
сотру́дник	sah-TROOD-neek	employee
рабо́тник	rah-BOHT-neek	worker
специали́ст (по компью́терам)	speh-TSEE-ah-leest (pah-kam-PYOO-ter-ahm)	expert (in computers)

You can now begin to field questions about your job and your position. Observe the following questions and try to respond. Remember, the noun that follows рабо́тать should be in instrumental case.

> Кто вы/ты по профе́ссии?
> Ktoh vwee/twee pah-prah-FES-see-ee?
> What is your profession?
>
> По како́й специа́льности вы/ты рабо́таете/рабо́таешь?
> Pah-kah-KOY speh-TSEE-ahl-nah-stee vwee/twee rah-BOH-tah-yet-yeh/rah-BOH-tah-yesh?
> What is your profession?
>
> Я рабо́таю до́ктором. Я помо́щник сейча́с.
> Yah rah-BOH-tah-yoo DOHK-tor-ahm. Yah pah-MOSCH-neek see-chas.
> I am a doctor. I am an assistant right now.
>
> [Я рабо́таю (I work as). Я сейча́с (Now I am).]

Professions

Profession	Pronunciation	English Meaning
врач	vrahch	doctor, physician
бизнесме́н	beez-ness-MYEN	business person
учи́тель(-ница)	oo-CHEEH-tehl(-nee-tsah)	teacher (female)
почтальо́н	poh-chtal-YOHN	mailman
медсестра́	med-SEH-strah	nurse
до́ктор	DOHK-tohr	doctor
адвока́т	ahd-vah-KAHT	lawyer
по́вар	POH-var	cook
официа́нт(-ка)	ah-feet-see-AHNT(-kah)	waiter (waitress)
вахтёр	vahk-TYOHR	security guard
дво́рник	DVOR-neek	custodian

continues

Professions (continued)

Profession	Pronunciation	English Meaning
парикмáхер	pah-REEK-mah-ker	hairdresser
нотáриус	nah-TAH-ree-oos	notary
страховóй агéнт	strak-ah-VOY ah-GYENT	insurance agent
манекéнщик(-щица)	mah-nyeh-KEN-sheek(-sheet-sah)	model (female)
худóжник	hoo-DOZH-neek	painter
актёр(актри́са)	ahk-TYOHR (ahk-TREE-sah)	actor (actress)
студéнт(-ка)	stoo-DYENT(-kah)	student (female)
элéктрик	eh-LEK-treek	electrician
шофёр	shah-FYOHR	driver

Now that you can tell your comrade what you do for a living, practice talking about other people by translating the sentences in the next exercise from English into Russian.

Exercise 10.1

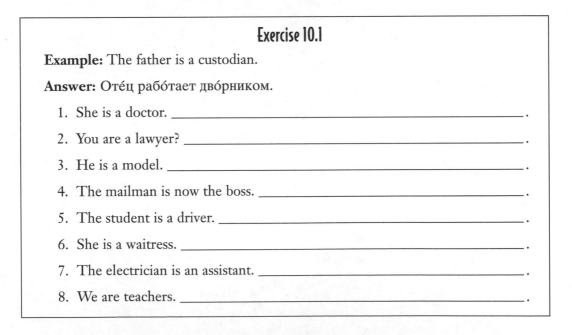

Example: The father is a custodian.

Answer: Отéц рабóтает двóрником.

1. She is a doctor. ______________________.
2. You are a lawyer? ______________________.
3. He is a model. ______________________.
4. The mailman is now the boss. ______________________.
5. The student is a driver. ______________________.
6. She is a waitress. ______________________.
7. The electrician is an assistant. ______________________.
8. We are teachers. ______________________.

Not only do you work as a professional in your field, you also have earned your position and pay through hard work and endurance. The following chart will help you brag (modestly) about your position in your company.

Job Descriptions

Russian	Pronunciation	English
Я рабо́таю на полста́вке.	Yah rah-BOH-tah-yoo nah-pal-STA-kee.	I work part-time.
Меня́ устро́или на рабо́ту.	men-YAH oo-STROH-eeh-lee nah rah-BOH-too.	I found a job.
Я пода́л(а) заявле́ние.	Yah pah-DAHL(AH) zah-yah-VLEH-nee-yeh.	I filed an application.
Я прохожу́ интервью́.	Yah prah-hah-ZHOO een-tehr-vyoo.	I am giving an interview.
Меня́ повы́сили в до́лжности.	men-YAH pah-VWEE-see-leeDOHL-zhnos—tee.	I received a promotion.
Мне повы́сили зарпла́ту.	Mneh pah-VWEE-see-lee zar-PLAH-too.	They raised my pay.
Я справля́юсь с обя́занностями.	Yah sprav-LYAH-yoos sab-YAH-zan-nast-yah-mee.	I handle my job responsibilities.
Я ве́даю отде́лом.	YahBYED-ah-yoo aht-DYEL-ahm.	I'm in charge of my department.

Memory Serves

To make a statement of fact, as in "I am a doctor," the Russian sentence remains in the nominative case. However, if you want to state your profession or job, you should use the correct form of the verb **работать** with the instrumental case.

Get Personal

If you have ever worked with or raised children, you know that they often learn by asking (what seems like) endless streams of questions. "What is that?" "What does it do?" and "Why?" are just a few. If you think of learning a new language like a second chance at being a child, you will go far. Asking questions is the easiest and most productive way to learn. If you don't understand, ask. Get nosy and make mistakes. The Russians that you meet will be eager to help you learn.

The first place to start is with the question words Кто (*who*) and Что (*what*). These words have a different declension for each case, but do not distinguish gender or number. The following chart will set you straight.

Asking Questions

Case	Russian	English	Russian	English
Nom.	Кто? Ktoh?	who?	Что? Shtoh?	what?
Prep.	(о) Ком? (ah) Kohm?	(about) whom?	(о) Чём? (ah) Chyom?	(about) what?
Acc.	Когó? kah-VOH?	whom?	Что? Shtoh?	what?
Gen.	Когó? kah-VOH?	(of) whom?	Чегó? chyeh-VOH?	(of) what?
Dat.	Комý? kah-MOO?	to whom?	Чемý chyeh-MOO?	to what?
Inst.	(с) Кем? (s) Kyem?	with whom?	(с) Чем? (s) Chyem?	with what?

Memory Serves

The words **Кто** and **Что** are interrogative pronouns, or pronouns used to ask questions. They decline only to match the noun they question in case. They do not change for gender or number. These pronouns usually appear at the beginning of the sentence to form a question.

Now that you know the different forms of these question words, you can begin to form basic questions and jump into your conversations with both feet. The following chart will show you these pronouns in use, with a few other key question words that you should know.

Key Question Words and Phrases

Russian	Pronunciation	English
О чём?	ah-chyohm?	about what?
О ком?	ah-kohm	about whom?
В какóе врéмя?	fkak-KOH-yeh VREHM-yah?	at what time?
Откýда?	aht-KOO-dah?	from where?
Как дóлго?	kahk DOHL-gah?	how long?
Скóлько?	SKOHL-kah?	how many?
Как?	kahk?	how?
Комý?	kah-MOO?	to whom?

Russian	Pronunciation	English
Зачéм?	zah-CHYEM?	what for?
Что?	shtoh?	what?
Когдá?	kahg-DAH?	when?
Кудá?	koo-DAH?	where to?
Где?	gdyeh?	where?
У когó?	oo-kah-VOH	who has …?
Кто?	ktoh?	who?
Почемý?	poh-chee-MOO?	why?
С кем?	skyem?	with whom?

The Easy Way to Finding Information

You've made it to your destination and said farewell to your airplane friends. Now, as you begin to explore the country, you find yourself traveling between cities next to an attractive young person. You realize that you will be sitting next to him or her for a couple of hours and decide to break the conversation barrier. The best course of action is to ask the obvious questions: "Where are you going?" and "How do you like it so far?" You put down your newspaper and begin to speak. Some of these phrases will help you get going.

Memory Serves

The question word **Где** (*where*) is used to speak about location. "Where is the library?" The question word **Кудá** expresses "where to" you are going to. "Where are you going (to)?"

Informational Questions

Formal (informal) Russian	English
Откýда вы (ты) éдете (éдешь)? Aht-KOO-duh vwee (twee) YEH-dyeh-tyeh (YEH-dyesh)	Where are you coming from?
Почемý вы (ты) тудá éдете (éдешь)? poh-chee-MOO vwee (twee) too-DAH YEH-dyeh-tyeh (YEH-dyesh)	Why are you going there?
Скóлько врéмени вы (ты) éдете (éдешь)? SKOHL-kuh VRE-me-nee vwee (twee) YEH-dyeh-tyeh (YEH-dyesh)	How long will you be traveling?
Где вы (ты) живëте (живëшь)? GDYEH vwee (twee) zhee-VYOH-tyeh (zhee-VYOSH)	Where do you live?

continues

Informational Questions (continued)

Formal (informal) Russian	English
Как вам (тебé) понрáвилась странá? kahk vahm (tee-BYEH) pah-NRAH-vee-lahs strah-NAH	How do you like the country?
Кудá вы (ты) éдете (éдешь)? koo-DAH vwee (twee) YEH-dyeh-tyeh (YEH-dyesh)	Where are you going?
О чём вы (ты) говорíте (говорíшь)? ah CHOM vwee (twee) guh-vah-REE-tyeh (guh-vah-REESH)	What are you talking about?
С кем вы (ты) éдете (éдешь)? SKYEHM vwee (twee) YEH-dyeh-tyeh (YEH-dyesh)	With whom are you traveling?
Когдá вы (ты) вернíтесь (вернёшься) домóй? kahg-DAH vwee (twee) vyehr-NYEE-tyehs (vyehr-NYOSH-suh) dah-MOY	When do you return home?
Скóлько у вас (тебя́) брáтьев и сестёр? SKOHL-kuh oo vahs (tee-BYAH) BRAH-tyekhff ee sees-TYOHR	How many brothers and sisters do you have?
У вас (тебя́) большáя семья́? oo vahs (tee-BYAH) bahl-SHAH-ya see-MYAH	Do you have a large family?

Conversationalist's Skills

The following two pieces of dialog are answers to the questions that you have learned in this chapter. The first is from your close (familiar) friend Ivan. The second is from a business acquaintance (formal) Sasha. Use the appropriate forms of address to direct as many questions as possible to their statements.

Example: Меня́ зову́т Борíс. **Question:** Как вас зову́т?

Familiar: Дóбрый день. Хорошó. Меня́ зову́т Ивáн. Я живу́ в Москвé. Я рабóтаю актёром. Я éду в Англию.

Formal: Дóбрый вéчер. Спасíбо не плóхо. Меня́ зову́т Сáша. Я рабóтаю инженéром. Я живу́ в Омске. Мы с брáтьями éдем во Фрáнцию.

The Least You Need to Know

- The greetings you use depend on your familiarity with a person. Don't use Ты with strangers or superiors!
- The verb жить ("to live") with the question word Где is used to ask someone where he or she lives. Or, you can always ask, "Откýда вы/ты" ("Where are you from?").
- For most professions, simply add a -ка or -ница to speak about a female. Remember that many professions do not change.
- You can easily get information by learning and asking a few simple questions.

Chapter 11

I'd Like to Get to Know You

In This Chapter

- Introducing your relatives
- Expressing possession
- Introducing yourself
- The verb звать ("to call, name")
- Using the idiom у когó ("to have")

You should now be able to breeze through your introductions, telling people your name, where you work, and what country or state you are from. But before you launch into a lengthy conversation with your new acquaintances, you should also introduce your guests to the members of your family who are standing around. In this chapter, you'll use what you learned from Chapter 10 to get the conversation moving. You will also learn how to use the appropriate possessive pronouns and experiment with the genitive case. But the first thing you will learn to do is to introduce your family and relatives.

Friends of the Family

Have you ever struggled for the correct label for a specific branch on the family tree? You refer to the woman standing in front of you as your mother's sister's daughter rather than cousin; meanwhile, everyone is scratching their heads. You can simplify your conversations by learning all the correct names for family members and relations in the following chart. You will notice that Russian does not have generic words such as *cousin.* All family members have gender-specific names. This chart will teach you everything you need to know.

Family Members

Male	English Meaning	Female	English Meaning
муж moozh	husband	жена́ zhe-NAH	wife
брат braht	brother	сестра́ sehs-TRAH	sister
сво́дный брат SVOHD-nee braht	step-brother	сво́дная сестра́ SVOHD-nah-yah –sehs-TRAH	step-sister
двою́родный брат dvah-YOO-rohdee braht	cousin	двою́родная сестра́ dvah-YOO- rohdnah-yah sehs-TRAH	cousin
оте́ц aht-YETS	father	мать maht	mother
ро́дственник ROHD-stven-neek	relative	ро́дственница ROHD-stven-neet-sah	relative
сын seen	son	дочь dohch	daughter
дя́дя DYAH-dyah	uncle	тётя TYOH-tyah	aunt
де́душка DEH-doosh-kah	grandfather	ба́бушка BAH-boosh-kah	grandmother
праде́душка prah-DEH-doosh-kah	great-grandfather	праба́бушка prah-BAH-boosh-kah	great-grandmother
племя́нник plehm-YAH-neek	nephew	племя́нница plehm-YAH-neet-sah	niece
внук vnook	grandson	вну́чка VNOOCH-kah	granddaughter
пра́внук PRAH-vnook	great-grandson	пра́внучка PRAH-vnooch-kah	great-granddaughter

Male	English Meaning	Female	English Meaning
супру́г soo-PROOK	spouse	супру́га soo-PROO-gah	spouse
вдове́ц vdah-VYETS	widower	вдова́ vdah-VAH	widow
свёкор SVYOH-kar	father-in-law	свекро́вь sveh-KROHV	mother-in-law
зять zyaht	son-in-law	неве́стка neh-VYEST-kah	daughter-in-law

You may have noticed that the prefix пра- ("prah") corresponds to the English prefix *great-*. Just as English speakers say *great-great-grandmother*, Russian speakers will also say прапрабабушка.

The words in the following chart are used in their plural form.

Family Members (Plurals)

Plural	Pronunciation	English Meaning
близнецы́	bleez-neht-SEE	twins
пре́дки	PREHT-kee	ancestors
роди́тели	rah-DEE-teh-lee	parents
родны́е	rahd-NEE-yeh	relatives
молодожёны	mah-lah-dah-ZHYOH-nee	newlyweds
де́ти	DHYEH-tee	children
пото́мки	pah-TOHM-kee	descendants

To Possess or to Be Possessed?

Possession makes the world go round. Arguing spouses might say, "He's your son!" or "She's your daughter!" To claim something as your own ("This is my car") or show someone else's ownership ("This is my father's car"), you need to use the genitive case and possessive adjectives.

Hot Topic

Showing **possession** in Russian requires a slight change of word order. The English phrase "the boy's dog" becomes "the dog of the boy" and the word *boy* takes the genitive case.

Showing Possession

In Chapter 8, you learned the plural forms of all the Russian cases, except genitive. You learned the declension patterns for genitive singular, but genitive plural requires a little patience and determination.

The plural form of genitive case has the largest number of exceptions in the Russian language. After you've learned these irregularities, you will have mastered the most difficult part of Russian grammar. Unlike other cases, genitive case makes a distinction between masculine, feminine, and neuter nouns in the plural. Here are the standard endings for the following regular nouns.

Masculine	Genitive Plural	Neuter	Genitive Plural	Feminine	Genitive Plural
дом	домóв	знáние	знáний	стенá	стен
dohm	dah-MOHF	ZNAH-nee-yeh	ZNAH-nee	steh-NAH	styehn
отéц	отцóв	тéло	тел	кни́га	книг
ah-TYETS	aht-SOHF	teh-LOH	tyel	KNEE-gah	kneeg

Observe the following examples. Notice that masculine nouns take the ending -OB/ -EB in the genitive plural. Neuter nouns take either -Й or no ending at all. Feminine nouns also drop their endings. Genitive case also has a number of irregularities in the plural form.

Genitive Plural

Nominative Singular	Genitive Singular	Genitive Plural	English Meaning
музéй mooz-YEY	музéя mooz-YEH-yah	музéев mooz-YEH-yef	of the museums
принц preents	при́нца PREEN-tsah	при́нцев PREEN-tsehf	of the princes
стол stohl	столá stah-LAH	столóв stah-LOHF	of the tables
лес lehs	лéса LEH-sah	лесóв leh-SOHF	of the forests
ключ klyooch	клю́ча KLYOO-chah	ключéй klooch-YEY	of the keys
словáрь slah-VAHR	словáря slah-VAHR-yah	словарéй slah-vahr-YEY	of the dictionaries

Nominative Singular	Genitive Singular	Genitive Plural	English Meaning
зда́ние ZDAH-nee-yeh	зда́ния ZDAH-nee-yah	зда́ний ZDAH-nee	of the buildings
ста́нция STAHN-tsee-yah	ста́нции STAHN-tsee-ee	ста́нций STAHN-tsee	of the stations
кни́га KNEE-gah	кни́ги KNEE-gee	книг kneek	of the books
ме́сто MYEH-stah	ме́ста MYEH-stah	мест myest	of the places

Irregular Genitive Plurals

Nominative Singular	Genitive Singular	Genitive Plural	English Meaning
муж moozh	му́жа MOOZH-ah	муже́й moozh-YEY	of the husbands
друг drook	дру́га DROO-gah	друзе́й drooz-YEY	of the friends
сын seen	сы́на SEE-nah	сынове́й see-nah-VYEY	of the sons
брат braht	бра́та BRAH-tah	бра́тьев BRAH-tyehv	of the brothers
челове́к cheh-lah-VYEK	челове́ка cheh-lah-VYEH-kah	люде́й lood-YEY	of the people
ребёнок rehb-YOHN-nahk	ребёнка reh-BYOHN-kah	дете́й deht-YEY	of the children
де́ньги (plural) DEHN-gee	—— ——	де́нег DEHN-ehg	of the money
сестра́ sehs-TRAH	сестры́ sehs-TREE	сестёр sehs-TYOHR	of the sisters
семья́ sehm-YAH	семьи́ sehm-YEE	семе́й sehm-YEY	of the families
мать maht	ма́тери MAH-teh-ree	матере́й mah-tehr-YEY	of the mothers
тётя TYOH-tyah	тёти TYOH-tee	тётей TYOH-tyey	of the aunts
дя́дя DYAH-dyah	дя́ди DYAH-dee	дя́дей DYAH-dyey	of the uncles

If the genitive plural seems overwhelming, don't despair! Few conversations require the plural form.

Your daily conversations will often call for genitive singular to express ownership and possession. The following chart shows some common examples of the genitive case in everyday use.

Examples of Genitive in Everyday Use

Russian Phrase	Pronunciation	English Meaning
Где маши́на бра́та?	gdyeh mah-SHEE-nah BRAH-tah?	Where is (my) brother's car (the car of my brother)?
Я ви́жу маши́ну бра́та.	yah VEEH-zhoo mah-SHEE-noo BRAH-tah.	I see my brother's car.
Я говорю́ о маши́не бра́та.	yah gah-vahr-YOO ah-mah-SHEEN-yeh BRAH-tah.	I am talking about my brother's car.
Это оте́ц де́вушки.	EH-tah aht-YETS DEH-voosh-kee.	This is the girl's father (the father of the girl).
Имя дру́га—Ива́н.	EEM-yah DROO-gah ee-VAHN.	My friend's name is Ivan (the name of my friend).
В како́е вре́мя дня ...?	fkah-KOH-yeh VREHM-yah dhyah?	At what time of day ...?
Это письмо́ до́чери.	EH-tah pees-MOH DOH-cheh-ree.	This is the daughter's letter (the letter of my daughter).

More for Me

The *possessive pronouns—his*, *her*, *your*, *their*, *my*, and *our*—also show ownership in Russian. As in English these words are actually adjectives, and like all Russian adjectives they must agree with the nouns they modify in gender, number, and case. The only exceptions to this are его́ (*his*), её (*her*), and их (*their*), which never change—ever. The declension of these adjectives follows the same rules that govern other adjectives.

Hot Topic

Possessive pronouns express a relationship between an object and the subject. "My book," "her car," and "his friend" are all examples of possessive pronouns.

The following examples show someone reading something. This "something" is a direct object and therefore takes the accusative case.

Russian	Pronunciation	English Phrase
Он читáет мою́ кни́гу.	Ohn chee-TAH-yet mah-YOO KNEE-goo.	He reads my book.
Они́ читáют егó кни́гу.	Ah-NEE chee-TAH-yoot yeh-VOH KNEE-goo.	They read his book.
Мы читáем вáшу кни́гу.	Mwee chee-TAH-yehm VAH-shoo KNEE-goo.	We read your book.
Я читáю её кни́гу.	Yah chee-TAH-yoo yeh-YOH KNEE-goo.	I read her book.

The complete list of possessive pronouns is shown in the following table.

Possessive Pronouns

Person	Singular	Meaning	Plural	Meaning
First	мой moy	my	наш nahsh	our
Second	твой tvoy	your (familiar)	Ваш vahsh	your (formal)
Third	егó/её yeh-VOH/ yeh-YOH	his/her	их eek	their

The following two tables show the declension patterns for *my* and *our*. Мой exactly mirrors Твой (*your*, familiar), and Наш exactly mirrors Ваш (*your*, formal). As you learned in Chapter 5, neuter and masculine adjectives take the same forms after nominative, so they are listed together in the following lists.

The Declension of the Possessive Adjective Мой (my)

Case	Masculine/Neuter	Feminine	Plural
Nom.	мой/моё moy/mah-YOH	моя́ mah-YAH	мои́ mah-YEE
Acc. (inan.)	мой/моё moy/mah-YOH	мою́ mah-YOO	мои́ mah-YEE
Acc. (anim.)	моегó mah-yeh-VOH	—— ——	мои́х mah-YEEKH
Prep.	моём mah-YOHM	моéй mah-YEY	мои́х mah-YEEKH

Case	Masculine/Neuter	Feminine	Plural
Gen.	моегó mah-yeh-VOH	моéй mah-YEY	моúх mah-YEEKH
Dat.	моемý mah-yeh-MOO	моéй mah-YEY	моúм mah-YEEM
Inst.	моúм mah-YEEM	моéй mah-YEY	моúми mah-YEE-mee

The Declension of the Possessive Adjective наш (*our*)

Case	Masculine/Neuter	Feminine	Plural
Nom.	наш/нáше nahsh/NAH-shyeh	нáша NAH-shah	нáши NAH-shee
Acc. (inan.)	наш/нáше nahsh/NAH-shyeh	нашу NAH-shoo	нáши NAH-shee
Acc. (anim.)	нáшего NAH-sheh-vah	—— ——	нáших NAH-sheekh
Prep.	нáшем NAH-shem	нáшей NAH-shey	нáших NAH-sheekh
Gen.	нáшего NAH-sheh-vah	нáшей NAH-shey	нáших NAH-sheekh
Dat.	нáшему NAH-sheh-moo	нáшей NAH-shey	нáшим NAH-sheem
Inst.	нáшим NAH-sheem	нáшей NAH-shey	нáшими NAH-shee-mee

Now that you know who's in charge of whom with the genitive case and your possessive pronouns, try to express the following relationships in Russian (see Appendix B for answers):

Exercise 11.1

Example: her brother

Answer: её брат

1. my father ____________________
2. his mother ____________________
3. our family ____________________

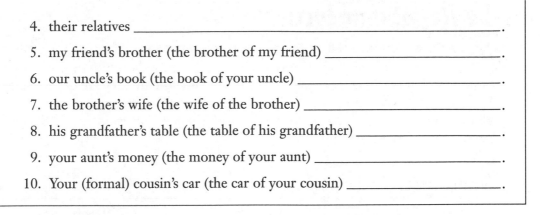

4. their relatives ______________________________.
5. my friend's brother (the brother of my friend) ______________________________.
6. our uncle's book (the book of your uncle) ______________________________.
7. the brother's wife (the wife of the brother) ______________________________.
8. his grandfather's table (the table of his grandfather) ______________________________.
9. your aunt's money (the money of your aunt) ______________________________.
10. Your (formal) cousin's car (the car of your cousin) ______________________________.

What Is Your Preference?

Everyone has a most valuable possession: a favorite pillow or recliner, a favorite movie or room of the house. The Russian adjective for *favorite* is люби́мый, and you will often use it with your possessive adjectives. Take a look at the following examples.

Мой люби́мый фильм—Ситизе́н Кайн.
Moy loo-BEE-mwee feelm—Citizen Kane.
My favorite film is *Citizen Kane*.

Люби́мый рестора́н моего́ бра́та—Алфре́йдос.
Loo-BEE-mwee peh-stah-RAHN mah-yeh-VOH BRAH-tah—Alfredo's.
My brother's favorite restaurant is Alfredo's.

Describe some of your favorite things with the following exercises.

Example: цвет, color

Answer: Мой люби́мый цвет—бе́лый.

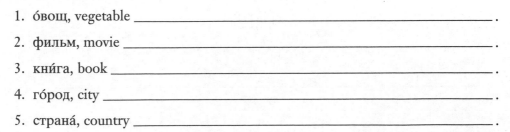

1. о́вощ, vegetable ______________________________.
2. фильм, movie ______________________________.
3. кни́га, book ______________________________.
4. го́род, city ______________________________.
5. страна́, country ______________________________.

In the Way of Introduction

The first part of a successful social event is the introductions. After you introduce yourself, you begin by introducing your friends to other guests. Although introductions are sometimes a more awkward part of communication, they are quite essential. Imagine trying to carry on a conversation between several different people without knowing anyone's name. The following phrases will help you avoid awkward moments of silence and embarrassment.

Introductions

Russian Phrase	Pronunciation	English Meaning
Хóчешь, я познакóмлю тебя́ с отцóм?	HOH-chyesh, yah pah-znah-KOHM-lyoo tehb-YAH saht-SOHM?	Let me introduce you (familiar) to my father.
Хоти́те, я познакомлю́ вас с му́жем?	Hah-TEET-yeh, yah pah-znah-KOHM-loo vahs SMOO-zhyem?	Let me introduce you (formal) to my husband.
Егó зову́т Андрéй.	Yeh-VOH zah-VOOT ahn-DREY.	His name is Andrey.
Её зову́т Ни́на.	Yeh-YOH zah-VOOT NEE-nah.	Her name is Nina.
Зна́ешь моегó бра́та Андрéя?	ZNAH-yesh mah-yeh-VOH BRAH-tah ahn-DREY-yah?	Do you (familiar) know my brother, Andrey?
Зна́ете мою́ сестру́ Ни́ну?	ZNAH-yet-yeh mah-YOO sehs-TROO NEE-noo?	Do you (formal) know my sister, Nina?
Это Андрéй/Ни́на.	EH-tah ahn-DREY/NEE-nah.	This is Andrey/Nina.
Очень прия́тно.	OH-chen pree-YAHT-nah.	It is a pleasure.

Культу́ра

Russian is spoken not only in Russia but also all across America. You don't need international plane tickets to speak with someone in Russian. New York and San Francisco have a huge Russian-speaking population, not including the many who live all across America's fruited plains.

Take the Plunge

Unlike learning new words or listening to a Russian radio station, conversation requires two people to practice. To really refine your skills, you should find a Russian speaker and strike up a conversation. Suppose you're riding to work on the subway or the bus. You could ask, "Кто́-нибудь здесь говори́т по-ру́сски?" ("Does anyone here speak Russian?") After two or three different people have excitedly responded "ДА!" you can make a couple of new friends. Try out some of the following:

1. Introduce yourself.
2. Tell them what you do in life.
3. Say where you live.
4. Ask your new Russian friend what they do and where they live.
5. Ask if he/she knows a member of your family.
6. Introduce someone to your new friend.
7. Say, "It's a pleasure meeting you."

Navigating Your Conversations

Perhaps the single most useful idiom in the Russian language is "у кого́" ("someone has"). Rather than the verb "to have," Russian uses the preposition У with a noun in the genitive case to express the same idea. You need only remember that the noun that follows У must be the name of a person or profession. For example, look at the following expressions:

У отца́ большо́й дом.
OO-aht-SAH balh-SHOY dohm.
The father has a large house.

У врача́ пацие́нт.
OO-vrah-CHAH pah-TSEE-yent.
The doctor has a patient.

У де́вушки краси́вая шля́па.
OO-DEH-voosh-kee krah-SEE-vah-yah SHLYAH-pah.
The girl has a pretty hat.

У ма́льчика стака́н молока́.
OO-MAHL-chee-kah stah-KAN mah-lah-KAH.
The boy has a glass of milk.

The "У кого́" phrase is frequently used with personal pronouns. The following chart shows the proper declension of these pronouns in the genitive with the preposition у.

The Idiomatic Expression У меня ("I have")

Person	Singular	Meaning	Plural	Meaning
First	у меня́ oo-men-YAH	I have	у нас oo-nahs	we have
Second	у тебя́ oo-tehb-YAH	you have (familiar)	у Вас oo-vahs	you have (formal)
Third	у него́/неё oo-nyeh-VOH/nyeh-YOH	he/she/it has	у них oo-neek	they have

The item being possessed or owned will always take the nominative case with the expression "to have." For example, observe the following exchanges:

> У кого́ есть ли́шный каранда́ш?
> Oo-kah-VOH yest LEESH-nee kah-ran-DASH?
> Who has a spare pencil?
>
> У кого́ есть ли́шная ру́чка?
> Oo-kah-VOH yest LEESH-nah-yah ROOCH-kah?
> Who has an extra pen?
>
> У них ли́щные карандаши́.
> oo-NEEK LEESH-nee-yeh kah-ran-dah-SHEE.
> They have (some) spare pencils.
>
> У него́ ли́шная ру́чка.
> Oo-nyeh-VOH LEESH-nah-yah pooch-kah.
> He has a spare pen.

What Do You Have?

Expressions of possession or ownership always require the idiom "у кого́," but Russian has some other ways to express the verb "to have." For example, "to have the right" or "to have the opportunity" uses the verb име́ть; "to be lucky" or "to have the luck" uses another idiom altogether. The following chart shows you some idioms that translate into *have* expressions:

"I Have" Expressions

Russian Idiom	Pronunciation	English Meaning
имéть прáво	eem-YET PRAH-vah	to have the right
имéть возмóжность	eem-YET vaz-MOZH-nahst	to have the possibility
имéть несчáстье	eem-YET neh-SHAST-yeh	to have the misfortune
у (меня́) врéмя	oo (mehn-YAH) VREHM-yah	(I) have time
у (меня́) желáние	oo (mehn-YAH) zheh-LAH-nee-yeh	(I) have desire
у (меня́) хрáбрость	oo (mehn-YAH) KRAHB-rahst	(I) have the courage
ви́деть сон	VEE-deht SOHN	to have a dream
не стóит	neh STOH-eet	there is no point
(мне) повезлó	(mnyeh) pah-vehz-LOH	(I) was lucky
(я) к э́тому не привы́к	(YAH) KEH-tah-moo neh pree-VWEEK	(I) am not accustomed to this
(не) собирáться	(neh) sah-bee-RAHT-syah	to (not) have the intention

So far you know how to express "I have" with the idiom "у когó," but to express "I do not have" you need to take the same idiom and add the genitive case. "У меня́ нет" means "I don't have." But instead of using the nominative case as you've been doing, you need to follow нет with the genitive case. For example, some of the idioms you learned in the chart above are repeated here in their negated form.

Expressions of Negation ("I do not have")

Russian Phrase	Pronunciation	English Meaning
у (меня́) нет врéмени	oo (mehn-YAH) nyet VREH-meh-nee.	(I) don't have time
у (меня́) нет желáния	oo (mehn-YAH) nyet zheh-LAH-nee-yah	(I) don't have the desire
у (меня́) нет хрáбрости	oo (mehn-YAH) nyet KRAHB-rah-stee	(I) don't have the courage
у (меня́) нет дóма	oo (mehn-YAH) nyet DOH-mah	(I) don't have a home

Practice your idioms in the following exercise (answers are listed in Appendix B). Transcribe the following expressions into Russian using the positive form ("I have") and also the negative form ("I do not have").

Exercise 11.4

Examples: He has a car (У него́ есть маши́на). He does not have a car (У него́ нет маши́ны).

1. They have a dog. ______________________.
2. She has a sister. ______________________.
3. We have the desire. ______________________.
4. He has a brother. ______________________.
5. You have a pencil. ______________________.
6. They have my dog. ______________________.

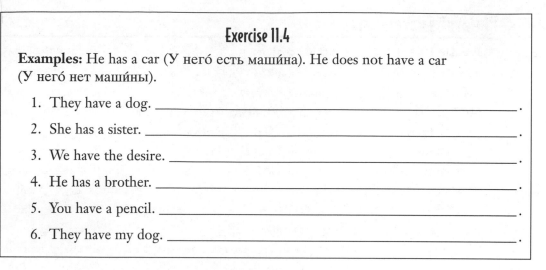

The Conversational Survival Guide

Not only do you spend time talking to other people, you will frequently talk about other people. Gossip is just as delicious in Russian as it is in English. Whether your friends and relatives are kind, troubled, or energetic, you need to expand your vocabulary to describe them. Adjectives will make light work of the process. In Chapter 8, you learned how to decline adjectives and make them agree with the nouns they modify in gender, number, and case. You can now begin to answer some of the following questions with the words in the next chart.

Како́й у него́/неё хара́ктер?
Kah-KOY oo-nyeh-VOH/nyeh-YOH hah-RAHK-tehr?
What kind of personality does he/she have?

Что он/она́ за челове́к?
Shtoh ohn/ah-NAH zah-cheh-lah-VYEK?
What sort of person is he/she?

Како́й он/она́ челове́к?
Kah-KOY ohn/ah-NAH cheh-lah-VYEK?
What is he/she like?

The following adjectives will help you answer these questions.

More Adjectives

Russian Phrase	Pronunciation	English Meaning
до́брый	DOHB-ree	kind
злой	zloy	mean
разгово́рчивый	raz-gah-VOHR-chee-vwee	talkative
ревни́вый	rev-NEE-vwee	jealous
и́скренний	EESK-rehn-nee	sincere
отзы́вчивый	aht-ZEEV-chee-vwee	sympathetic
оби́дчивый	ah-beed-CHEE-vwee	sensitive
ла́сковый	LAHS-kah-vwee	affectionate
скро́мный	SKROHM-nee	modest
самолюби́вый	sah-mah-loo-BEE-vwee	proud
самоуве́ренный	sah-mah-oo-VEH-ren-nee	self-confident
трудолюби́вый	troo-dah-loo-BEE-vwee	hard-working
энерги́чный	eh-nehr-GEECH-nee	energetic
лени́вый	leh-NEE-vwee	lazy
тала́нтливый	tah-LAHN-tlee-vwee	talented
любозна́тельный	loo-bah-ZHAH-tehl-nee	curious
у́мный	OOM-nee	intelligent
остроу́мный	ahs-trah-OOM-nee	witty, clever
нахо́дчивый	nah-HOHD-chee-vwee	resourceful
споко́йный	spah-KOY-nee	calm
ти́хий	TEE-kee	quiet
весёлый	veh-SYOH-lee	merry
че́стный	CHEST-nee	honest

Try to answer the following questions using the adjectives you have just learned.

1. Како́й он по отноше́нию к други́м лю́дям?

   What is his attitude toward others?

   Он ______________________________.

2. Како́й он по отноше́нию к са́мому себе́?

   What is his attitude toward himself?

   Он ______________________________.

3. Кака́я она́ по отноше́нию к труду́?

   What is her attitude toward work?

   Она́ ______________________________.

4. Кака́я она́ по спосо́бностям (интелле́кту)?

   What are her abilities (intellect)?

   Она́ ______________________________.

5. Каки́е они́ по темпера́менту (привы́чкам)?

   What are their temperaments (habits) like?

   Они́ ______________________________.

The Least You Need to Know

- To show possession in Russian, use the genitive case and possessive adjectives. Rearrange the phrase "boy's dog" to "dog of the boy."
- "У меня́" ("I have") isn't just another idiom; it's required to express possession, corresponding to "I have" in English.
- "I do not have" is expressed by using "У меня́ нет" + the genitive case.
- You can describe people quickly and easily by learning some adjectives.

Chapter 12

Finally, You're at the Airport

In This Chapter

- Airports, airplanes, traveling
- Verbs of motion
- How to give and receive directions
- The help of prepositions

You made reservations for your international vacation, drove to the airport, checked your bags, and got onto the plane. As you enjoy the long flight across the ocean, you manage to have an interesting conversation with a Russian nuclear physicist, who seems a bit distant but gives you the names of some good restaurants and hotels for your stay.

While your plane begins its descent for landing, you think about navigating the foreign airport. You need to collect your bags, go through customs and exchange some currency, hail a taxi, and get directions to your hotel. If you have concerns about accomplishing any of these tasks, don't worry. By the end of this chapter, you will be able to breeze through these and other tasks in Russian.

Onboard the Plane

No international flight is complete without crying babies and eccentric fellow passengers wanting to show you their personal collection of bottle caps. Sometimes the in-flight movie isn't enough to make you comfortable. Whether your seat is too close to the engine or you feel claustrophobic, you can ask your flight attendant to change your seating assignment or make an inquiry about the flight. This section offers you the right words and phrases to smooth the wrinkles out of your flight.

Assistance, Please

Improving your in-flight conditions is as simple as reviewing a few key terms. The words in the following chart will help you make the most of your experience.

Inside the Plane

Russian Word	Pronunciation	English Meaning
авиакомпáния	ah-vee-ah-kahm-PAH-nee-yah	airline
самолёт	sah-mahl-YOHT	airplane
прохóд (самолёта)	prah-HOHD sah-mahl-YOH-tah	aisle (of the airplane)
мéсто у прохóда	MYES-tah oo-prah-HOH-dah	aisle seat
багáж	bah-GASH	baggage
кнóпка вы́зова	KNOH-pkah VWEE-zah-bah	call button
ручнáя клáдь	pooch-NAH-yah klahd	carry-on bag
экипáж	eh-kee-PASH	crew
запаснóй вы́ход	zah-pas-NOY VWEE-hat	emergency exit
бортпроводни́к (-ница)	bart-prah-vahd-NEEK (-NEET-sah)	flight attendant
курéние запрещенó	koo-REH-nee-yeh zah-preh-sheh-NOH	no smoking
вéрхнее багáжное отделéние	VEHR-knyeh-yeh bah-GAZH-nah-yeh aht-deh-LEH-nee-yeh	overhead luggage compartment
пилóт	pee-LOHT	pilot
привязнóй ремéнь	pree-vyah-ZNOY peh-MYEN	seat belt
чемодáн	chem-ah-DAHN	suitcase
сади́ться на самолёт	sah-DEET-syah nah-sah-mahl-YOHT	to board a plane
высáживаться из самолёта	vwee-SAH-zhee-vaht-syah issh-mahl-YOH-tah	to deplane

Russian Word	Pronunciation	English Meaning
иллюмина́тор (окно́)	eel-loo-mee-NAH-tahr (ahk-NOH)	window
ме́сто у иллюмина́тора (окна́)	MYES-tah oo-eel-loo-mee-NAH-tah-rah (ahk-NAH)	window seat
крыло́	kree-LOH	wing

Inside the Airport

After a lengthy conversation with your nuclear physicist friend, you feel exhausted mentally and physically. As the plane lands, you can't wait to deplane and find your baggage. After the crowd disperses through the airport terminal, you grab your bags and wonder where you should go next. Do you want to find a hotel or would you rather grab a quick sandwich first? As you walk down the terminal, airport signs and store windows greet you everywhere. Already tired from the flight, you must now try to determine which direction to go.

Which Words Are Right for You?

You may want to stop at the nearest "спра́вочное бюро́" ("information office") and ask for directions, or glance at an airport ка́рта (*map*) to get your bearings. In either case the words in the following table will help you find what you are looking for.

Inside the Airport

Russian Word	Pronunciation	English Meaning
аэропо́рт	aeh-rah-PORT	airport
прилёт	pree-LYOHT	arrival
теле́жка	tehl-YESH-kah	baggage cart
вы́дача багажа́	VWEE-dah-chah bah-gah-ZHAH	baggage claim
туале́т	too-ahl-YET	bathroom
поса́дочный тало́н	pah-SAH-dach-nee tah-LOHN	boarding pass
остано́вка авто́буса	ah-stah-NOHV-kah ahv-TOH-boo-sah	bus stop
прока́тный пункт	prah-KAHT-nee poonkt	car rental
сто́йка	STOY-kah	counter
тамо́жня	tah-MOZH-nyah	customs
лифт	leeft	elevator

Russian Word	Pronunciation	English Meaning
вход	fhoht	entrance
вы́ход	VWEE-haht	exit
спра́вочное бюро́	SPRAH-vach-nah-yeh byoo-ROH	information office
носи́льщик	nah-SEEL-sheek	porter
ме́ры безопа́сности	MYEH-ree bez-ah-PAHS-nah-stee	security measures
биле́т	beel-YET	ticket
биле́тная ка́сса	beel-YET-nah-yah KAH-sah	ticket office

Signs and Directories

Airline security constantly increases, and the policies of foreign airports sometimes differ from those in the United States. Pay attention to all signs featured in red and yellow, and don't be afraid to use your pocket dictionary to define any words you don't know. Although you will often find security guards friendly, you want to avoid being searched as much as possible. Try to match the following airport warnings with their English translations in the following exercises.

Exercise 12.1

A. Внима́ние! Нельзя́ носи́ть ору́жие в аэропорту́!

B. Все су́мки и бага́ж подлежа́т о́быску!

C. Не принима́йте паке́ты от незнако́мцев.

D. Не оставля́йте бага́ж без присмо́тра.

E. Воспреща́ется кури́ть в аэропорту́.

Identify the sign that tells you:

_____ 1. Do not leave bags unattended.

_____ 2. All bags are subject to search.

_____ 3. Smoking is not permitted in the airport.

_____ 4. Attention! You may not carry weapons in the airport.

_____ 5. Do not take any packages from strangers.

Going Places

As you make your way around the airport, you will find the terminals packed with business people and tourists alike rushing to their flights, casually strolling, and walking here and there. In fact, you will notice that nearly everyone is moving somewhere. The whole airport is in motion. To express movement or motion in Russian, you need some *verbs of motion* or verbs that express movement toward a goal or destination.

Hot Topic

Verbs of motion come in pairs, and they express movement toward a destination. The indefinite verb expresses habitual or regular movement, and the definite verb expresses a one-time movement.

Russian verbs of motion sometimes cause problems for English speakers for two reasons. First, motion verbs come in pairs of *definite* and *indefinite motion.* The indefinite motion indicates a regular action, such as "Alex goes to the store every morning" and "Sue goes to school every day." Definite motion verbs express an action that occurs only one time, as in "Alex is going to the store right now" or "Sue is going to the park after school today." Second, Russian does not have a verb that means "to go." Instead, verbs of motion in Russian indicate the method of travel—by foot, by vehicle, by plane, by boat.

Hot Topic

Indefinite motion indicates a regular or habitual activity. Phrases such as *often, every day,* or *regularly* usually accompany indefinite motion verbs.

Definite motion indicates an activity or movement that is happening right now or happens only once. Definite motion can always be translated using the verb "to be" as in "he is going" or "they are walking."

For now you'll learn the motion verbs for walking and flying, and in Chapter 13 you will learn the verb pair for "to drive." Although the following two verbs may not appear to be related, they are directly connected to each other. The verb pair ходи́ть/идти́ means "to go by foot" or "to walk."

The Verb ходи́ть (indefinite: "to go by foot, walk")

Person	Singular	English	Plural	English
First	хожу́ hah-ZHOO	I walk	хо́дим HOH-deem	We walk
Second	хо́дишь HOH-deesh	You walk (familiar)	хо́дите HOH-deet-yeh	You walk (formal)
Third	хо́дит HOH-deet	He/She walks	хо́дят HOH-dyat	They walk

Па́вел хо́дит домо́й (ка́ждый день).
PAH-vehl HOH-deet dah-MOY (KAZH-dee dehn).
Pavel walks home (every day).

Анна (ча́сто) хо́дит в кино́.
AHN-nah (CHAS-tah) HOH-deet fkee-NOH.
Anna (often) goes to the movies.

The Verb идти́ (definite: "to go by foot, walk")

Person	Singular	English	Plural	English
First	иду́ ee-DOO	I am walking	идём eed-YOHM	We are walking
Second	идёшь eed-YOHSH	You are walking (familiar)	идёте eed-YOHT-yeh	You are walking (formal)
Third	идёт eed-YOHT	He/She is walking	иду́т ee-DOOT	They are walking

Па́вел идёт домо́й (сейча́с).
PAH-vehl eed-YOHT dah-MOY (see-CHAS).
Pavel is going home (right now).

Анна идёт в кино́ (сего́дня ве́чером).
AHN-nah eed-YOHT fkee-NOH (she-VOHD-nyah VEH-cheh-rahm).
Anna is walking to the movies (tonight).

Getting in Motion

The verb pair ходи́ть/идти́ is usually followed by the preposition в or на with the accusative case. Verbs of motion do not take direct objects (nouns in the accusative case), but using the prepositions в or на with the accusative marks the destination, or goal of motion. Do you remember the declension patterns for nouns in the accusative case from Chapter 7? Inanimate masculine nouns do not change and feminine nouns add у or ю in the accusative. To express where you are headed, remember this simple formula:

ходи́ть/идти́ + в/на + accusative case

When forming questions, the interrogative pronoun кудá is used. For example:

Кудá вы идёте (ты идёшь)?
Koo-DAH vwee eed-YOH-tyeh (twee eed-YOHSH)?
Where are you going?

In response you might answer:

Я идý на рабóту, а онá идёт в теáтр.
Yah ee-DOO nah-rah-BOH-too, ah ah-NAH eed-YOHT fteh-AH-ter.
I am going to work, and she is going to the theater.

Мы идём в парк.
Mwee eed-YOHM vpark.
We are going to the park.

To ask someone where they usually go (after work, in the mornings, and so on), you might ask:

Кудá вы хóдите по утрáм?
Koo-DAH vwee HOH-deet-yeh pah-oot-RAHM?
Where do you usually go in the mornings?

In response you might answer:

По утрáм я хожý в кафé.
Pah-oot-RAHM yah hah-ZHOO vkah-FYEH.
In the mornings I go to a café.

The verb pair летáть/летéть ("to go by air, fly") works the same way as the verb pair ходи́ть/идти́. Remember, летáть is indefinite, and летéть is definite. They also require the prepositions в and на to express the goal of motion.

The Verb летáть (indefinite: "to go by air, fly")

Person	Singular	English	Plural	English
First	летáю leh-TAH-yoo	I fly	летáем leh-TAH-yem	We fly
Second	летáешь leh-TAH-yesh	You fly (familiar)	летáете leh-TAH-yet-yeh	You fly (formal)
Third	летáет leh-TAH-yet	He/She flies	летáют leh-TAH-yoot	They fly

Мы лета́ем в Бо́стон (ка́ждое у́тро).
Mwee leh-TAH-yem fBOH-stahn (KAZH-dah-yeh OOT-rah).
We fly to Boston (every morning).

Они́ лета́ют в Евро́пу (ка́ждый год).
Ah-NEE leh-TAH-yoot vyeh-VROH-poo (KAZH-dee GOHD).
They fly to Europe (every year).

The Verb лететь (definite: "to go by air, fly")

Person	Singular	English	Plural	English
First	лечу́ leh-CHOO	I am flying	лети́м leh-TEEM	We are flying
Second	лети́шь leh-TEESH	You are flying (familiar)	лети́те leh-TEEH-tyeh	You are flying (formal)
Third	лети́т leh-TEET	He/She is flying	летя́т leh-TYAHT	They are flying

Я лечу́ в Нью-Йорк (за́втра).
Yah leh-CHOO vnoo-YORK (ZAF-trah).
I am flying to New York (tomorrow).

Он лети́т в Евро́пу (сего́дня).
Ohn leh-TEET vyeh-VROH-poo (she-VOHD-hyah).
He is flying to Europe (today).

Where Is …?

If the red "you are here" arrow has left you a little confused about where *here* is, exactly, you may want to ask someone for directions. You can easily get information by asking someone the following:

Где тамо́жня (туале́т)?
Gdyeh tah-MOZH-nyah (too-ah-LYET)?
Where is the customs office (bathroom)?

Как попа́сть на тамо́жню (в туале́т)?
Kahk pah-PAHST nah-tah-MOZH-nyoo (vtoo-ahl-YET)?
How do you get to the customs office (to the bathroom)?

Где нахóдится вы́ход?
Gdyeh nah-HOH-deet-cyah VWEE-haht?
Where is the exit located?

If you're uncertain and want to form a question about the existence of something, you can use the word есть to form your question. Remember, you are literally asking, "Does a restaurant exist near here?"

Есть ресторáн бли́зко отсю́да?
Yest reh-stah-RAHN BLEES-kah aht-CYOO-dah?
Is there a restaurant near here?

Да, есть ресторáн.
Dah, yest reh-stah-RAHN.
Yes, there is a restaurant.

If someone's answer has left you a little unclear, you can ask in reply:

Объясни́те мне подрóбно, как попáсть тудá.
Ahb-yahs-NEET-yeh mnye pah-DROH-bnah, kahk pah-PAHST too-DAH.
Explain to me, in detail, how to get there.

An answer might be:

Иди́те пря́мо, поверни́те налéво (напрáво).
Ee-DEET-yeh PRYAH-mah, pah-vehr-NEET-yeh nah-LYEH-vah (nah PRAH-vah)
Go straight ahead, and then turn left (right).

If your journeys take you to someone's office (lawyer's office, doctor's office), you should use the preposition к + the name of the professional in the dative case. For example:

Он идёт к врачу́ (к медсестрé).
Ohn eed-YOHT kvrah-CHOO (kmed-sehs-STREH).
He is going to the doctor's office (to the nurse's office).

In the same way, if you visit family or friends, you also use the preposition к with the dative case. For example:

Онá идёт к отцу́ (к мáме).
Ah-NAH eed-YOHT kaht-SOO (KMAH-myeh).
She is going to (her) father's house (to her mother's house).

Go Straight Ahead and Hang a Left

Finding your way through unfamiliar places can be difficult. Fortunately, you can always ask someone for directions. If the directions are more complicated than "go thatta way," you may find some of the following verbs helpful.

Verbs Used When Giving Directions

Russian Word	Pronunciation	English Meaning
повернýть налéво/напрáво	pah-vehr-NOOT nahl-YEH-vah/nah-PRAH-vah	to turn left/right
проходи́ть (чéрез)	prah-hah-DEET (CHEH-rez)	to approach
подходи́ть к …	pod-hah-DEET k …	to walk up to
доходи́ть до …	doh-hah-DEET doh …	to continue, walk (through) …

A Prefixed Situation

Learning new vocabulary can be as easy as learning a few syllables to attach to your verbs. Rather than creating new words for every movement, Russians add prefixes to existing verbs to change their meanings. Check out some of these examples.

Как входи́ть в здáние (вы́ходить из здáния)?
Kahk vhah-DEET VZDAH-nee-yeh (VWEE-hah-deet eez ZDAH-nee-yah)?
How do you enter the building (exit from the building)?

Когдá самолёты прилетáют (улетáют)?
Kahg-DAH sah-mahl-YOH-tee pree-leh-TAH-yoot (oo-leh-TAH-yoot)?
When are the planes arriving (departing)?

I Am at Your Command

Receiving directions is an exercise in obeying commands. When telling someone what to do or how to do it, the imperative mood takes charge. As in English, the subject (you) is invisible in the imperative sentence. "Go!" and "Sit down!" each have the invisible subject *you*. As Russian has two forms of the pronoun *you*, it also has two imperative forms: familiar and formal. Try to determine which of the following two commands corresponds to ты and вы.

A. Поверни́ нале́во.
Pah-vehr-NEE nahl-YEH-vah.
Turn left.

B. Поверни́те напра́во.
Pah-vehr-NEET-yeh nahp-RAH-vah.
Turn right.

If you guessed that A was the familiar (ты) form, you are correct. Did you notice that B (the formal вы form) looked identical to the вы conjugation of the verb? In second-type (и-type) conjugations (see Chapter 9), the imperative plural will often be the same as the вы conjugation. Using the imperative in Russian is the same as in English with the exception of the form of address. But how is it formed?

You will study the perfective form of verbs in Chapter 22. Until then, set your mind at rest. The imperative forms of verbs are provided for you. Simply learn to recognize them and distinguish between the familiar and formal forms of address.

Taking Commands

Not all Russian verbs can be used in the *imperative* mood. In Russian you can't command someone to live, to see, to hear, or to know. Most intransitive verbs, verbs that reflect abilities or states of being, are not used in the imperative. In the same fashion, most transitive verbs, verbs that indicate action on something or movement toward some object, are used. Some of the verbs that you already know (or learned in this lesson) are listed in their imperative forms in the following chart. Pay attention to the difference between the positive (do this!) and the negative (don't do that!) forms. You will learn why this peculiarity occurs in Chapter 23.

Hot Topic

Imperatives are used to give commands or instructions, or to make requests. The imperative form reflects either **ты** or **вы**.

Imperatives

Verb	Positive	English	Negative	English
идти́ eed-TEE	пойди́(те) pah-ee-DEE (tyeh)	Go!	Не ходи́(те) neh hah-DEE (tyeh)	Don't go!
входи́ть vhah-DEET	войди́(те) vay-DEE (tyeh)	Enter!	Не входи́(те) neh vhah-DEE (tyeh)	Don't enter!

continues

Imperatives (continued)

Verb	Positive	English	Negative	English
выходи́ть vwee-hah-DEET	вы́йди(те) VWEE-dee (tyeh)	Exit!	Не выходи́(те) neh vwee-hah-DEE (tyeh)	Don't exit!
повора́чивать pah-vah-RAH-chee-vaht	поверни́(те) pah-vehr-NEE (tyeh)	Turn!	Не повора́чивай(те) neh pah-vah-RAH-chee-vay (tyeh)	Don't turn!
смотре́ть smah-TRET	посмотри́(те) pah-smah-TREE (tyeh)	Look!	Не смотри́(те) neh smah-TREE (tyeh)	Don't look!

Prepositions: The Little People

In the world of directions, prepositions make communication possible. The difference between *around* and *through* can be the difference between walking through wet cement or finding the right detour. You've encountered prepositions from the beginning, in idioms in Chapter 5 and onward.

Each preposition serves a specific function in Russian, and a few of them are interchangeable with one another (as you may have noticed already). The following chart lists the most common prepositions and the cases they can be used with.

Prepositions

Russian Preposition	Pronunciation	Required Case(s)	English Meaning(s)
о	ah	prepositional	about
в	v	prepositional accusative	in, at to, toward
на	nah	prepositional accusative	at, on to, toward
из	ees	genitive	from
с	suh	genitive instrumental	from with
че́рез	CHEH-res	accusative	through
ме́жду	MEZH-doo	instrumental	between
до	doh	genitive	before, until
по́сле	POH-slee	genitive	after
над	naht	instrumental	above

Russian Preposition	Pronunciation	Required Case(s)	English Meaning(s)
под	ohd poht	instrumental	below
за	zah	accusative	for (in exchange for)
за	zah	instrumental	behind
для	dlyah	genitive	for (intended for)
у	oo	genitive	by, at (a person's home)
óколо	OH-kah-lah	genitive	near, around
к	kah	dative	to, toward

Of the Noun, by the Noun, for the Noun

In the process of translating or conversing, sometimes it's difficult to keep track of which prepositions mean what, what cases they require, and even how to use them. You can simplify the whole mess by categorizing your prepositions this way:

- The prepositional prepositions refer to a static location (in, at, on).
- Accusative prepositions reflect movement to, toward, or through.
- Genitive prepositions refer to movement away from or location.
- Dative has one preposition (to go to someone's place or office).
- Instrumental prepositions cover above, below, behind, and between.
- Nominative has no prepositions.

These guidelines are general, and they don't cover every preposition. But if you can remember those six building blocks you can easily build a strong foundation. Let's take a look at the prepositions of each case in detail.

Prepositional Prepositions

Russian Word	Use	English Meaning
О	Он тóлько дýмает о деньгáх.	He thinks only *about* money.
	Они́ чáсто говоря́т о дóме.	They often talk *about* the house.
В	В кармáне монéта.	*In* the pocket there is a coin.
На	На кры́ше кóшка.	There is a cat *on* the roof.

Now try to fill in the blanks of the following sentences using the correct case (see answers in Appendix B):

Exercise 12.2

1. Она́ ду́мает о ____________________. (She thinks about her *friend.*)
2. Мно́гие рабо́тают в ____________. (Many people work in *this building.*)
3. На __________ де́ти игра́ют. (In the *street* [outside] children are playing.)

The two most common Russian prepositions, в and на, can also be used in the accusative case. Pay attention to the differences in use.

Accusative Prepositions

Russian Word	Use	English Meaning
в	Он идёт в магази́н.	He is going *to* the store.
на	Мы идём на по́чту.	We are going *to* the post office.
че́рез	Я хожу́ че́рез мост ка́ждый день.	I go *across* the bridge every day.

This exercise should be a breeze after all your walking practice so far. Complete the following phrases with the missing word (answers are in Appendix B):

Exercise 12.3

1. Они́ нашли́ доро́гу че́рез____________________.
2. Отнеси́те меня́ в ____________________.
3. Мы лю́бим ходи́ть на ____________________.

You will see these common genitive prepositions appear from time to time.

Genitive Prepositions

Russian Word	Use	English Meaning
до	До рабо́ты я за́втракаю.	*Before* work I eat breakfast.
по́сле	По́сле у́жина он ложи́тся спать.	*After* dinner he goes to sleep.
с	Она идёт домо́й с рабо́ты.	She is going home *from* work.

Russian Word	Use	English Meaning
из	Они́ из Калифо́рнии.	They are *from* California.
для	Я купи́л шля́пу для бра́та.	I bought a hat *for* my brother.

Use the genitive case to complete the following prepositional phrases (see Appendix B for answers):

Exercise 12.4

1. Что вы де́лаете по́сле ________________? (What are you doing after *work?*)
2. Я с ________________. (I am from the *south.*)
3. До ________________, моя́ са́мая люби́мая пье́са была́ Отэ́лло. Before *Hamlet* (Гамле́т) my favorite play was *Othello.*)
4. Он идёт домо́й из ________________. (He is going home from the *library.*)
5. Мы покупа́ем сви́тер для ________________. (We are buying a sweater for the *teacher.*)

Here are the three most common instrumental *prepositions.*

Instrumental Prepositions

Russian Word	Use	English Meaning
С	Я рабо́таю с други́ми людьми́.	I work *with* other people.
Ме́жду	Отноше́ния ме́жду Аме́рикой и Росси́ей хоро́шие.	The relationship *between* America and Russia is good.
Под	У него́ пробле́ма под контро́лем.	He has the problem *under* control.

One more exercise and you have finished! (See answers in Appendix B.)

Exercise 12.5

1. Он живёт под ________________. (He lives under a *bridge.*)
2. Помоги́те мне с ________________. (Help me with this *problem.*)
3. Магази́н нахо́дится ме́жду двумя́ ________________. (The store is located between two *big buildings.*)

Hot Topic

Prepositions show the connection between a phrase and the rest of the sentence.

Are You Lost Already?

Sometimes your luck just runs out. Not only do the signs confuse you, but the person you asked for help speaks fluent Swahili and knows Russian only as a second language. Even though you don't understand each other, at least he's sympathetic. You tighten your belt and give it your best. These phrases will help you smooth out the potholes.

Tired and Confused

Russian Phrase	Pronunciation	English Meaning
Извини́(те)	eez-veh-NEE(tyeh)	Excuse me.
Прости́(те)	prah-STEE(tyeh)	Forgive me.
Прости́те, я не понима́ю.	prah-STEE-tyeh, yah neh pah-nee-MAH-yoo.	I'm sorry. I don't understand (you).
Я не всё по́нял(а́).	YAH neh fsyoh POH-nyahl(AH).	I didn't understand everything.
Пожа́луйста, говори́те помедленне́е.	Pah-ZHAH-loo-stah, gah-vah-REET-yeh pah-med-lehn-YEH-yeh.	Please, speak more slowly.
Что вы сказа́ли?	SHTOH vwee skah-ZAH-lee?	What did you say?
Пожа́луйста, повтори́те э́то.	pah-ZHAH-loo-stah, pah-vtah-REET-yeh EH-tah.	Please, repeat that.

The Least You Need to Know

- Learning a few useful vocabulary words will help you figure out airport signs in Russian.
- Verbs of motion are either definite or indefinite, and they refer to the mode of motion.

- Commands are formed from the definite motion verb; and commands need to match your familiarity with a person.
- Prepositions are useful tools in expressing direction. Russian has prepositions from all cases (besides the nominative), and some prepositions even share cases.
- If you don't understand what to do or where to go, ask someone "Как попáсть в ...?" ("Kahk pah-PAHST v ...?"); or, if you don't understand what someone is telling you, tell that person "**Я** не понимáю" (Yah neh pah-nee-MAH-yoo).

Chapter 13

Get There Without Delay

In This Chapter

- Out and about
- The rental car
- Which or what, any or every?
- Cardinal numbers and counting
- Telling time

You have bravely endured the international flight, fought your way through baggage claim and customs, and now you face your second challenge—getting to the hotel. As you stroll down the airport terminal toward the street, you realize that you need to find some public transportation to reach your hotel. If you're lucky, transportation from the airport was provided with your travel package, and someone is waiting to escort you away. If not, you need to decide whether to travel by taxi, bus, streetcar, or metro. This chapter explains how to get from here to there, and accomplish your tasks quickly and efficiently.

Planes, Trains, and Automobiles

Now that you've arrived at your destination, you think about the many things to do and places to go. You can walk anywhere, of course, but it takes time and energy that you may want to expend on other ventures. A taxi will take you directly to your destination, but it is the most expensive means of travel. Scheduled taxis, buses, and streetcars give you a view of the whole city and expose you to the everyday lives of Russian people. The metro is speedy and reliable, but extremely crowded. If you choose to rent a car, you should try to brush up on your knowledge of European traffic laws. Whatever your needs or preference may be, you should learn the best words to make the journey.

Buy the Ticket

Finding transportation is as simple as poking your head outside the door of the hotel. You have decided how you want to travel. Now all you need to know is the right word. You will recognize most of these forms of public transportation from Chapter 5. Riding on any of the following modes of transportation is expressed with the prepositional case ("на авто́бусе").

Transportation

Russian Word	Pronunciation	English Meaning
авто́бус	ahv-TOH-boos	bus
маши́на	mah-SHEE-nah	car
автомоби́ль	ahv-tah-mah-BEEL	car
микроавто́бус	meek-roh-ahv-TOH-boos	minibus
маршру́тное такси́	marsh-ROOT-nah-yeh tahk-SEE	shuttle bus
трамва́й	trahm-VAY	streetcar
метро́	meh-TROH	subway
такси́	tahk-SEE	taxi

Take the Ride

In Chapter 12, you learned the verb pair ходи́ть/идти́, which means "to walk, go." Russian does not have a single word that means "to go." Instead, different verbs are used depending on the means of travel—"to go by foot" and "to go by vehicle." To express how you are going to get to where you are going (other than by walking), you need to use the verb pair éздить/éхать, "to go, drive." The same rules at work with ходи́ть/идти́ are at work here. Éздить is an indefinite verb of motion, and can be used to express round trip or regular actions, whereas éхать is definite and expresses one-time motion. Observe the conjugation patterns and examples in the following chart.

The Verb éздить (indefinite: "to go, drive")

Person	Singular	English	Plural	English
First	éзжу YEH-zhoo	I drive	éздим YEZ-deem	We drive
Second	éздишь YEZ-deesh	You drive (familiar)	éздите YEZ-deet-yeh	You drive (formal)
Third	éздит YEZ-deet	He/She drives	éздят YEZ-dyat	They drive

Он всегдá éздит на рабóту.
Ohn vsehg-DAH YEZ-deet nah-rah-BOH-too.
He (always) drives to work.

Они́ éздят в теáтр кáждую пя́тницу.
Ah-NEE YEZ-dyat fteh-AH-ter KAZH-doo-yoo PYAT-neet-soo.
They drive to the theater (every Friday).

The Verb éхать (definite: "to go, drive")

Person	Singular	English	Plural	English
First	éду YEH-doo	I am driving	éдем YEH-dyem	We are driving
Second	éдешь YEH-desh	You are driving (familiar)	éдете YEH-deht-yeh	You are driving (formal)
Third	éдет YEH-deht	He/She is driving	éдут YEH-doot	They are driving

Онá éдут на рабóту.
Ah-NAH YEH-deht nah-rah-BOH-too.
She is going to work (right now).

Они́ е́дут в теа́тр (сего́дня ве́чером).
Ah-NEE YEH-doot fteh-AH-ter (she-VOHD-nyah VEH-cher-ahm).
They are driving to the theater (tonight).

Do you remember your idioms for travel? If not, refer to Chapter 5 and refresh your memory. Pay attention to the use of these idioms in the following exercise. Fill in the blanks with the appropriate verb (correctly conjugated, of course).

Exercise 13.1

1. Он ________________ на маши́не на рабо́ту ка́ждый день.

   He <u>goes</u> to work by car every day.

2. Мы ________________ на авто́бусе в музе́й.

   We <u>are going</u> to the museum by bus.

3. Вы лю́бите ________________ на велосипе́де?

   Do you like <u>to go</u> by bicycle?

4. Они́ сейча́с ________________ на метро́ к нам.

   They <u>are going</u> to our house by metro right now.

Which Is Better?

As you stand outside the lobby of your hotel, you notice the abundance of options for your daily transportation. Taxis, buses, and streetcars pass by in every direction. You ask a porter to arrange a ride for you to downtown Moscow, and he replies, "Which one, or what kind?" When asking questions such as "Which taxi?" or "What building?" you need to call upon the adjective како́й, the word for *what* or *which*. Like all good adjectives, it must agree with the noun it modifies in gender, number, and case. Fortunately, it is a regular adjective and has an ordinary declension pattern.

Memory Serves

To make an exclamation, such as "What a beautiful day!" or "What a nice car!" the adjective **како́й** is often used. For example: "**како́й прекра́сный день!**" and "**Кака́я хоро́шая маши́на!**"

Како́й with Nouns

When used to form a question, како́й begins the sentence, followed by the noun it modifies. Similar to other adjectives such as любо́й (*any*), ка́ждый (*every*), такóй (*such*), and весь (*all*), какóй follows a regular declension pattern. The following table reviews the declension of какóй and the slightly irregular весь.

The Declension of какóй and весь

Case	Masculine/Neuter	Feminine	Plural
	which (house)	which (car)	which (people)
Nom.	какóй (дом) kah-KOY какóе (здáние) kah-KOY	какáя (машúна) kah-KAH-yah	какúе (лю́ди) kah-KEE-yeh
Prep.	какóм (дóме) kah-KOHM	какóй (машúне) kah-KOY	какúх (лю́дях) kah-KEEKH
Acc. (inan.)	какóй (дом) kah-KOY	какýю (машúну) kah-KOO-yoo	какúе (машúны) kah-KEE-yeh
Acc. (anim.)	какóго (отца) kah-KOH-vah	— —	какúх (людéй) kah-KEEKH
Gen.	какóго (дóма) kah-KOH-vah	какóй (машúны) kah-KOY	какúх (людéй) kah-KEEKH
Dat.	какóму (дóму) kah-KOH-moo	какóй (машúне) kah-KOY	какúм (лю́дям) kah-KEEM
Inst.	какúм (дóмом) kah-KEEM	какóй (машúной) kah-KOY	какúми (людьмú) kah-KEE-mee

Case	Masculine	Feminine	Neuter	Plural
	the whole (house)	the whole (car)	the whole (sea)	all (people)
Nom.	весь (дом) vyes	вся (машúна) vsyah	всё (мóре) vsyoh	все (лю́ди) vsyeh
Prep.	всём (дóме) vsyohm	всей (машúне) vsyey	всём (мóре) vsyohm	всех (лю́дях) vsyekh
Acc. (inan.)	весь (дом) vyes	всю (машúну) vsyoo	всё (мóре) vsyoh	все (машúны) vsyeh
Acc. (anim.)	всегó (отцá) vsyeh-VOH	— —	— —	всех (людéй) vsyekh
Gen.	всегó (дóма) vsyeh-VOH	всей (машúны) vsyey	всегó (мóря) vsyeh-VOH	всех (людéй) vsyekh
Dat.	всемý (дóму) vsyeh-moo	всей (машúне) vsyey	всемý (мóрю) vsyeh-moo	всем (лю́дям) vsyehm
Inst.	всем (дóмом) vsyehm	всей (машúной) vsyey	всем (мóрем) vsyehm	всеми (людьмú) VSYEH-mee

As you already know, anything can happen while you travel. You might even be asked a question that uses какóй in a declined form. To be fully prepared, you should pay attention to a few of the ways it might appear in questions.

Какýю машúну вы берёте напрокáт?
Kah-KOO-yoo mah-SHEE-noo vwee behr-YOHT-yeh nah-prah-KAHT?
What kind of car are you renting?

На какóм автóбусе ты éздишь в цéнтр?
Nah-kah-KOHM ahv-TOH-boos tee YEZ-deesh ftsehntr?
Which bus are you taking downtown?

Отéц какóго человéка там ждёт?
Ah-tyets kah-KOH-vah cheh-lah-VYEH-kah tahm zhdyoht?
Which person's father is waiting there?

На какóм самолёте вы летúте?
Nah kah-KOHM sah-mahl-YOH-tyeh vwee leh-TEE-tyeh?
On which plane are you flying?

Using Which with What?

Sometimes carrying on a conversation can be an exercise in frustration if the person with whom you're speaking assumes that you already know all the details. Try to make sense of the following statements by asking questions using the adjective какóй.

Example: Мы смóтрим картúну.

(Какýю картúну?)

Красúвую картúну.Questions Using какóй

Russian Phrase	Pronunciation	English Meaning
Мы éздим на автóбусе.	Mwee YEZ-deem nah-ahv-TOH-boos-yeh.	We go by bus.
Онá éдет в гóрод.	Ah-NAH YEH-deht VGOH-rahd.	She is driving into town.
Онú берýт напрокáт машúну.	Ah-NEE beh-ROOT nah-prah-KAHT mah-SHEE-noo.	They are renting a car.
Я встречáюсь с дрýгом.	Yah vstreh-CHAH-yoos SDROO-gahm.	I am meeting with a friend.

Russian Phrase	Pronunciation	English Meaning
Он идёт в музéй.	Ohn eed-YOHT vmoo-ZEY.	He is going to a museum.
Эта кни́га занятá у человéка.	EH-tah KNEE-gah zahn-yah-TAH oo-cheh-lah-VYEH-kah.	This book is borrowed from a person.
Я читáю кни́гу.	Yah chee-TAH-yoo KNEE-goo.	I am reading a book.

The Best Way to Go

If your journeys take you outside the city limits, the bus will only take you so far. You will probably want to rent a car to ensure complete freedom of movement. As you walk into the rental agency, you may want to keep some of the following questions in mind.

Каки́е у вас мáрки маши́н?
Kah-KEE-yeh oo-vahs MAR-kee mah-SHEEN?
What kind of cars do you have?

Скóлько стóит арéнда за день?
SKOHL-kah STOH-eet ah-REN-dah zah dehn?
What is the rate per day?

Бензи́н тóже включён в цéну?
Ben-ZEEN TOH-zheh vkloo-CHYOHN VTSEH-noo?
Is gas also included?

Включенá ли в страхóвку компенсáция жéртвам в слýчае авáрии?
Vkloo-cheh-NAH lee vstrah-KOHV-koo kahm-pehn-SAHT-see-yah ZHERT-vahm FSLOO-chay-yeh ah-VAHR-ee-ee?
Does the insurance policy cover personal liability?

Memory Serves

Russians, like many other Europeans, don't have as many personal cars as Americans. You will find most Russian cities designed for public transportation, and rarely see people driving by themselves. Also, remember to find out in advance where the gas stations are located. If you plan to travel long distances, you may need to bring extra gas with you.

To help you keep your bearing as your drive, you should know the cardinal directions and how to express them in motion.

на се́вер (nah-SEH-vehr)	to the north
на юг (nah-YOOK)	to the south
на за́пад (nah-ZAH-paht)	to the west
на восто́к (nah-vah-STOHK)	to the east

They've Called Your Number

People count every day, from Wall Street brokers to customers fishing for spare change. Numbers are needed for scheduling appointments, telling time, counting sheep as you go to sleep, measuring, and weighing. Grab your pocket calculator and start crunching numbers!

I'm Accounted For

Hot Topic

Cardinal numbers are the numbers used to count: one, two, three ….

To understand the responses to your questions "How much?" or "How many?" you need to learn the Russian numbers listed in the following chart. The following nouns are *cardinal numbers*, or numbers that express quantity. Before you can tell time or negotiate prices, you need to become familiar with the Russian number system.

Cardinal Numbers

Russian Word	Pronunciation	English Meaning
ноль	nohl	0
оди́н/одна́/одно́	ah-DEEN/ahd-NAH/ahd-NOH	1
два/две/два	dvah	2
три	tree	3
четы́ре	cheh-TEE-reh	4
пять	pyaht	5
шесть	shest	6
семь	sehm	7
во́семь	VOH-sehm	8
де́вять	DEH-vyaht	9
де́сять	DEH-syaht	10

Russian Word	Pronunciation	English Meaning
оди́надцать	ah-DEE-nahd-tsat	11
двена́дцать	dveh-NAD-tsat	12
трина́дцать	tree-HAD-tsat	13
четы́рнадцать	cheh-TEER-nad-tsat	14
пятна́дцать	pyat-NAD-tsat	15
шестна́дцать	shest-NAD-tsat	16
семна́дцать	sehm-HAD-tsat	17
восемна́дцать	voh-sehm-NAD-tsat	18
девятна́дцать	dehv-yaht-NAD-tsat	19
два́дцать	DVAD-tsat	20
два́дцать оди́н	DVAD-tsat ah-DEEN	21
два́дцать два/две	DVAD-tsat dvah/dveh	22
два́дцать три	DVAD-tsat tree	23
два́дцать четы́ре	DVAD-tsat cheh-TEE-reh	24
два́дцать пять	DVAD-tsat pyaht	25
два́дцать шесть	DVAD-tsat shest	26
два́дцать семь	DVAD-tsat sehm	27
два́дцать во́семь	DVAD-tsat VOH-sehm	28
два́дцать де́вять	DVAD-tsat DEH-vyaht	29
три́дцать	TREED-tsat	30
со́рок	SOH-rahk	40
пятьдеся́т	pyat-dehs-YAHT	50
шестьдеся́т	shest-dehs-YAHT	60
се́мьдесят	SEHM-dehs-yaht	70
во́семьдесят	VOH-sehm-dehs-yaht	80
девяно́сто	dehv-yah-NOH-stah	90
сто	stoh	100
сто оди́н/одна́/одно́	stoh ah-DEEN/ahd-NAH/ahd-NOH	101
сто два/две	stoh dvah/dveh	102
две́сти	DVEH-stee	200
три́ста	TREE-stah	300
четы́реста	cheh-TEE-reh-stah	400
пятьсо́т	pyat-SOHT	500
ты́сяча	TEES-yah-chah	1,000
две ты́сячи	dveh TEES-yah-chee	2,000

continues

Cardinal Numbers (continued)

Russian Word	Pronunciation	English Meaning
сто ты́сяч	stoh TEES-yach	100,000
миллио́н	meel-lee-OHN	1,000,000
два миллио́на	dvah meel-lee-OH-nah	2,000,000
миллиа́рд	meel-lee-AHRT	1,000,000,000
два миллиа́рда	dvah meel-lee-AHR-dah	2,000,000,000

After you have mastered the fundamentals of counting in Russian, you should remember these few details.

- The number 1 (оди́н) changes to match the gender of the noun it modifies. For example: "оди́н стол" ("one table"), "одна́ маши́на" ("one car"), "одно́ колесо́" ("one wheel"). The number 2 (два) also changes, but you will learn how to attach numbers to nouns in Chapter 18.
- The number 40 (со́рок) and 90 (девяно́сто) are unusual and must be memorized, because they do not follow the normal pattern.
- Remember that Russian numbers have only one (if any) ь. In the teens (11–19) the ь moves to the end of the word. In the numbers 50 through 80, the ь moves to the middle.
- Compound numbers are formed the same way in Russian as in English. "One hundred seventy-five" becomes "сто се́мьдесят пять." Russians do not use *one* or *and* in their compound numbers.

Do You Have the Time?

You've been working so hard at mastering Russian numbers that you've completely lost track of time. Is it dinnertime already, or is it still early afternoon? You can quickly solve this dilemma by asking someone one of these simple questions.

Hot Topic

The preposition в usually means *in* or *to*, but in time expressions it means *at*.

Кото́рый час сейча́с?
Kah-TOH-ree chas see-CHAS?
What time is it?

Сейча́с …
See-CHAS …
It's … (+ the time).

The phrases in the following table will help you tell what time it is.

Telling Time

Russian Word	Pronunciation	English Meaning
час но́чи/дня	chas NOH-chee/dnyah	1:00 A.M./P.M.
два часа́	dvah chah-SAH	2:00
три часа́	tree chah-SAH	3:00
четы́ре часа́	cheh-TEE-reh chah-SAF	4:00
пять часо́в	pyaht chah-SOHF	5:00
шесть часо́в, пять мину́т утра́/ве́чера	shest chah-SOHF, pyaht mee-NOOT oot-RAH/VEH-cheh-rah	6:05 A.M./P.M.
семь часо́в, де́сять мину́т	sehm chah-SOHF, DEHS-yaht mee-NOOT	7:10
во́семь часо́в, пятна́дцать мину́т	VOH-sehm chah-SOHF, pyat-NAD-tsat mee-NOOT	8:15
де́вять часо́в, три́дцать мину́т	DEHV-yaht chah-SOHF, TREED-tsat mee-NOOT	9:30
де́сять часо́в, со́рок одна́ мину́та	DEHS-yaht chah-SOHF, SOH-rahk ahd-NAH mee-NOO-tah	10:41
оди́ннадцать часо́в, со́рок пять мину́т	ah-DEEN-nad-tsat chah-SOHF, SOH-rahk pyaht mee-NOOT	11:45
двена́дцать часо́в, пятьдеся́т две мину́ты	dveh-NAD-tsat chah-SOHF, pyaht-dehs-YAHT dveh mee-NOO-tee	12:52
по́лночь	POHL-nohch	midnight
по́лдень	POHL-dehn	noon

In addition, just as Americans will say "half past" or "a quarter till," Russians separate time into quarter and half-hour segments.

Halves and Quarters

Russian Word	Pronunciation	English Meaning
полови́на тре́тьего	pah-lah-VEE-nah TREH-tyeh-vah	half past 2:00
че́тверть четвёртого	CHET-vehrt chet-VYOHR-tah-vah	a quarter past 3:00
без че́тверти четы́ре	bez CHET-vehr-tee cheh-TEE-reh	a quarter till 4:00
полови́на шесто́го	pah-lah-VEE-nah shes-TOH-vah	half past 5:00
без десяти́ шесть	bez dehs-yah-TEE shest	ten till 6:00
два́дцать мину́т восьмо́го	DVAD-tsat mee-NOOT vahs-MOH-vah	twenty past 7:00

Keep the following in mind when telling time:

- Time expressions are as simple as stating the hour and minute. Watch closely, however. The hours 2, 3, and 4 take часа́, whereas the hours 5 and higher require часо́в.
- Time expressions involving terms such as "half past" or "ten till" are frequently used in passing remarks but not in regular conversation. You should recognize them if spoken, but you do not need to learn them.
- To express "at what time" you plan to do something, use the preposition **в** + the time. For example: "Они иду́т в теа́тр в семь часо́в." ("They are going to the theater at 7.)
- The terms for A.M. and P.M. differ pending on the time of the day. Russians divide the day into four parts. 12 midnight to 4 A.M. is *night* (ночь). 4 A.M. to 11 A.M. is *morning*. 11 A.M. to 5 P.M. is *day* or *afternoon*. 5 P.M. to 12 midnight is *evening*.

Memory Serves

To suggest *when* you plan to do something, use the preposition **в** + the time.

You should also be able to give some more general estimates of time. Not everyone wears a watch, or if they do their watch may not keep exact time. Sometimes less information is more. The following time expressions will round out your speech.

Time Expressions

Russian Word	Pronunciation	English Meaning
секу́нда	seh-KOON-dah	second
мину́та	mee-NOO-tah	minute
час	chas	hour
день	dehn	day
у́тро	OOT-rah	morning
у́тром	OOT-rahm	in the morning
день	dehn	afternoon
днём	dnyohm	in the afternoon
ве́чер	VEH-chehr	evening
ве́чером	VEH-cheh-rahm	in the evening
ночь	nohch	night
но́чью	NOH-chyoo	at night
в кото́ром часу́?	fkah-TOH-ram chah-SOO?	at what time?

Russian Word	Pronunciation	English Meaning
о́коло ча́са	OH-kah-lah chah-SAH	around one
че́рез час	CHEH-res chas	in an hour
че́рез полтора́ часа́	CHEH-res pahl-tah-RAH chah-SAH	in an hour and a half
че́рез полчаса́	CHEH-res pahl-chah-SAH	in half an hour
час наза́д	chas nah-ZAHT	an hour ago
ка́ждый час	KAZH-dee chas	every hour
ра́но	RAH-nah	early
по́здно	POHZ-nah	late
вчера́	vcheh-RAH	yesterday
сего́дня	seh-VOHD-nyah	today
за́втра	ZAHF-trah	tomorrow

The Least You Need to Know

- You can use the verb е́здить/е́хать to indicate that you are being transported somewhere, and by what means of transportation by using the prepositional case.
- Како́й is the pronoun for *which* and *what*, and it is declined as an adjective.
- Regardless of how you use the Russian language, you will need to know cardinal numbers at some point in the future.
- The preposition в usually means *in* or *to*, but when telling time it means *at*.

Chapter 14

A Room with a View

In This Chapter

- Making the most of the hotel
- A handful of ordinal numbers
- Thinking and knowing
- Prefixing verbs

You have successfully navigated the baggage claim, found an appropriate method of transportation, and are now standing in front of your hotel. As you put your bags down inside the lobby, you glance around the hotel's interior and decide that you've chosen an excellent hotel.

As you wait for the hotel employee to locate your reservation, you think about room service and relaxing in the hot tub. What kind of room do you want? Perhaps a bed and shower alone will suffice. Or maybe you want something a little more extravagant. From cable TV to a balcony view, this chapter will help you settle into your hotel room in style.

This Hotel Has Everything and a Kitchen Sink

As you check into your room, you want to be doubly sure that they have the features you're looking for. The following chart outlines the basics, and, remember, if you're uncertain, you can always ask:

У вас есть …?

oo-VAHS yest …?

Do you have …?

At the Hotel

Russian Word	Pronunciation	English Meaning
бар	bahr	bar
портье́	pahr-TYEH	desk clerk
швейца́р	shvay-TSAR	doorman
лифт	leeft	elevator
лифтёр	leeft-YOHR	elevator man
гости́ница	gah-STEE-neet-sah	hotel
химчи́стка	heem-CHEEST-kah	laundry and dry-cleaning service
регистра́ция	reh-gee-STRAH-tsee-yah	registration
рестора́н	reh-stah-RAHN	restaurant
обслу́живание в но́мере	ahb-SLOO-zhee-vah-nee-yeh VNOH-mer-yeh	room service
бассе́йн	bah-SAYN	swimming pool

No matter where you choose to stay, you want to know what kind of service you're paying for. Are the walls thick and insulated? Are there noisy activities nearby late at night? Which floor are you on: smoking or nonsmoking? Does your room have a view of the ocean or an alleyway? Don't be fooled by the luxurious lobby of the hotel, but be certain that your room meets your expectations by learning a few of the words in the following chart.

Hotel Basics

Russian Word	Pronunciation	English Meaning
но́мер с ви́дом …	NOH-mehr SVEE-dahm …	a room with a view …
… на го́род	… nah-GOH-raht	… of the city
… на двор	nah-DVOHR	… of the courtyard
… на мо́ре	nah-MOHR-yeh	… of the sea
с кондиционе́ром	skahn-deet-see-ah-NEH-rahm	with air conditioning
буди́льник	boo-DEEL-neek	alarm clock
балко́н	bahl-KOHN	balcony

Russian Word	Pronunciation	English Meaning
ва́нна	VAH-nah	bathtub
двухме́стный но́мер (с двумя́ крова́тями)	dvook-MYEST-nee NOH-mehr (sdvoom-YAH krah-VAHT-yah-mee)	double room (with twin beds)
ключ	klooch	key
но́мер	NOH-mehr	room
сейф	sayf	safe
душ	doosh	shower
одноме́стный но́мер (с двухспа́льной крова́тью)	ahd-nah-MYEST-nee NOH-mehr (sdvook-SPAHL-noy krah-VAHT-yoo)	single room (with a double bed)
но́мер-люкс	NOH-mehr-lyooks	suite
телефо́н	the-leh-FOHN	telephone
(цветно́й) телеви́зор	(sveht-NOY) teh-leh-VEE-zahr	television (color)
с пита́нием	spee-TAH-nee-yehm	with meals
без пита́ния	bez pee-TAH-nee-yah	without meals

Культу́ра

Many European countries (including Russia) have two different "bathrooms." The **ва́нная** usually has the **ва́нна** and **душ** (bathtub and shower), whereas the **туале́т** has the toilet and sink. Be certain you know which room to ask for while traveling around.

Now that you've unpacked and begun to relax, use some of the vocabulary that you've learned. Fill in the blanks in the following exercise.

Exercise 14.1

1. У меня́ жена́ и дво́е детей. Я хочу́ ________________ но́мер. (I have two children. I want ________________ room.)
2. Мой муж лю́бит мо́ре. У вас но́мер ________________? (My husband likes the sea. Do you have a room with ________________?)
3. Он хо́чет но́мер-люкс ________________. (He wants a suite __________.)

Get Some Room Service

Even the presidential suite sometimes lacks something important. Whether it's too cold for your liking and you want an extra blanket, or you have the late-night munchies, you should know how to call the front desk and ask for the appropriate goods and services. Don't be afraid to pick up that phone! Glance over the words in the next chart and make your life a little more comfortable.

Necessities

Russian Word	Pronunciation	English Meaning
ада́птер	ah-DAHP-tehr	adapter (power converter)
пе́пельница	PEH-pehl-neet-sah	ashtray
кусо́к мы́ла	koo-SOHK mee-lah	bar of soap
одея́ло	ah-deh-YAH-lah	blanket
открыва́лка для консе́рвов	aht-kree-VAHL-kah dlyah kahn-SEHR-vahf'	can opener
што́пор	SHTOH-pahr	corkscrew
ве́шалка	VEH-shal-kah	hanger
куски́ льда́	koos-KEE lldah	ice cubes
спи́чки	SPEECH-kee	matches
минера́льная вода́	meen-eh-RAHL-nah-yah vah-DAH	mineral water
поду́шка	pah-DOOSH-kah	pillow
полоте́нце	pah-lah-TYEN-tsyeh	towel

The following phrases will help you start communicating your needs. Notice how the adverb ну́жен changes to match the noun that is needed. Review the phrases and try to complete the exercise that follows.

Я бы хоте́л(а) …
Yah bwee hah-TYEHL(ah) …
I would like ….

Мне нужна́ (поду́шка).
Mnyeh noozh-NAH (pah-DOOSH-kah).
I need (a pillow).

Мне нужны́ (куски́ льда́).
Mnyeh noozh-NEE (koos-KEE LDAH).
I need (ice cubes).

Мне ну́жен (ада́птер).
Mnyeh NOOZH-yen (ah-DAHP-tyehr).
I need (an adapter).

Exercise 14.2

1. I need a room. ______________________________.
2. I would like a key. ______________________________.
3. I need a blanket. ______________________________.
4. I need some matches. ______________________________.

Внима́ние

One of the classic "tourist mistakes" that Americans make while traveling in European countries is to mistake the tiny "bathtub" next to the toilet for a convenient way to wash clothes. It's not a bathtub; it's a bidet.

You're Going Places—Up!

You checked into the hotel, requested some extra towels, and spent a long relaxing hour in the hot tub. But as you dry off and make your way back to your room, you realize that all the hallways look the same. Is your room on the second or the third floor? Is your room the fourth or fifth door on the left? To get your navigational skills back on track, you should learn how to form *ordinal numbers.* Study the numbers in the following chart, and you'll be back in your room before you find any of that stress you left in the hot tub.

Ordinal Numbers

Russian Word	Pronunciation	English Meaning
пе́рвый	PEHR-vwee	first
второ́й	ftah-ROY	second
тре́тий	TREH-tee	third
четвёртый	cheht-VYOHR-tee	fourth
пя́тый	PYAH-tee	fifth

continues

Ordinal Numbers (continued)

Russian Word	Pronunciation	English Meaning
шестóй	shes-TOY	sixth
седьмóй	sehd-MOY	seventh
восьмóй	vahs-MOY	eighth
девя́тый	dehv-YAH-tee	ninth
деся́тый	dehs-YAH-tee	tenth
оди́ннадцатый	ah-DEEN-nad-tsah-tee	eleventh
двенáдцатый	dveh-NAD-tsah-tee	twelfth
двадцáтый	dvad-TSAH-tee	twentieth
тридцáтый	treed-TSAH-tee	thirtieth
сороковóй	cah-rah-kah-VOY	fortieth
пятидеся́тый	pyah-tee-dehs-YAH-tee	fiftieth
сóтый	SOH-tee	hundredth
ты́сячный	TEE-syahch-nee	thousandth
миллиóнный	meel-lee-OH-nee	millionth

A few notes on ordinal numbers:

- Forming ordinal numbers is as simple as adding the adjectival ending -ый or -ой to the end of the cardinal number. A slight change occurs in ordinal numbers 50 through 80. For example, пятьдеся́т (cardinal) becomes пятидеся́тый (ordinal). The -ь is replaced with -и in the ordinal form.
- Трéтий (*third*) is the only ordinal number oddball. In its feminine, neuter, and plural forms, it mutates to become трéтья, тéтье, and трéтьи respectively.
- Remember, like other adjectives, ordinal numbers must always match the nouns they modify in gender (masculine, feminine, neuter), number (singular, plural), and case.

Hot Topic

Ordinal numbers are the adjectival forms of cardinal numbers. They answer the question **котóрый** or *which?*

Declension of Ordinal Numbers

Like all other adjectives, ordinal numbers have to match the nouns they modify. They decline like any other adjective, with the exception of the oddball трéтий. You can review your declension patters from Chapter 8 in the following charts.

Case	Masculine	Feminine	Neuter	Plural
Nom.	пéрвый PEHR-vwee	пéрвая PEHR-vah-yah	пéрвое PEHR-vah-yeh	пéрвые PEHR-vwee-yeh
Prep.	пéрвом PEHR-vahm	пéрвой PEHR-voy	пéрвом PEHR-vahm	пéрвых PEHR-vweekh
Acc. (Inan.)	пéрвый PEHR-vwee	пéрвую PEHR-voo-yoo	пéрвое PEHR-vah-yeh	пéрвые PEHR-vwee-yeh
Acc. (Anim.)	пéрвого PEHR-vah-vah	—— ——	—— ——	пéрвых PEHR-vweekh
Gen.	пéрвого PEHR-vah-vah	пéрвой PEHR-voy	пéрвого PEHR-vah-vah	пéрвых PEHR-vweekh
Dat.	пéрвому PEHR-vah-moo	пéрвой PEHR-voy	пéрвому PEHR-vah-moo	пéрвым PEHR-vweem
Inst.	пéрвым PEHR-vweem	пéрвой PEHR-voy	пéрвым PEHR-vweem	пéрвыми PEHR-vwee-mee

Case	Masculine	Feminine	Neuter	Plural
Nom.	трéтий TREH-tee	трéтья TREH-tyah	трéтье TREH-tyeh	трéтьи TREH-tee
Prep.	трéтьем TREH-tyehm	трéтьей TREH-tyay	трéтьем TREH-tyem	трéтьих TREH-teekh
Acc. (Inan.)	трéтий TREH-tee	трéтью TREH-tyoo	трéтье TREH-tyeh	трéтьи TREH-tee
Acc. (Anim.)	трéтьего TREH-tyeh-vah	—— ——	—— ——	трéтьих TREH-teekh
Gen.	трéтьего TREH-tyeh-vah	трéтьей TREH-tyay	трéтьего TREH-tyeh-vah	трéтьих TREH-teekh
Dat.	трéтьему TREH-tyeh-moo	трéтьей TREH-tyay	трéтьему TREH-tyeh-moo	трéтьим TREH-teem
Inst.	трéтьим TREH-teem	трéтьей TREH-tyay	трéтьим TREH-teem	трéтьими TREH-tee-mee

Was It the First or the Second Floor?

Put your numbers into action by filling in the blanks of the following exercise. Remember to use the appropriate endings.

Exercise 14.3

1. Я ищу _______________ этáж. I am looking for _______________ floor.
2. У _____ брáта моя́ кни́га. _______________ brother has my book.
3. Кто знáет, кто был _______________ президéнтом? Who knows, who was the _______________ president?
4. С _______________ момéнта, я люби́л её. From the _______________ moment I loved her.

Verbs Get More Action

Verbs are the meat and potatoes of every language including Russian. Without a well-balanced diet of verbs, your language skills will be anemic. You learned the fundamental aspects of verb use in Chapter 9. You know that verbs express action, motion, and states of being. You know they have tense (past, present, future), aspect (perfective and imperfective), and can be either transitive or intransitive. Right now you know the imperfective aspect of verbs in the present tense. In Parts 5 and 6 you will learn how to use verbs in the past and future tenses and start putting together some really complex sentences.

The best-kept secret of the Russian language is that the number of verbs is very small. That's right. The number of root verbs is extremely limited. So how does the Russian language have thousands of verbs? Russians use prefixes to expand the meanings of their verbs. Whereas English has several words for "to talk" and "to convince," Russians see a connection between the two ideas and shape the verb using prefixes. This section introduces you to the world of prefixes.

What I Think I Know I Did

Before exploring the world of *prefixes*, you should become familiar with two common Russian verbs: "to know" and "to think." They are straightforward first-conjugation verbs, so there are no surprises or consonant mutations to deal with. The Russian verb знать, "to know," can be used in almost all the ways that it is used in English. People, places, ideas, and things can be "known" in the sense conveyed by this verb. Remember, this verb is transitive (requiring a direct object), and it requires the accusative case.

The Verb знать ("to know")

Person	Singular	English	Plural	English
First	зна́ю ZNAH-yoo	I know	зна́ем ZNAY-yehm	We know
Second	зна́ешь ZNAY-yesh	You know (familiar)	зна́ете ZNAY-yet-yeh	You know (formal)
Third	зна́ет ZNAY-yet	He/She knows	зна́ют ZNAY-yoot	They know

The verb ду́мать ("to think") is more limited in use. This verb is almost always used with the preposition о (*about*) + the prepositional clause.

The Verb думать ("to think")

Person	Singular	English	Plural	English
First	ду́маю DOO-mah-yoo	I think	ду́маем DOO-mah-yehm	We think
Second	ду́маешь DOO-mah-yesh	You think (familiar)	ду́маете DOO-mah-yet-yeh	You think (formal)
Third	ду́мает DOO-mah-yet	He/She thinks	ду́мают DOO-mah-yoot	They think

Он то́лько ду́мает о еде́.
Ohn TOHL-kah DOO-mah-yet ah-yehd-YEH.
He thinks only about food.

Она́ ду́мает о до́ме.
Ah-NAH DOO-mah-yet ah-DOHM-yeh.
She thinks about home.

Prefixes

You have, thus far, been introduced to root verbs, or the original verbs. Think of root verbs as a piece of bread. By itself it has its own texture and flavor. But by adding other foods to it, you can change its taste or even make it into something altogether different, like a sandwich. Root verbs can be changed or modified by the addition of certain prefixes that alter the meaning of the verb.

Hot Topic

Prefixes in Russian are words or syllables joined to the beginning of a verb. Prefixes expand or qualify the meaning of the verbs to which they are joined.

The most common prefixes that you will see are в, вы, на, по, раз, про, у, за, and пере. You may recognize a few of these from common prepositions that you have been using so far. However, do not be tricked by their function as prepositions! When these prefixes are attached to a verb, they lose any meaning that they might have by themselves. For instance, you know that на means *at* or *on*, and ходи́ть means "to walk." But находи́ть means "to find."

The Ties That Bind

Unfortunately, there is no method of learning to teach you every word of a foreign language. Think of how many English words you don't know! The value of recognizing prefixes and root verbs is that you can reduce your time memorizing new words by focusing on the words you already know.

How does that work? Suppose you glance at a newspaper and notice that an important senator is разгова́ривают. Before you grab your dictionary, you can try to take the verb apart piece by piece. You know that раз- is a verb prefix, so you set it aside for the moment. You then notice that гова́ривать looks similar to говори́ть ("to talk"), a verb that you'll learn later. If you were in a pinch and had to guess, you could say that the senator is "talking." You wouldn't be far wrong. The verb разгова́ривать really means "to narrate" or "to discuss in full," but you can grasp the meaning without the dictionary.

Memory Serves

Prefixes do not, generally, change the conjugation pattern of the verbs to which they are attached. They also do not change the stress, with the exception of the prefix вы́-, which is almost always stressed.

The following chart outlines some common prefixed verbs. Pay attention to the changes in meaning from the root verb to the prefixed verb.

Common Verbs with Prefixes

Russian Verb	English Meaning	Prefixed Verb	English Meaning
быва́ть bwee-VAHT	to be, occur	забыва́ть zah-bwee-VAHT	to forget
ходи́ть hah-DEET	to go, walk	находи́ть nah-hah-DEET	to find
по́мнить POH-mneet	to remember	напомина́ть nah-pah-mee-NAHT	to remind

Russian Verb	English Meaning	Prefixed Verb	English Meaning
брать braht	to take	собира́ть sah-bee-RAHT	to collect
ходи́ть hah-DEET	to go, walk	входи́ть fhah-DEET	to enter
ходи́ть hah-DEET	to go, walk	выходи́ть vwee-hah-DEET	to exit
реша́ть reh-SHAHT	to solve	разреша́ть raz-reh-SHAT	to allow, permit
говори́ть gah-vah-REET	to talk	уговори́ть oo-gah-vah-REET	to persuade

Express Yourself

Now that you've had a taste of prefixes, try to complete the sentences in the following exercise by using the verbs you have just learned. Remember, the conjugation for prefixed verbs does not change from the root verb.

Exercise 14.4

Example: Я ча́сто ________________ но́мер. (I often forget the number.)

1. Он ________________ ма́рки. (He collects stamps.)
2. Ми́ша ________________ в зда́ние. (Misha is entering the building.)
3. Роди́тели ________________ ей по́здно возвраща́ться домо́й. (The parents allow her to return home late.)
4. Он всегда́ ________________ свой ключ до́ма. (He always forgets his keys at home.)
5. Его́ брат ________________ их под кре́слом ка́ждое у́тро. (His brother finds them under the armchair every morning.)

The Least You Need to Know

- Rest and relaxation in your hotel room is as simple as learning a few key words and phrases.
- Ordinal numbers give you a limitless number of adjectives to modify nouns. They are all formed regularly and decline normally, except тре́тий.
- If you're thinking about thinking or knowing, you should use the verbs ду́мать and зна́ть.
- You can navigate magazines and newspapers without a dictionary if you know how to recognize root verbs and prefixes and if you're willing to do a little guess work.

Part 4 The Fun Stuff

Learning Russian doesn't always involve stress and hard work—sometimes you need to relax and have a good time. The chapters in Part 4 will give you a relaxing break, time for shopping or sightseeing, for dinner and a movie, and for sports and games. All the possibilities lie before you!

As you relax, you'll also learn some important notes about the weather and Russian culture. You will learn how to express yourself, saying what you want to do and when you want to do it, and describe how much fun you're having.

Chapter 15

A Date with the Weather

In This Chapter

- Your local weather conditions
- Days of the week
- Months and seasons of the year
- What day is it?

Your first night in Moscow has been lazy and relaxed, and you decide that you'd like to do a little sightseeing tomorrow. But before you begin laying out your clothes for the next day, have you thought about the weather conditions? Although summer in Moscow is usually clear skies and sun, anything can happen. Regardless of your plans for your vacation, you need to know how to dress. This means that you need to turn on the Weather Channel or take a glance at the morning paper. In this chapter, you will learn how to prevent disaster with the right words for weather conditions, and along the way you'll learn how to make plans accordingly.

They're Swimming and It's Only 40 Degrees Outside!

You faithfully listened to the radio, and you even put on an extra pair of long underwear to be safe. But as you step outside, you'd swear it was 80 degrees and not 30 degrees. Why is that? You didn't hear the radio incorrectly. Russians use the Celsius scale and not the Fahrenheit scale. This means that you need to do a little math in your head before you step outside. The easiest way to keep your temperatures in check is to remember that 0 degrees Celsius equals 32 degrees Fahrenheit, and 30 degrees Celsius equals 86 degrees Fahrenheit. The words in the following chart will keep you straight.

Weather Expressions

Russian Word	Pronunciation	English Meaning
Какáя сегóдня погóда?	Kah-KA-yah seh-VOHD-nyah pah-GOH-dah?	How is the weather today?
Какóй прогнóз погóды?	Kah-KOY prahg-NOHZ pah-GOH-dee?	What is the weather forecast?
Какóй прекрáсный день!	Kak-KOY preh-KRAH-snee dehn!	What a beautiful day!
Сейчáс хорóшая погóда.	See-CHAS hah-ROH-shah-yah pah-GOH-dah.	The weather is great.
Сейчáс ужáсная погóда.	See-CHAS oo-ZHAS-nah-yah pah-GOH-dah.	The weather is terrible.
Сейчáс прохлáдная погóда.	See-CHAS prah-KLAD-nah-yah pah-GOH-dah.	The weather is cool.
Сейчáс тёплая погóда.	See-CHAS TYOH-plah-yah pah-GOH-dah.	The weather is warm.
Идёт мéлкий дождь.	Eed-YOHT MEHL-kee dohzhd.	It's drizzling.
Дýет вéтер.	DOO-yet VET-her.	The wind is blowing.
Сегóдня пáсмурно.	Seh-VOHD-nyah PAS-moorah.	It's cloudy.
Сегóдня ненáстье.	Seh-VOHD-nyah neh-NAH-styeh.	It's stormy.
Сóлнце свéтит.	SON-tsyeh SVEH-teet.	The sun is shining.
Сейчáс гром и мóлния.	See-CHAS grohm ee MOHL-nyah.	There is lightning and thunder now.
Идёт дождь.	Eed-YOHT dohzhd.	It is raining.
Сейчáс влáжная погóда.	See-CHAS VLAH-zhnah-yah pah-GOH-dah.	It is humid now.
Похóже, что бýдет дождь.	Pah-HOH-zhyeh shtoh BOO-det dohzhd.	It looks like it will not be raining.

Russian Word	Pronunciation	English Meaning
Сего́дня хо́лодно.	Seh-VOHD-nyah HOH-lahd-nah.	It is cold today.
Сего́дня тепло́.	Seh-VOHD-nyah tehp-LOH	It is warm today.

What's the Temperature?

You have your mini-calculator working overtime as you wander the streets downtown, but you can't seem to find the current temperature flashing on any bank signs. Your best bet is simply to stop someone and ask. You can also respond when people ask you about the weather.

Кака́я сейча́с температу́ра?
Kah-KAH-yah see-CHAS tehm-peh-rah-TOO-rah?
What's the temperature?

Сейча́с де́сять гра́дусов моро́за.
See-CHAS DEHS-yaht GRAH-doo-sahv mah-ROH-sah.
It is negative 10 degrees.

Сейча́с нуль.
See-CHAS nool.
It is zero.

Сейча́с шестьдеся́т гра́дусов тепла́.
See-CHAS shest-dehs-YAHT GRAH-doo-sahv tehp-LAH.
It is 60 degrees.

You can use the words in the following chart to expand your weather vocabulary.

Wind, Rain, and Fog

Russian Word	Pronunciation	English Meaning
тума́н	too-MAHN	fog
облака́	ahb-lah-KAH	clouds
дождь	dohzhd	rain
снег	snek	snow
гроза́	grah-SAH	thunderstorm
со́лнце	SOHN-tseh	sun
бу́ря	BOOR-yah	storm

continues

Wind, Rain, and Fog (continued)

Russian Word	Pronunciation	English Meaning
ве́тер	VEH-tehr	wind
моро́з	mah-ROHS	frost
хо́лод	HOH-laht	cold (noun)
жара	zhah-RAH	heat
вла́жность	VLAZH-nahst	humidity
о́ттепель	OHT-tehp-yehl	thaw
роса́	pah-SAH	dew
хоро́ший/я́сный	hah-ROH-see/YAHS-nee	fine/fair
плохо́й/ужа́сный	plah-KOY/oo-ZHAS-nee	poor/awful
па́смурный/тума́нный	PAHS-moor-nee/too-MAH-nee	overcast/foggy
сыро́й/дождли́вый	see-ROY/dahzh-DLEE-vwee	wet/rainy
со́лнечный/жа́ркий	SOHL-nech-nee/ZHAR-kee	sunny/hot
прохла́дный/холо́дный	prah-KLAHD-nee/hah-LOHD-nee	cool/cold

The Forecast for Tomorrow

As you try to make plans for the weekend, you glance at the morning paper. Just for practice, glance at a handful of American cities and describe what their current weather conditions are.

Example: Сего́дня в Чика́го. (Today in Chicago.)

Answer: Хо́лодно. Идёт снег. (It is snowing.) Температу́ра 25 гра́дусов. (The temperature is 25 degrees.)

1. Сего́дня в Нью-Йо́рке.
2. Сего́дня в Атла́нте.
3. Сего́дня в Лос-Анджелесе.
4. Сего́дня в Бо́стоне.
5. Сего́дня в Вашингто́не.

Calendar Language

You've arrived in Moscow, recovered from jetlag, and spent a few days relaxing on your vacation. The week has been a blur of activity from the airport to the hotel to the restaurant to the theater, and you're so involved with activities that you lose track of time. You wander down the streets and wonder why the stores are closed. Is it a holiday? What day of the week is it? The business days of many of the stores and shops you see differ. Eventually you stop a fellow pedestrian and ask, "What day is it?" To properly understand his answer, you should learn the names of the days of the week.

Can You Tell Me What Day It Is?

The following chart will help you fill in your weekly calendar. You may want to remember that the term for *weekend* ("выходны́е дни") literally means "free days." The same words can be used if you have a day off work or an unofficial holiday. "Выходно́й день" can be any day that you are not working.

Days of the Week

Russian Word	Pronunciation	English Meaning
день	dehn	day
неде́ля	neh-DEHL-yah	week
понеде́льник	pah-neh-DEHL-neek	Monday
вто́рник	FTOR-neek	Tuesday
среда́	sreh-DAH	Wednesday
четве́рг	chet-VERK	Thursday
пя́тница	PYAHT-neet-sah	Friday
суббо́та	soo-BOH-tah	Saturday
воскресе́нье	vahs-kree-SEHN-yeh	Sunday
выходны́е (дни)*	vwee-hahd-NEE-yeh dnee	weekend
Како́й сего́дня день?	Kah-KOY seh-VOHD-nyah dehn?	What day is today?

*дни *(Days) is usually omitted in conversational language.*

Внима́ние

The Russian calendar, unlike the American calendar, begins on Monday. Be sure you have the correct day when you glance at the calendar. In addition, Russians do not capitalize the names of the days or months. They will always appear in lowercase unless they begin a sentence.

If you do something on a certain day, you need to use the Russian preposition в where you would use *on* in English. To put your days to work, use в + the day of the week in the accusative case.

Я иду́ в теа́тр в пя́тницу.
Yah ee-DOO fteh-AHTR VPYAHT-neet-soo.
On Friday I am going to the theater.

Suppose you do the same thing every Friday. You should use the preposition по + the day of the week in the dative case, plural form.

Я хожу́ в теа́тр по пя́тницам.
Yah hah-ZHOO fteh-AHTR POH-PYAHT-neet-sahm.
I go to the theater on Friday.

Memory Serves

To speak about what you are doing on a specific day, use the preposition **в** + the accusative case. To speak about what you do regularly on a certain day, use the preposition **по** + the dative plural.

Try responding to the following phrases:

Како́й день был вчера́?
Kah-KOY dehn bweel fcheh-RAH?
What day was yesterday?

Како́й день бу́дет за́втра?
Kah-KOY dehn BOO-det ZAHF-trah?
What day is tomorrow?

These Months Are a Mouthful

Now that you have the days of the week and the weather conditions tucked under your belt, you can begin to speak about the weather during specific months. For instance, you could ask, "Кака́я пого́да быва́ет в ию́не?" ("What is the weather like in June?"), or talk about your plans for summer vacation or holiday leave. The following table lists the months of the year.

Months of the Year

Russian Word	Pronunciation	English Meaning
ме́сяц	MEHS-yats	month
год	gohd	year
янва́рь	yahn-VAHR	January
февра́ль	fehv-RAHL	February
март	mart	March
апре́ль	ahp-REHL	April
май	mahy	May
ию́нь	ee-YOON	June
ию́ль	ee-YOOL	July

Russian Word	Pronunciation	English Meaning
áвгуст	AHV-goost	August
сентя́брь	sent-YAH-behr	September
октя́брь	ahk-TYAH-behr	October
ноя́брь	nah-YAH-behr	November
декáбрь	deh-KAH-behr	December

The names of the months in Russian are all masculine, which is important to remember when speaking about your plans. If you want to say that you are doing something (or that something is happening) in a certain month, use the preposition в + the prepositional phrase masculine form. Remember, months are not capitalized.

Я поéду в Росси́ю в мáе.
Yah pah-YEH-doo vrah-SEE-yoo VMAH-yeh.
I am going to Russia in May.

The same is true when speaking about the year. Use the preposition в + the prepositional phrase.

Я учу́сь (в коллéдже) в э́том году́.
Yah oo-CHOOS (vkah-LEHD-zhyeh) VEH-tahm gah-DOO.
I am studying (in college) this year.

Культу́ра

Russians typically celebrate New Year's Day in the same way that Americans celebrate Christmas. New Year's marks the beginning of winter break for students. May 9 is the Russian "Victory Day," the day World War II victory is celebrated with fireworks and parades.

Get Into the Season

No weather talk is complete without some seasonal variety. Or, perhaps you're engaging in an inquiry about which sports are played in summer and which are played in winter.

The Seasons of the Year

Russian Word	Pronunciation	English Meaning
врéмя гóда	VREHM-yah GOH-dah	season
зимá, зимóй	zee-MAH, zee-MOY	winter, in winter
веснá, веснóй	vehs-NAH, vehs-NOY	spring, in spring
лéто, лéтом	LEH-tah, LEH-tahm	summer, in summer
óсень, óсенью	OH-sehn, OH-sehn-yoo	fall, in the fall

Культу́ра

As the largest country in the world, Russia has no typical climate. Like the United States, some areas are colder; others, warmer. If you plan to focus your visit in the Golden Ring, or the cities surrounding Moscow, you should find the seasons comparable to states like Pennsylvania and New York.

To express *in* with the seasons, use the fixed adverbs listed in the following chart. Remember your adverbs from the time of day: Утром ("in the morning"), днём ("in the afternoon"), ве́чером ("in the evening"), and но́чью ("at night")? These adverbs function the same way, and they literally mean "during summer" or "in the time of summer."

Я пое́ду в Росси́ю зимо́й/ле́том.
Yah pah-YEH-doo vrah-SEE-yoo zee-MOY/LEH-tahm.
I am going to Russia in the winter/summer.

Remember to modify these adverbs using other adverbs.

Зимо́й хо́лодно.
Zee-MOY HOH-lahd-nah.
It is cold during winter.

You can easily use the seasons as adjectives as in the following examples:

Хокке́й (бе́йсбол) зи́мний (ле́тний) спорт.
Hah-KYEY (BAYS-bahl) ZEEM-nee (LET-nee) spohrt.
Hockey (baseball) is a winter (summer) game.

Волейбо́л (баскетбо́л) весе́нний (осе́нний) спорт.
Vah-ley-BOOHL (bahs-kyet-BOOHL) veh-SEHN-nee (ah-SEHN-nee) spohrt.
Volleyball (basketball) is a spring (autumn) game.

Scheduling Your Activities

Whether it's that big promotion or your next vacation, you don't want to deal with general terms like "in a few months" or "soon," you want to specify the exact date. Remind people of your birthday, your anniversary, or any day that is special. Before we start speaking with precision, let's recap the basics.

Finding Time

Russian Word	Pronunciation	English Meaning
час	chas	hour
день	dehn	day
неде́ля	hen-DEHL-yah	week
ме́сяц	MEHS-yats	month
год	goht	year
на про́шлой неде́ле	nah-PROH-shloy neh-DEHL-yeh	last week
на сле́дующей неде́ле	nah-sleh-DOO-you-see neh-dehl-yeh	next week
в про́шлом году́	VPROH-slahm gah-DOO	last year
в бу́дущем году́	VBOO-doo-shyem gah-DOO	next year

What's the Date?

So you finally made time for that big date? Before you start making dinner reservations, you should know how to form the date correctly in Russian. To answer the question "What's the date?" you use the ordinal numeral in the nominative singular neuter and the month in the genitive. Here's the formula:

> Ordinal number (in nominative case neuter) + month (in genitive case) + year (the last number in genitive case) + the word *year* (in genitive case).

To express the date on which something is taking place, you should familiarize yourself with your ordinal numbers and the genitive case once more. Here's the formula:

> Ordinal number (in genitive case) + month (in genitive case) + the year (the last number in genitive case) + year (in genitive case).

If this seems a little complicated, the following phrases will help you keep it straight:

> Сего́дня восемна́дцатое февраля́ две ты́сячи пе́рвого (четвёртого) го́да.
> Seh-VOHD-nyah voh-sehm-NAHD-tsah-tah-vah fehv-rahl-YAH, dveh TEES-yah-chee PEHR-vah-vah (cheet-VYOR-ta-va) GOH-dah.
> Today is February 18, 2004.

> Это случи́лось два́дцать девя́того ма́я, ты́сяча девятьсо́т девяно́сто седьмо́го го́да.
> EH-tah sloo-CHEE-lahs DVAHD-tsat dehv-RAH-tah-vah MAH-yah, TEES-yah-chah dehv-yaht-SOHT dehv-yah-NOH-stah sehd-MOH-vah GOH-dah.
> This happened on May 29, 1997.

When saying the full date, only the last number of the year declines in the genitive case. However, when referring to only the year, the last number of the year declines in the prepositional case.

> У меня́ биле́ты на соревнова́ние на пе́рвенство ми́ра в две ты́сячи второ́м (пя́том) году́.
> oo-mehn-YAH bee-LYEH-tee nah-sah-rev-nah-VAH-nee-yeh nah-PEHR-vehn-stvah MEER-ah vdveh TEES-yah-chee vtah-ROHM (PYA-tahm) gah-DOO.
> I have tickets to the World Series in 2005.

To refer to the date and the month alone, the genitive case is standard.

> Мой день рожде́ния седьмо́го апре́ля.
> Moy dehn pazh-DEH-nee-yah sehd-MOH-vah ahp-REHL-yah.
> My birthday is April 7th.

How is your memory? Do you remember important doctor's appointments or the date of the Super Bowl? Practice your knowledge of dates with the following exercise.

Exercise 15.1

Example: Christmas ____________________

Answer: два́дцать пя́того декабря́

1. New Year's Eve ____________________
2. Victory Day ____________________
3. Valentine's Day ____________________
4. 23 April, 1942 ____________________

Time Expressions

Sometimes it's best to be less specific. Perhaps you don't know the exact date, or perhaps you don't want to commit to a certain time. You can speak more vaguely as in "in a week" or "soon." You will already be familiar with some of these expressions from previous chapters.

Finding Time

Russian Word	Pronunciation	English Meaning
ско́ро	SKOH-rah	soon
сейча́с	see-CHAS	now
неда́вно	neh-DAHV-nah	recently
сего́дня	seh-VOHD-nyah	today
вчера́	fcheh-RAH	yesterday
звтра	ZAHF-trah	tomorrow
позавчера́	poh-zah-fcheh-RAH	the day before yesterday
послеза́втра	pohs-lee-ZAHV-trah	the day after tomorrow
в бу́дущем	VBOO-doo-shyem	in the future
в про́шлом	VPROH-shlahm	in the past
че́рез неде́лю	CHEH-rehz neh-DEHL-yoo	in a week
че́рез ме́сяц	CHEH-rehz MEHS-yats	in a month
на э́той неде́ле	nah-EH-toy neh-DEHL-yeh	this week

Put your skills to use by translating the following sentences:

Exercise 15.2

1. В бу́дущем году́ я пое́ду на Супер-Боль. ______________________.
2. Мой день рожде́ния четы́рнадцатого ма́я. ______________________.
3. Что вы де́лаете в выходны́е? ______________________.
4. В сре́ду он идёт в парк. ______________________.

The Least You Need to Know

- Mastering a handful of expressions for weather conditions will keep you high and dry.
- The Russian days of the week begin with понеде́льник and continue through вто́рник, среда́, четве́рг, пя́тница, суббо́та, and воскресе́нье.
- Months are easy to remember if you can say янва́рь, февра́ль, март, апре́ль, май, ию́нь, ию́ль, а́вгуст, сентя́брь, октя́брь, ноя́брь, and дека́брь.
- Seasons, in order of appearance, are зима́, весна́, ле́то, and о́сень.

Chapter 16

Sightseeing Is Fun

In This Chapter

- Get the most out of sightseeing
- It's a zoo out there
- How to make suggestions and plans
- Using the adverbs мóжно and нельзя́ to react
- Including other countries

As you wake up in your hotel room, you see the sun shining in through the windows. It's the perfect time to grab your camera and see the sights. If downtown Moscow is your destination, you can begin with a brisk stroll down Tverskaya ulitsa (Tver Street). From there, you can head to the Kremlin and tour Крáсная Плóщадь (Red Square), noting St. Basil's Cathedral and the towering monuments that line the walkways.

As you ride the metro toward the достопримечáтельности (*sights*), you can flip through your guidebook to check which museums are open and how to get there. Armed with a city map and your guidebook, you are prepared to see everything that the city has to offer. In this chapter, you will find a selection of places to go and things to do there; and you will learn how to express some suggestions or general opinions about the things you see.

The Sights to See

From Omsk to Vladivostok, you can find a thousand ways to spend your time. Do you like ancient architecture? You can satisfy your cravings for towering cathedrals and vast palaces in almost any Russian city. Perhaps you want to see huge collections of priceless artwork? There are museums, galleries, and the artists to support them everywhere you go. Whether you seek a leisurely stroll or a guided tour, the words and phrases in the following chart will help you find a way to relax.

Я поéду в …
Yah pah-YEH-doo v …
I am going to …

Places and Activities

The Place	English Meaning	The Activity	English Meaning
собóр	cathedral	чтóбы вúдеть щéдевры искýсства	to see the artwork
цéрковь	church	чтóбы вúдеть архитектýру	to see the architecture
цирк	circus	чтóбы вúдеть акробáтов	to see the acrobats
вы́ставка	exhibition	чтóбы вúдеть картúны	to see the pictures
кремль	Kremlin	чтóбы вúдеть дворцы́	to see the palaces
ры́нок	market place	чтóбы смотрéть на товáры	to look at the goods
музéй	museum	чтóбы смотрéть на скульптýры	to look at the sculptures
плóщадь	square	чтóбы вúдеть пáмятник	to see the monument
теáтр	theater	чтóбы вúдеть спектáкль	to see a performance
прúстань	wharf	чтóбы смотрéть на корáбли	to look at the ships
зоопáрк	zoo	чтóбы наблюдáть живóтных	to watch the animals

Культýра

Russians love the water, and many spend the majority of their vacations on the beaches of Lake Baikal, the Black and Caspian seas, or along the shores of any of the numerous lakes in Russia. As a general rule, the closer you get to a body of water, the more recreational activities, like amusement parks and carnivals, you will find.

What Shall We See?

What has your day been like so far? Have you seen anything that strikes your fancy? Perhaps it would be easier to take in all the sights if you could actually ви́деть (*see*). The verb ви́деть ("to see") can help you express what sights you want to take in. If you want to watch a show, or look at a painting, you may also want to learn the verb смотре́ть ("to watch, look") to express those actions. These two verbs work almost identically in Russian as they do in English.

The Verb ви́деть (imperfective: "to see")

Person	Singular	English	Plural	English
First	ви́жу VEE-zhoo	I see	ви́дим VEE-deem	We see
Second	ви́дишь VEE-deesh	You see (familiar)	ви́дите VEE-deet-yeh	You see (formal)
Third	ви́дит VEE-deet	He/She sees	ви́дят VEE-dyaht	They see

Я ви́жу кора́бль. Они́ ви́дят меня́.
Yah VEE-zhoo kah-RAHBL. Ah-NEE VEE-dyaht mehn-YAH.
I see the boat. They see me.

The Verb смотре́ть (imperfective: "to look, watch")

Person	Singular	English	Plural	English
First	смотрю́ smah-TROO	I look/ watch	смо́трим SMOH-treem	We look/ watch
Second	смо́тришь SMOH-treesh	You look (familiar)	смо́трите SMOH-treet-yeh	You look … (formal)
Third	смо́трит SMOH-treet	He/She looks	смо́трят SMOH-tryaht	They look …
Imperative	Смотри́! smah-TREE!	Look!	Смотри́те! smah-TREET-yeh	Look!

Я смотрю́ накора́бль. Они́ смо́трят наменя́.
Yah smah-TROO kah-RAH-behl. Ah-NEE SMOH-tryaht mehn-YAH.
I am looking at the boat. They are looking at me.

Let's Go Already

The English language grows more widespread every year; unfortunately, not everyone likes to speak it. Consider France; many French-speaking people can speak English, but they prefer to speak their native language. However, France and Russia have diplomatic and economic ties dating back hundreds of years. You will often find the French delighted to speak with you in Russian. The same can be said for Germany, and many other European nations. Although not everyone you meet will speak Russian, almost everywhere you travel in Europe and throughout the globe, you will find people who do. To make your journeys lighter on the shoulders, you may want to learn the names of some of the countries and the continents.

Continents and Countries

Russian Word	English Meaning	Russian Word	English Meaning
Африка AHF-ree-kah	Africa	Голла́ндия gah-LAHN-dee-yah	Netherlands
Азия AH-zee-yah	Asia	Норве́гия nahr-VEH-gee-yah	Norway
Австрия AHV-stree-yah	Austria	По́льша POHL-shah	Poland
Бе́льгия BEHL-gee-yah	Belgium	Португа́лия pahr-too-GAH-lee-yah	Portugal
Кана́да kah-NAH-dah	Canada	Румы́ния roo-MEE-nee-yah	Romania
Кита́й kee-TIY	China	Росси́я rah-SEE-yah	Russia
Еги́пет yeh-GEE-peht	Egypt	Испа́ния ees-PAH-nee-yah	Spain
Англия AHN-glee-yah	England	Шве́ция SHVEHT-see-yah	Sweden
Финля́ндия feen-LAHN-dee-yah	Finland	Швейца́рия shveyt-SAH-ree-yah	Switzerland
Фра́нция FRAHN-tsee-yah	France	Соединённые Шта́ты sah-yeh-deen-YOH-nee-yeh SHTAH-tee	United States
Герма́ния gehr-MAH-nee-yah	Germany		
Гре́ция GREH-tsee-yah	Greece		
Ве́нгрия VEHN-gree-yah	Hungary		

Russian Word	English Meaning	Russian Word	English Meaning
Индия EEN-dee-yah	India		
Изра́иль eez-RAH-eel	Israel		
Ита́лия ee-TAH-lee-yah	Italy		

Going and Coming

Where will your travels take you? Are you aiming for any place in Europe, or do you hope to reach a specific country? Where will you stay when you arrive—with relatives or in a hotel? To express all of these plans, use the preposition по and the dative case. Here is another verb for traveling: путеше́ствовать.

The Verb путеше́ствовать (imperfective: "to travel")

Person	Singular	English	Plural	English
First	путеше́ствую poo-teh-SHEHST-voo-yoo	I travel	путеше́ствуем poo-teh-SHEHST-voo-yehm	We travel
Second	путеше́ствуешь poo-teh-SHEHST-voo-yehsh	You travel (familiar)	путеше́ствуете poo-teh-SHEHST-voo-yet-yeh	You travel (formal)
Third	путеше́ствует poo-teh-SHEHST-voo-yet	He/She travels	путеше́ствуют poo-teh-SHEHST-voo-yoot	They travel

Они́ ре́дко путеше́ствуют по Росси́и.
Ah-nee PEHD-kah poo-teh-SHEHST-voo-yootpah-Rahss-EE-yee.
They rarely travel abroad.

Вы мно́го путеше́ствуете?
Vwee MNOH-gah poo-teh-SHEHST-voo-yet-yeh?
Do you travel a lot?

If you plan to stay with friends or family during your travels, you will want to use the preposition y + the genitive case. For example:

Я путеше́ствую по Евро́пе и живу́ у ро́дственников.
Yah poo-teh-SHEHST-voo-yoo payehv-ROH-pp ee zhee-VOO oo-ROHD-stveh-nee-kaf.
I am traveling to Europe and staying with relatives.

Я путеше́ствую по Росси́и и живу́ у друзе́й.
Yah poo-teh-SHEHST-voo-yoo pah-rah-SEE-yee ee zhee-VOO oo oo-droo-ZYEY.
I am traveling to Russia and staying with friends.

What Brings You Here?

No matter what your final destination might be, you always have to go *through* (че́рез) somewhere to arrive there. And after you have arrived, you're always coming *from* (из or с) somewhere else. To talk about your experiences while traveling, or to simply tell someone where you are from, you need to use these three handy prepositions.

Memory Serves

The preposition **че́рез** means *through,* and it requires the accusative case. The prepositions **из** and **с** mean *from,* and require the genitive case.

If your accent confuses someone, you can answer questions about yourself by telling them where you're from using из or с.

Я—из Нью-Йо́рка. Я—из Москвы́.
Yah—eez Nyoo-YORK-ah. Yah—eez Mahsk-VWEE.
I am from New York. I am from Moscow.

Я—с Се́вера. Я—с Юга.
Yah—SSEH-veh-rah. Yah—SYOO-gah.
I am from the North. I am from the South.

Suppose you decided to drive across the country or hike across Europe. To tell the people along the way where you have been before, you can use из and с as well, and to make things more clear, you can use the preposition через to indicate which places you have traveled through.

Я е́ду в Нью-Йо́рк на маши́не из Вирджи́нии че́рез Пенсильва́нию.
Yah YEH-DOO vNyoo-YORK nah-mash-EE-neh eez Veer-JEE-nee-ee CHEH-rehz Pehn-seel-VAH-nee-yoo.
I am driving to New York, from Virginia, through Pennsylvania.

Я иду́ от ле́са домо́й че́рез по́ле.
Yah ee-DOO at LYEH-sa dah-MOY CHEH-rez POH-lyeh.
I am going from the woods home through the field.

The Power of Suggestion

You've been walking all day long, but your friends continue to drag you along to exhibit after exhibit. You love to sightsee, but you have different opinions about power-walking across the city. It may be time to suggest to your friends that you take a break for lunch, or just slow down and take it easy. To give those tired legs a break, you need to make a suggestion to your friends. Your friend, the adverb, arrives to save the day. Russian has a few key *impersonal* adverbs, which create suggestions. They indicate the ideas "is it possible to," "may I," or "I must, it is necessary."

Hot Topic

Impersonal sentences are sentences that have no logical subject. They are translated using the pronoun *it*. The adverbs **мóжно** ("it is possible") and **нельзя́** ("it is not possible," "one may not") can be used to create such impersonal sentences.

The following chart lists the common impersonal adverbs, or adverbs that are used to create impersonal sentences.

Common Impersonal Adverbs

Russian Word	Pronunciation	English Meaning
возмóжно	vahs-MOHZH-nah	it is possible
мóжно	MOHZH-nah	it is possible, one may
нельзя́	nehlz-YAH	it is not possible, one may not
нáдо	NAH-dah	it is important to, one needs to
нýжно	NOOZH-nah	it is necessary to, one must

The only exception to this group is the adverb должен, which does require a subject. Должен changes to agree with the subject.

The Adverb должен

Russian Word	Pronunciation	English Meaning
Я/Ты дóлжен/должнá	Yah/Tee DOHL-zhehn/dahl-ZHNAH	I/you must
Он дóлжен	Ohn DOHL-zhehn	He must
Онá должнá	Ah-NAH dahl-ZHNAH	She must
Онó должнó	Ah-NOH dahl-zhnoh	It must
Мы/Вы/Они́ должны́	Mwee/Vwee/Ah-NEE dahl-ZHNEE	We/you/they must

Unlike normal adverbs, these impersonal adverbs cannot stand alone. They require an infinitive verb following them to complete a sentence. With the exception of the adverb до́лжен, they do not require subjects; however, the dative case is used to indicate "to whom" the adverb applies. Take a look at these examples:

Что (мне) на́до сде́лать по́сле рабо́ты?
Shtoh (mnyeh) NAH-dah ZDEH-laht POHS-lee rah-BOH-tee?
What (do I) need to do after work?

Мо́жно води́ть маши́ну без колёс?
MOHZH-nah vah-DEET mah-SHEE-noo behz kahl-YOHS?
Is it possible to drive a car without wheels?

Нет, нельзя́ так води́ть маши́ну.
Nyeht, nehlz-YAH tahk vah-DEET mah-SHEE-noo.
No, it is not possible to drive a car that way.

Мы должны́ бо́льше чита́ть.
Mwee dahl-ZHNEE BOHL-sheh chee-TAHT.
We need to read more.

Make Me an Offer I Can't Refuse

Your feet are tired, but you don't want to seem impolite by simply demanding that your friends slow down. You can use your impersonal adverbs with the particle ли to form some polite, thoughtful suggestions that will keep the whole crowd in a pleasant mood.

Нельзя́ ли идти́ немно́го помедлене́е?
Nehlz-YAH lee ee-TYEE nehm-NOH-gah pah-mehd-lehn-YEH-yeh?
Would it be possible to walk a little slower?

Нельзя́ ли пойти́ в кино́ и́ли в рестора́н сейча́с, а на бале́т немно́го по́зже?
Nehlz-YAH lee pay-TEE vkee-NOH EE-lee vreh-stah-RAHN see-CHAHS, ah nah bah-LYET nehm-NOH-gah POHZ-zheh?
Would it be possible to go to the movies or a restaurant now, and to the ballet a little bit later?

Мо́жно ли э́то ви́деть в друго́й день?
MOHZH-nah lee EH-tah VEE-deht vdroo-GOY dehn?
Couldn't we see this another day?

Memory Serves

The adverbs **Мо́жно** and **Нельзя́** mean "it is possible" and "it is not possible, not allowed."

Мóжно ли отдыхáть немнóго?
MOHZH-nah lee aht-deeh-KAHT nehm-NOH-gah?
Couldn't we rest a little bit?

Say Yes, No, Absolutely Not

Rather than reply to your friends' suggestions with a curt "yes" or "no," let them know what you really think of their ideas. Some of the following phrases will help.

Да, э́то мне нрáвится.
Dah, EH-tah mnyeh NRAH-veet-syah.
Yes, I like that.

Нет, э́то мне не нрáвится.
Nyeht, EH-tah mnyeh neh NRAH-veet-syah.
No, I don't like that.

Это кáжется подóбно шýтке.
EH-tah KAH-zheht-syah pah-DOHB-nah SHOOT-kyeh.
That seems like a joke.

Я бы хотéл(а) …
Yah bwee hah-TYEHL(ah) …
I would like …

Я предпочитáю не …
Yah prehd-pah-chee-TAH-yoo neh …
I prefer not to …

Это скýчно.
Eh-tah SKOOSH-nah.
This bores me.

In My Opinion

If someone suggests an idea or activity that immediately strikes a chord with you—perhaps the Super Bowl or the county garlic festival—you can immediately respond with enthusiasm. The following chart has some words to get you started.

That's a Great Idea

Russian Word	Pronunciation	English Meaning
По-мóему …	pah-MOH-yeh-moo …	In my opinion …
Я бы сказáл(а) …	Yah bwee skah-ZAHL(ah) …	I would say …
Отли́чно!	Aht-LEECH-nah!	Excellent!
Прекрáсно!	Preh-KRAHS-nah!	Wonderful!
Хорошó!	Hah-rah-SHOH!	Good!

What Do You Think?

You have become a "Рýсская звездá" ("Russian star")! Everyone and their distant relatives are standing in line to spend time with you. Respond to their suggestions, both positively and negatively.

Exericse 16.1

Example: Давáйте смотрéть фильм.

Answer: Отли́чно! Я люблю́ смотрéть фи́льмы.

Нет, я не хочý смотрéте фильм.

1. Хоти́те пойти́ в кинó сегóдня? ______________________________.
2. Давáй игрáть в мяч во дворé. ______________________________.
3. Хóчешь поéхать со мной в библиотéку, чтóбы читáть немнóго. ______________________________.
4. Есть нóвый фильм по телеви́зору. Давáйте посмóтрим. ______________________________.

The Least You Need to Know

- You can navigate any Russian city by knowing some key phrases and words for what you want to do and see.
- To suggest an activity, use the formal Давáйте (*let's*) or familiar Давáй (*let's*) + the infinitive or first person plural form of a verb.
- Simple phrases can express your interest or satisfaction.

Chapter 17

Shop 'Til You Drop

In This Chapter

- Stores and what they sell
- Clothing, colors, sizes, materials, and designs
- How to носи́ть ("to wear") your clothes
- Getting what you want
- Demonstrate this, that, these, and those

You've seen the sights and visited the museums, but you want something to remember them by. Perhaps you want to prove to your doubting friends that you visited the Kremlin, or maybe you just want to add a few postcards to your collection. Did you want to experiment with some popular Russian fashions? Whatever your needs, this chapter will help you start shopping, find the right colors and sizes, and talk about your personal tastes.

Now That's My Kind of Store

Whether you're strolling through St. Petersburg or Little Odessa, flipping through the latest advertisements or watching infomercials, you can do the bulk of your shopping by simply browsing selections and sales. The following table will get you going to the right outlets. Remember that if you want to say that you're going to a store or shop, use пойти́ with в + the accusative case.

Я пойду́ в …
Yah pah-ee-DOO v …
I'm going to …

What's in Store?

The Store	English Meaning	The Merchandise	English Meaning
кни́жный магази́н	bookstore	кни́ги, журна́лы, литерату́ра	books, serials, literature
магази́н оде́жды	clothing store	оде́жда космети́ческие принадле́жности	clothes
универма́г	department store	това́ры, электротова́ры (почти́ всё)	goods, electronics (nearly everything)
апте́ка	drug store	гигиени́ческие това́ры	hygiene articles
цвето́чный магази́н	florist	цветы́	flowers
магази́н пода́рков	gift shop	сувени́ры, безделу́шки, матрёшки, откры́тки	souvenirs, trinkets, matroshkas, postcards
ювели́рный магази́н	jewelry store	ювели́рные изде́лия, часы́	jewelry, watches
магази́н ко́жаного това́ра	leather goods	ремни́, ко́жаный пиджа́к, бума́жники	belts, leather jacket, wallets
музыка́льный	music store	сиди, кассе́ты, магази́н	CDs, tapes
кио́ск	newsstand	газе́ты, путеводи́тель	newspapers, guidebook
канцеля́рские принадле́жности	office supply store	почто́вая бума́га, ру́чки, бума́га	stationery, pens, paper
парфюме́рия	perfume store	духи́, одеколо́н	perfume, cologne
апте́ка	pharmacy	лека́рства	medicine
спорти́вные това́ры	sports store	спорти́вная оде́жда, кроссо́вки, спорти́вные това́ры	sports clothing, sneakers, sports equipment
таба́чный магази́н	tobacconist	сигаре́ты, сига́ры, зажига́лки	cigarettes, cigars, lighters

Clothes

Whether you want to change out of your American attire and blend in or just pick up some fashionable Russian clothing, you will eventually find yourself seeking out some of the latest trends. The following chart will give you some ideas on how to dress yourself.

Я хочу́ купи́ть … Покажи́те мне …
Yah hah-CHOO koo-PEET … Pah-kah-ZHEET-yeh mnyeh …
I want to buy … Show me a …

Clothes Make the Man (and Woman)

Russian Word	Pronunciation	English Meaning
по́яс	POH-yahs	belt
блу́зка	BLOOS-kah	blouse
сапоги́	sah-pah-GEE	boots
бюсга́лтер	byoos-GAHL-tehr	bra
пальто́	pahl-TOH	coat
пла́тье	PLAH-tyeh	dress
перча́тки	pehr-CHAT-kee	gloves
носово́й плато́к	nah-sah-VOY plah-TOHK	handkerchief
шля́па	SHLYH-pah	hat
пиджа́к	pid-ZHAK	jacket
джи́нсы	JEEN-see	jeans
пижа́мы	pee-ZHAH-mee	pajamas
тру́сики	TROO-see-kee	panties
брю́ки	BRYOO-kee	pants
колго́тки	kahl-GOHT-kee	pantyhose
су́мка	SOOM-kah	purse
сви́тер	SVEE-tyehr	sweater
плащ	plahsh	raincoat
хала́т	hah-LAHT	robe
шарф	sharf	scarf
руба́шка	poo-BASH-kah	shirt
ту́фли	TOOF-lee	shoes
кроссо́вки	KYEH-dee kras-SOHV-kee	sneakers
носки́	nahs-KEE	socks

continues

Clothes Make the Man (and Woman) (continued)

Russian Word	Pronunciation	English Meaning
мужскóй костю́м	moozh-SKOY kah-STYOOM	suit (men)
жéнский костю́м	ZHEHN-skee kah-STYOOM	suit (women)
гáлстук	GAHL-stook	tie
мáйка	MAY-kah	sleeveless shirt
футбóлка	Food-BOHL-ka	T-shirt
зóнтик	ZOHN-teek	umbrella
ни́жнее бельё	NEEZH-nyeh-yeh behl-YOH	underwear

After making one or two purchases, you will want to glance at yourself in the mirror. As you look at that sleek, attractive reflection staring back at you, you can now begin to describe your appearance. To get started, you'll want to grab the useful verb носи́ть, "to wear."

The Verb носи́ть (imperfective: "to wear")

Person	Singular	English	Plural	English
First	ношу́ nah-SHOO	I wear	нóсим NOH-seem	We wear
Second	нóсишь NOH-seesh	You wear (familiar)	нóсите NOH-seet-yeh	You wear (formal)
Third	нóсит NOH-seet	He/She wears	нóсят NOH-syaht	They wear
Imperative	носи́ nah-SEE	Wear (it)!	носи́те nah-SEET-yeh	Wear (it)!

Он нóсит си́нюю рубáшку.
Ohn NOH-seet SEEN-yoo-yoo poo-BASH-koo.
He is wearing a blue shirt.

Онá чáсто нóсит орáнжевый.
Ah-NAH CHAS-tah NOH-seet ah-RAHN-zheh-vwee.
She often wears orange.

If you're simply describing someone's appearance, you may want to avoid the verb носи́ть altogether, and use the preposition в + the prepositional case. Russians often choose the latter method to describe other people. For example:

Он в джи́нсах. Они́ в си́них руба́шках.
Ohn VJEEN-sahk. Ah-NEE VSEE-neek roo-BASH-kahk.
He is wearing jeans. They are wearing blue shirts.

What do you normally wear? Check your vocabulary in the following exercise (answers are listed in Appendix B). You should either use the correct form of the verb носи́ть or a prepositional phrase. Be careful not to combine the two!

Exercise 17.1

Example: He is wearing a yellow vest.

Answer: Он но́сит жёлтый жиле́т/Он в жёлтом жиле́те.

1. They go to the store in sneakers. ______________________.
2. We wear suits to church. ______________________.
3. He often wears black. ______________________.
4. Do you like to wear a raincoat? ______________________.
5. I am wearing a pink undershirt. ______________________.

A Little Color

Part of the appeal of the Russian culture is the richness of the language; but, sometimes, this richness makes the language a bit of a headache for students of Russian. For instance, you learn that кра́сный means *red* and can be used to describe the color of objects. However, if you wanted to describe someone's hair as red, you would need to use the word ры́жий. They have identical meanings in English, but different uses in Russian. Although you may be able to describe someone's mood as blue in English, the same is not true of Russian. Different words are used for different situations, and must be learned accordingly. The words in the following chart will help you describe the color of clothes or most ordinary objects.

A Dash of Color

Russian Word	Pronunciation	English Meaning
голубо́й	gah-loo-BOY	blue (light)
чёрный	CHYOHR-nee	black

continues

A Dash of Color (continued)

Russian Word	Pronunciation	English Meaning
си́ний	SEE-nee	blue (navy)
кори́чневый	kah-REECH-neh-vwee	brown
се́рый	SYEH-ree	gray
зелёный	zehl-YOH-nee	green
ора́нжевый	ah-RAHN-zheh-vwee	orange
ро́зовый	POH-zah-vwee	pink
лило́вый	li-LOH-vwee	lilac
фиале́товый	fiah-LEH-tovwee	violet
кра́сный	KRAHS-nee	red
бе́лый	BYEH-lee	white
жёлтый	ZHYOHL-tee	yellow

If you want to find a lighter or darker shade of your favorite color, just add све́тло- (*light*) or тёмно- (*dark*) to the color you need. Look over these compound adjectives to get the idea.

све́тло-зелёный, тёмно-зелёный
SVET-lah-zehl-YOH-nee, TYOHM-nah-zehl-YOH-nee
light green, dark green

све́тло-кра́сный, тёмно-кра́сный
SVET-lah-KRAHS-nee, TYOHM-nah-KRAHS-nee
light red, dark red

You can add a little more color to your descriptions by using some of the adjectives in the following chart.

Я ищу́ …
Yah ee-SHOO …
I'm looking for a …

Fashionable Adjectives

Russian Word	Pronunciation	English Meaning
мо́дный	MOHD-nee	fashionable
у́зкий	OOZ-kee	narrow
узо́рчатый	oo-ZOHR-chah-tee	patterned

Russian Word	Pronunciation	English Meaning
клéтчатый	KLET-chah-tee	plaid
однотóнный	ahd-nah-TOH-nee	solid color
полосáтый	pah-lah-SAH-tee	striped
ширóкий	shee-ROH-kee	wide

What suits you best? Are you looking for stripes or solids? Use the phrases and words that you've just learned to ask your salesperson a few questions. Remember that the phrases you've learned so far are transitive, meaning they require direct objects. This means that the nouns that follow them should be in the accusative case. (Answers are listed in Appendix B.)

Exericse 17.2

Example: I'm looking for gray shoes.

Answer: Я ищý сéрые тýфли.

1. Please, show me a solid pink skirt. ____________________.
2. I'd like to buy blue jeans. ____________________.
3. I'm looking for a black overcoat. ____________________.
4. Please, show me a red hat. ____________________.

Object of My Affection

You send a picture of yourself in a sharp new outfit to your brother back home. A few days later, you receive a reply from him saying, "I like those pants. Where did you find those pants? I'd like to buy a pair just like those pants. Those pants look good on you." You scratch your head and think, "What's wrong with this letter?" Rather than repeating *those pants* over and over, it would sound much better to say, "I like those pants. Where did you find them? They look good on you."

Hot Topic

A **direct object** answers the questions *whom* or *what*. You meet *whom;* you hit *what;* or you see *what* or *whom*.

The phrase "those pants" is a *direct object* noun in English. When you replace that phrase with *them* you have substituted the noun for a direct object pronoun. In Chapter 7, you learned how to form and use nouns as direct objects, and you've been happily using them ever since. Rather than repeating clumsy phrases, you can streamline your speech by grabbing some direct object pronouns, or pronouns in the accusative case. But you needn't stop there; you can replace your indirect object nouns with pronouns as well.

To begin, nouns or pronouns in the accusative case answer the questions кто (*what*) or кого́ (*whom*). The following chart shows some easy ways to get started.

кто (*what*) or кого́ (*whom*)

	Nominative (Subj.)	Verb	Acc. (Direct Obj.)
With noun	Я yah (I)	ношу́ nah-SHOO (wear)	бе́лые носки́. BEH-lee-yeh nah-SKEE (white socks)
With pronoun	Я yah (I)	ношу́ nah-SHOO (wear)	их. eek (them)
With noun	Мы mwee (We)	хоте́ли бы hah-TYEH-lee bwee (would like)	вечери́нку. veh-cheh-REEN-koo (a party)
With pronoun	Мы mwee (We)	хоте́либы hah-TYEH-lee bwee (would like)	её. yeh-YOH (it)

Indirect object nouns or pronouns answer the questions кому́ ("to whom") and чему́ ("to what"), and they are in the dative case. They specify what action the verb takes upon which person or thing.

кому́ ("to whom") and чему́ ("to what")

	(Subject)	Nom. Verb	Dat. (Indirect Object)	Acc. (Direct Object)
With noun	Они́ ah-NEE (They)	даю́т dah-YOOT (give)	учи́телю oo-CHEE-tehl-yoo (the teacher)	бума́гу boo-MAH-goo (the paper)
With pronoun	Они́ ah-NEE (They)	даю́т dah-YOOT (give)	ему́ yeh-MOO (him)	бума́гу boo-MAH-goo (the paper)
With noun	Она́ ah-NAH (She)	пи́шет PEESH-yet (writes)	ма́тери MAH-teh-ree (her mother)	письмо́ pees-MOH (a letter)
With pronoun	Она́ ah-NAH (She)	пи́шет PEESH-yet (writes)	ей yey (her)	письмо́ pees-MOH (a letter)

Any noun, in any of the six Russian cases, can be replaced by a pronoun in the appropriate case. The following table shows you the declension patterns of each of the personal pronouns. You should be familiar with each form of the following pronouns, but don't worry about memorizing all of them. Your primary focus should be the accusative and dative pronouns, because you will use them every day.

Declension Patterns of Personal Pronouns

Person	Nom.	Prep.	Acc.	Gen.	Dat.	Inst.
I	я yah	мне mnyeh	меня́ mehn-YAH	меня́ mehn-YAH	мне mnyeh	мной mnoy
You	ты tee	тебе́ tehb-YEH	тебя́ tehb-YAH	тебя́ tehb-YAH	тебе́ tehb-YEH	тобо́й tah-BOY
He/It	он/оно́ ohn/ah-NOH	нём NYOM	его́ yeh-VOH	его́ yeh-VOH	ему́ yeh-MOO	им eem
She	она́ ah-NAH	ней NYEY	её yeh-YOH	её yeh-YOH	ей yey	ей yey
We	мы mwee	нас nahs	нас nahs	нас nahs	нам hahm	на́ми HAH-mee
You	вы vwee	вас vahs	вас vahs	вас vahs	вам vahm	ва́ми VAH-mee
They	они́ ah-NEE	них neekh	иих eekh	их eekh	им eem	и́ми EEH-mee

Step up to the plate and try to replace the following direct object nouns, shown in underline, with the appropriate accusative case pronouns (see Appendix B for answers).

Exercise 17.3

Example:

Он покупа́ет большу́ю су́мку. (He is buying a big bag.)

Answer: Он покупа́ет её.

1. Мы смо́трим (watching) телеви́зор (TV). ______________________.
2. Она́ лю́бит му́жа. ______________________.
3. Я люблю́ мои́ джи́нсы. ______________________.
4. Он постро́ил (built) э́ту шко́лу (this school). ______________________.

Direct Me to You, Them, and Us

As you stroll through the Nevski Prospect, you stop in a store that catches your eye and try on a few different items of clothing. You converse with the salesperson, asking him to recommend something for your frame and build. He makes several suggestions. You should respond by using some of the same direct object pronouns that you have already practiced (answers are listed in Appendix B).

Exercise 17.4

Example: Вы лю́бите э́ту руба́шку? ____________________.

Answer: Да, я люблю́ её. ____________________.

1. Ты хо́чешь пече́нье? ____________________.
2. Вы де́лаете дома́шнюю рабо́ту (homework)? ____________________.
3. Ты купи́л (bought) маши́ну? ____________________.
4. Вы лю́бите свои́х (your) родителей? ____________________.

Indirectly to Us, to You, to Them

You have made the bulk of your purchases; but, as you sit down at home to look over your gifts, you can't decide what to give whom. Use the following exercise to replace the indirect object nouns with the appropriate pronouns. Put your dative case pronouns to work with the following suggestions (answers in Appendix B).

Exericse 17.5

Example: Да́йте ____________________ (me) оде́жду.

Answer: Да́йте мне оде́жду.

1. Разреши́те (allow) ____________________ (her) пойти́ в магази́н.
2. Это меша́ет (bothers) ____________________ (him).
3. Напиши́ (write) ____________________ (them) письмо́!
4. Говори́те (speak) ____________________ (to me), не ____________________ (to him).

Talk to the Salesperson

Shopping can be as interactive as you need it to be. Sometimes you simply want to window-shop, to browse the selections of new fashions, or to compare prices from store to store. If you find yourself attracted to a particular item, or if you want a salesperson to do your browsing for you, you may want to engage them in a small conversation. Some of the typical questions and answers are provided here.

Мóжно вам помóчь?
MOHZH-nah vahm pah-MOHCH?
May I help you?

Что вы хотúте? Что вы úщите?
Shtoh vwee hah-TEET-yeh? Shtoh vwee EE-shee-tyeh?
What would you like? What are you looking for?

Нет, спасúбо, я прóсто присмáтриваюсь.
Nyeht, spah-SEE-bah, yah PROH-stah pree-SMAH-tree-vah-yoos.
No, thank you, I'm just looking.

Я бы хотéл(а) вúдеть …
Yah bwee hah-TYEHL(ah) VEE-deht …
Yes, I would like to see …

Я ищý …
Yah ee-SHOO …
I'm looking for …

Вы дéлаете скúдки?
Vwee DEH-lah-yet-yeh SKEED-kee?
Do you have any sales?

Мóжно э́то примéрить?
MOHZH-nah EH-tah pree-MYEH-reet?
May I try this on?

Let's Wrap It Up!

As you narrow down your selection, your salesperson will ask you, "Какóй вы предпочитáете?" ("Which do you prefer?") You learned how to work with the interrogative pronoun какóй (*which*, *what*) in Chapter 8. To answer the question specifically, you will want to say э́тот (*this*) or тот (*that*) one.

Hot Topic

Demonstrative pronouns enable you to distinguish between two or more items (that is, this and that).

These *demonstrative pronouns* perform like adjectives; and, as always, they agree in gender, number, and case with the nouns they modify. The patterns for these two words follow the regular rules and decline normally.

You can quickly respond to the salesperson by saying the following:

Я предпочита́ю...
Yah prehd-poh-chee-TAH-yoo ....
I prefer ....

Demonstrative Pronouns—This and These

Case	Masculine	Feminine	Neuter	Plural
Nom.	э́тот EH-taht	э́та EH-tah	э́то EH-tah	э́ти EH-tee
Prep.	э́том EH-tahm	э́той EH-toy	э́том EH-tahm	э́тих EH-teekh
Acc. (inan.)	э́тот EH-toht	э́ту EH-too	э́то EH-tah	э́ти EH-tee
Acc. (anim.)	э́того EH-tah-vah	—— ——	—— ——	э́тих EH-teekh
Gen.	э́того EH-tah-vah	э́той EH-toy	э́того EH-tah-vah	э́тих EH-teekh
Dat.	э́тому EH-tah-moo	э́той EH-toy	э́тому EH-tah-moo	э́тим EH-teem
Inst.	э́тим EH-teem	э́той EH-toy	э́тим EH-teem	э́тими EH-tee-mee

Demonstrative Pronouns—That and Those

Case	Masculine	Feminine	Neuter	Plural
Nom.	тот toht	та tah	то toh	те tyeh
Prep.	том tohm	той toy	том tohm	тех tyehkh
Acc. (inan.)	тот toht	ту too	то toh	те tyeh

Case	Masculine	Feminine	Neuter	Plural
Acc. (anim.)	тогó tah-VOH	——— ———	—— ——	тех tyehkh
Gen.	тогó tah-VOH	той toy	тогó tah-VOH	тех tyehkh
Dat.	томý tah-MOO	той toy	томý tah-MOO	тем tyem
Inst.	тем tyem	той toy	тем tyem	тéми tyeh-mee

What Are You Looking For?

You made the mistake of taking your fashion-conscious friend with you to shop. Whereas you would normally have made a purchase within a few minutes and left, she has you second-guessing yourself and double-checking every shirt-and-tie combination in the mirror. When you finally find the selections right for you, you may want to tell your salesperson something from the following chart.

Opinionated Responses

Russian Word	Pronunciation	English Meaning
Мне э́то нрáвится.	Mnyeh EH-tah NRAH-veet-syah.	I like it.
Это мне не подхóдит.	Eh-tah mnyeh neh pahd-HOH-deet.	That suits me.
Это прия́тно.	EH-tah pree-YAHT-nah.	It's nice.
Это элегáнтно.	EH-tah eh-leh-GAHNT-nah.	It's elegant.
Мне э́то не нрáвится.	Mnyeh EH-tah neh NRAH-veet-syah.	I don't like it.
Это не подхóдит по размéру.	EH-tah neh pahd-HOH-deet pah-pahz-MEH-roo.	It doesn't fit me.
Сли́шком мáленький.	SLEESH-kahm MAH-lehn-kee.	It's too small.
Сли́шком большóй.	SLEESH-kahm bahl-SHOY.	It's too big.
Сли́шком ýзкий.	SLEESH-kahm OOZ-kee.	It's too tight.
Сли́шком дли́нный.	SLEESH-kahm DLEEN-nee.	It's too long.
Сли́шком корóткий.	SLEESH-kahm kah-ROHT-kee.	It's too short.

I Prefer ...

Many of your shopping experiences will involve your personal preference. Why choose a lighter color over dark, or vice versa? You have certain needs that are specific to you.

Sometimes you can't explain it any further than:

> Я бы предпочита́л(а) ...
> Yah bwee prehd-poh-chee-TAHL(ah) ....
> I would prefer ....

A salesperson might ask you:

> Каки́е руба́шки вам бо́льше всего́ нра́вятся?
> Kah-KEE-yeh roo-BAHSH-kee vahm BOHL-shyeh vsyeh-VOH NRAHV-yaht-cyah?
> Which shirts do you like best?

You could answer:

> Бо́льше всего́ я люблю́ э́ту/ту руба́шку.
> BOHL-shyeh vsyeh-VOH yah loob-LOO EH-too/too roo-BAHSH-koo.
> I like this/that shirt best.

Before you rush headlong into your nearest department store, take a moment to reflect on what you have learned, and practice it for a few minutes in the following exercise. The following questions use the interrogative pronoun како́й. Use the correct form of a demonstrative pronoun to respond.

Example: Каку́ю су́мку вы лю́бите? (Which purse do you like?)

Answer: Эту су́мку. (This purse.)

1. Како́е пальто́ вы лю́бите? (What kind of coat do you like?)
2. С каки́ми туфля́ми вы но́сите пла́тье? (With what kind of shoes do you wear the dress?)
3. Каки́е трусы́ вам подхо́дят? (What kind of underwear suits you?)
4. Како́го цве́та блу́зку вы предпочита́ете? (What color blouse do you prefer?)

The Least You Need to Know

- To shop, you need to know the names of Russian stores and what items they sell.
- To describe what you, or someone else, are wearing, you can use the verb носи́ть ("to wear") + the accusative case or the subject in the nominative case + в + the prepositional case.
- Russian personal pronouns take the accusative case if they function as direct objects, or they take the dative case if they function as indirect objects.
- The Russian demonstrative pronouns э́тот (*this*) and тот (*that*) will help you express this or that. The interrogative pronoun како́й (*which*) will help you clarify conversations.

Chapter 18

Restaurant Hopping

In This Chapter

- Appease your pallet
- How to order food in a restaurant or café
- Getting exactly what you want
- Special diets

The evening lights of Kiev have begun to blaze, and you're staring out your hotel window at the streets below. Although your day has been peaceful and relaxing, you soon realize that you are "голóден как волк" ("hungry as a wolf"). You immediately head to the elevator and begin to prowl the shop windows for a restaurant that looks appealing.

Russians are well known for their love of food—in mass quantities and delicious. You will find the opportunities to satisfy your hunger both numerous and filling. Before you order appetizers and meals, you should know the proper phrases. At the end of this chapter, you will be able to order your meals in Russian, even if you have special dietary needs, and send them back if you don't like them.

Time to Wine and Dine

When you begin your search for the appropriate restaurant, you will not only need to search for what kind of foods they serve, but also what types of restaurants they are. You may be looking for a restaurant that serves only зáавтрак (*breakfast*), обéд (*lunch*), or ýжин (*dinner*); or you may be in the mood for a self-service buffet or the luxury of a 4-star restaurant. Russian has several different words to define where you wish to dine; one of these should help you.

My Stomach Is Growling

Russian Word	Pronunciation	English Meaning
ресторáн	reh-stah-RAHN	restaurant
столóвая	stah-LOH-vah-yah	dining room
кафé	kahf-YEH	informal restaurant
кафетéрий	kah-feh-THE-ree	first-class self-service restaurant, cafeteria
закýсочная	zah-KOO-sahch-nah-yah	snack bar
пирожкóвая	pee-rohsh-KOH-vah-yah	small café specializing in pirozhki (small pies)
бистрó	bees-TROH	fast-food restaurant

Note: The term ресторáн *does not refer to any restaurant. It applies only to full-service restaurants featuring three-course meals, live entertainment, and dancing.*

Культýра

The typical Russian meal features an appetizer and three courses. **закýска** (*appetizers*) are usually followed with a shot of vodka. The first and second courses are always soup or salad, and the third course is the actual meal. Unless you specify otherwise, your Russian waiter will probably assume you want a traditional Russian meal—which will always be good, but maybe not what you had in mind.

When Do We Eat?

Before taking the plunge and committing yourself to a restaurant, you may want to wander the streets of Kiev a bit and glance at the menus. While considering, you should also think about the popularity of the restaurant. Will reservations be required? Or perhaps you're simply perusing the newspaper and you need to call and ask for directions. The following list will provide you with some useful phrases for dining out.

Dining Out

Russian Word	Pronunciation	English Meaning
Я хотéл(а)бы заказáть стóлик …	Yah hah-TYEHL(ah) bwee zah-kah-ZAHT stah-LEEK…	I would like to reserve a table …
… на сегóдняшний вéчер	… nah-she-VOHD-nyah-shnee VEH-chehr	… for tonight
… на зáвтрашний вéчер	… nah ZAHV-trash-nee VEH-chehr	… for tomorrow night
… на вéчер пя́тницы	… nah-VEH-chehr PYAHT-neet-see	… for Friday night
… на двои́х	… nah-dvah-EEK	… for two people
… на откры́том вóздухе	… nah-aht-KREE-tahm VAHZ-dook-yeh	… out side
… у окнá	… oo-ahk-NAH	… at the window
… в углý	… voog-LOO	… in the corner
… в мéсте для куря́щих	… VMEST-yeh dlyah koor-YAH-sheek	… in a smoking section
… в мéсте для некуря́щих	… VMEST-yeh dlyah neh-koor-YAH-sheek	… in a nonsmoking section

Notice the difference between use of the prepositions в and на. Although the same preposition is used throughout, the case changes. "Time" expressions ("For Saturday; for tonight") and expressions of purpose ("For two [people]") require the accusative case. The location expressions require the prepositional case.

Я бы хотéл(а) заказáть стóлик на сегóдняшний вéчер на откры́том вóздухе.
Yah bwee hah-TYEHL(ah) zah-kah-ZAHT STOH-leek nah-she-VOHD-nyah-shnee VEH-chehr nah aht-KREE-tahm VOHZ-dook-yeh.
I would like to reserve a table for tonight, in the outside.

Я бы хотéл(а) заказáть стóлик на двои́х (трои́х) на вéчер пя́тницы.
Yah bwee hah-TYEHL(ah) zah-kah-ZAHT STOH-leek nah-dvah-EEK (trah-EEK) nah VEH-chehr PYAHT-neet-see.
I would like to reserve a table for two (three) on Friday night.

At the Restaurant

You know that Friday night in Kiev will be crowded and lively, so you decide to make your dinner reservations in advance—just to be safe. You've arranged for a dinner by firelight in a nonsmoking restaurant. The following exchange might occur next.

Question:

> Ско́лько вас бу́дет?
> SKOHL-kah vahs BOO-deht?
> How many will be at your table?

You might answer:

> Пожа́луйста, сто́лик на пя́терых.
> Pah-ZHAH-loo-stah, STOH-leek nah-PYAH-teh-reek.
> Please, a table for five.

You arrived at the restaurant to find everything prepared for you; the table, the fireplace, and the mood were just as you expected them to be. You're seated at the table, and have been glancing over the menu items. You are ready to order, but where is your server? You may notice him busily serving other tables; no doubt he's very busy, but your stomach has certain needs. To get his attention and place your order, you may need to become slightly more aggressive. Certainly you don't want to be rude, but you shouldn't hesitate to grab his attention and let him know that you are hungry. Here are some useful phrases for speedy results.

In the Restaurant

Russian Word	Pronunciation	English Meaning
Прими́те, пожа́луйста, зака́з.	pree-MEET-yeh, pah-ZHAH-loo-stah, zah-KAHZ	I (we) would like to order.
Что бы вы посове́товали…?	Shtoh bwee vwee pah-cah-VYEH-tah-vah-lee …?	What would you recommend for …?
… на заку́ску?	… nah-zah-KOOS-koo?	… an appetizer?
… на пе́рвое?	… nah-PEHR-vah-yeh?	… the first course?
… на второ́е?	… nah-ftah-ROH-yeh?	… the second course?
… на тре́тье?	… nah-TREH-tyeh?	… the third course?
Я хочу́ …	Yah hah-CHOO …	I want …
Не могли́ бы вы э́то убра́ть?	Neh mahg-LEE bwee vwee EH-tah oob-RAHT?	Could you take these away?
Еда́ и обслу́живание бы́ли отли́чны.	Yeh-DAH ee ahb-SLOO-zhee-vah-nee-yeh BWEE-lee aht-LEECH-nee.	The meal and service were excellent.
Принеси́те, пожа́луйста, счёт.	Pree-neh-SEET-yeh, pah-ZHAH-loo-stah, chyoht.	Check, please.

Memory Serves

You should always find out the tipping policy before entering a restaurant. Under the former Soviet Union, tips were strictly prohibited; and many restaurants still discourage the practice of tipping (although their prices may be slightly higher), whereas others encourage it. You should ask a native before dining, just to be certain, because the practice of tipping may vary from region to region.

The food arrives, piping hot, and it smells great. But as you reach down to grab your fork, you realize that you have no silverware. You'll need to ask the waiter to bring you a replacement. You can use the phrases "У меня́ нет …" ("I don't have …") and "Принеси́те мне пожа́луйста …" ("Please bring me …") to solve this problem.

У меня́ нет + genitive case
Oo-mehn-YAH nyeht …
I don't have …

Принеси́те мне, пожа́луйста + accusative case
Pree-neh-SEET-yeh mnyeh, pah-ZHAH-loo-stah …
Please, bring me …

Setting the Table

Russian Word	Pronunciation	English Meaning
глубо́кая таре́лка	gloo-BOH-kah-yah tah-REHL-kah	bowl (deep plate)
ча́шка	CHASH-kah	cup
таре́лка	tah-REHL-kah	plate
ви́лка	VEEL-kah	dinner plate
стака́н	stah-KAHN	glass
нож	NOHSH	knife
меню́	mehn-YOO	menu (indeclinable) it remains unchanged in all cases
салфе́тка	sahl-FYET-kah	napkin
пе́речница	PEH-rehch-neet-sah	pepper shaker
прибо́р	pree-BOHR	place setting
соло́нка	sah-LOHN-kah	salt shaker
блю́дце	BLOOH-dtseh	saucer
сто́пка	STOHP-kah	shot glass

continues

Setting the Table (continued)

Russian Word	Pronunciation	English Meaning
ма́ленькая таре́лка	MAH-lehn-kah-yah tah-REHL-kah	small plate
официа́нт	ah-feet-see-AHNT	waiter
официа́нтка	ah-feet-see-AHNT-kah	waitress
бока́л	bah-KAHL	wine glass
ло́жка	LOHSH-kah	spoon

Remember, the phrase "У меня́ нет" ("I don't have") requires the genitive case:

У меня́ нет таре́лки.
Oo-mehn-YAH nyeht tah-REHL-kee.
I don't have a plate.

У неё нет ви́лки.
Oo-nyeh-YOH nyeht VEEL-kee.
She doesn't have a fork.

But the phrase "Пожа́луйста, принеси́те мне" ("Please bring me") requires the accusative case for *what* and the dative case for *to whom:*

Принеси́те ему́, пожа́луйста, таре́лку.
Pree-neh-SEET-yeh yeh-MOO, pah-ZHAH-loo-stah tah-REHL-koo.
Please bring him a plate.

Принеси́те ей, пожа́луйста, ви́лку.
Pree-neh-SEET-yeh yehy, pah-ZHAH-loo-stah, VEEL-koo.
Please bring her a fork.

Service, Please

You've been practicing your newfound restaurant terms; but now you're at the restaurant, and something is missing! To impress your date, and, more importantly, to start eating, you need to tell the server what is wrong. This exercise will help you maintain top form (answers are listed in Appendix B). Remember to use the proper cases:

У + genitive, нет, the missing item + genitive

Exercise 18.1

Example: I don't have a glass.

Answer: У меня́ нет стака́на.

1. She doesn't have a knife. ________________________________.
2. We don't have silverware. ________________________________.
3. He doesn't have a small plate. ________________________________.
4. I don't have a salt shaker. ________________________________.

My Needs Are on Order

You passed the first test with flying colors. You told the waiter what was missing. What if he simply looks at you, and agrees that you don't have any silverware? You'll need to ask him to bring you some. Remember to use the following phrase:

Пожа́луйста, принеси́те (мне), ________________________________.

Пожа́луйста, принеси́те + dative case (мне), the missing item + accusative case.

See Appendix B to check your answers.

Exercise 18.2

Example: Please bring us a plate.

Answer: Принеси́те нам, пожа́луйста, таре́лку.

1. Please bring her a menu. ________________________________.
2. Please bring him a spoon. ________________________________.
3. Please bring me a napkin. ________________________________.
4. Please bring us glasses. ________________________________.

What Would You Recommend?

You won't be able to order the staples of the traditional Russian meal without the words in the following two tables. Learn them by heart!

I Have a Soup in Mind

Russian Word	Pronunciation	English Meaning
борщ	borshch	borscht
бульóн	bool-YOHN	clear soup, bouillon
щи	shchee	cabbage soup
уxá	ooh-KAH	fish soup
рассóльник	pahs-SOHL-neek	fish/meat and cucumber soup
солянка	sahl-YAHN-kah	thick soup with (fish) meat, olives
суп	soop	soup

Meats for the Occasion

Russian Word	Pronunciation	English Meaning
колбасá	kahl-bah-SAH	sausage
яи́чница	yah-EECH-neet-sah	fried eggs
ветчинá	veht-chee-NAH	ham
мя́со	MYAH-sah	meat
говя́дина	gahv-YAH-dee-nah	beef
свини́на	svee-NEE-nah	pork
бара́нина	bah-RAH-nee-nah	lamb
ку́рица	KOO-reet-sah	chicken
индéйка	eend-YAHY-kah	turkey
котлéта	kaht-LEH-tah	hamburger
бифштéкс	beef-SHTEHKS	beefsteak

Культу́ра

Russians enjoy eating beef, but they don't have the passion for it that Americans do. Fish is the real Russian staple; you will find that Russians' knowledge of fish far exceeds the average American's. To experience the best of Russian cuisine, you will want to try several varieties of fish during your visit.

A Dietary Dilemma

Does eggplant make your head ache, or are you allergic to shellfish? Perhaps your doctor has prescribed a special diet heavy in iron or fiber, or maybe you're watching your cholesterol. Whatever your dietary needs, you should know how to get the right food for your body. These phrases will help you trim the fat.

Special Diets

Russian Word	Pronunciation	English Meaning
Я на дие́те.	Yah nah dee-EHT-yeh.	I am on a diet.
Я вегетариа́нец.	Yah veh-geh-tah-ree-AH-nets.	I'm a vegetarian.
Я не могу́ есть еду́ с …	Yah neh mah-GOO yehst yeh-DOO s …	I can't eat foods with …
… с моло́чными проду́ктами.	… smah-LOHCH-nee-mee prah-DOOK-tah-mee.	… any dairy products.
… с алкого́лем.	… sahl-kah-GOHL-yehm.	… any alcohol.
… с морски́ми проду́ктами.	smahr-SKEE-mee prah-DOOK-tah-mee.	… any seafood.
Я хочу́ что́-то …	Yah hah-CHOO SHTOH-tah …	I'm looking for a dish …
… не жи́рное.	… neh ZHEER-nah-yeh.	… low in fat.
… с ма́лым коли́чеством на́трия.	… SMAH-leem kah-LEECH-yehst-vahm NAHT-ree-yah.	… low in sodium.
… без мя́са.	… behz MYAH-sah.	… without meat.
… без припра́в.	… behz pree-PRAHV.	… plain.
… без консерва́нтов.	… behz kahn-sehr-VAHN-tahv.	… without preservatives.

A Raw Deal

Did you receive a soup instead of a salad? Perhaps your filet mignon was well done instead of medium rare. Whatever the case, if your food is not up to your standards, you should be able to explain the problem to your server.

Sending It Back

Russian Word	Pronunciation	English Meaning
(э́то)… холо́дное	(EH-tah)… hah-LOHD-nah-yeh	… is cold
… недожа́ренное	… neh-dah-ZHAH-reh-nah-yeh	… is too rare

continues

Sending It Back (continued)

Russian Word	Pronunciation	English Meaning
… пережа́ренное	peh-reh-ZHAH-reh-nah-yeh	… is overcooked
… сли́шком жёсткое	… SLEESH-kahm ZHOST-kah-yeh	… is tough
… сли́шком сухо́е	… SLEESH-kahm sooh-KOH-yeh	… is dry
… сли́шком солёное	… SLEESH-kahm sah-LOH-nah-yeh	… is too salty
… сли́шком сла́дкое	… SLEESH-kahm SLAHT-kah-yeh	… is too sweet
… сли́шком о́строе	… SLEESH-kahm OHST-rah-yeh	… is too spicy
… испо́рченное	… ees-POHR-chehn-nah-yeh	… is spoiled
… го́рькое	… GOHR-kee	… is bitter
… гря́зное	… GRYAHZ-nah-yeh	… is dirty

My Sweet Tooth Is Aching

Does your heart yearn for something sweet? When the dessert menu arrives, you will have to start choosing between heavenly chocolates and sinful cavities. Russians love pastries and include them in their appetizers, their meals, and their desserts. Not all Russian pastries are sweet; but when it comes to the desserts, they are exactly what you would expect.

For a Fancy Finale

Russian Word	Pronunciation	English Meaning
варе́ники	vah-REH-nee-kee	dumpling filled with cheese or fruit
запека́нка	zah-peh-KAHN-kah	casserole
моро́женное	mah-ROH-zhen-nah-yeh	ice-cream
пече́нье	peh-CHEHN-yeh	cookies
пиро́г	pee-ROHK	pie
пломби́р	plahm-BEER	ice-cream bar
по́нчик	POHN-cheek	filled pastry (doughnut)
торт	tohrt	cake
экле́р	ehk-LEHR	éclair
пиро́жное	pee-ROHZH-nah-yeh	pastry
пирожо́к	pee-rah-ZHOHK	small pie
компо́т	kahm-POHT	stewed fruit

Quench My Thirst!

Russians have world renown for their champagne and, of course, their vodka. The typical Russian drinks some kind of alcoholic beverage with dinner. Here are some of the most common drinks you would find on a Russian menu.

Beverages

Russian Word	Pronunciation	English Meaning
во́дка	VOHT-kah	vodka
конья́к	kahn-YAHK	cognac
ви́ски	VEES-kee	whiskey
пи́во	PEE-vah	beer
шампа́нское	shahm-PAHN-skah-yeh	champagne
кра́сное вино́	KRAHS-nah-yeh vee-NOH	red wine
бе́лое вино́	BEH-lah-yeh vee-NOH	white wine

If you prefer not to drink or, perhaps, want to save the wine until the end, you can order any number of different beverages to drink during the meal. Some of the drinks you may enjoy during or after your meal are listed here.

Russian Word	Pronunciation	English Meaning
ко́фе …	KOH-fyeh …	coffee …
… с молоко́м	… smah-lah-KOHM	… with milk
… со сли́вками	… sah-SLEEV-kah-mee	… with cream
… чёрный	… CHYOHR-nee	… black
… без кофейна	… behz kah-feh-EE-nah	… decaffeinated
чай …	chay …	tea …
… с лимо́ном	… slee-MOH-nahm	… with lemon
… с са́харом	… SSAH-kah-rahm	… with sugar
… травяно́й	… trahv-yah-NOY	… herbal
минера́льная вода́	mee-neh-RAHL-nah-yah vah-DAH	mineral water

Культу́ра

You will find that the American "doggie bag" is nowhere to be found in Russia. Russians anticipate eating everything that they order in a restaurant, and you will not find take-out boxes in Russian restaurants. Should you dine out, if you want to know how big the portion is, you should ask the waiter "**Это мно́го?**" ("Is it a lot?").

It Was Delicious

If the meal has surpassed and exceeded your expectations, by all means, don't hold back. You can use some of the following phrases to boldly proclaim your happiness.

Memory Serves

One of the many similarities between English and Russian is the word-building system. For instance, to change *happy*, an adjective, into a noun, you add "-ness." *Happiness, sadness, thoughtfulness* are all examples of this pattern. Although Russian doesn't use "-ness," it does use **-ность** to perform the same task. You can change many adjectives into nouns with the same strategy.

Еда́ была́ отли́чна!
Yeh-DAH bwee-LAH aht-LEECH-nah!
The food was excellent!

У вас бы́ло превосхо́дное обслу́живание.
Oo-vahs BWEE-lah preh-vahs-HOHD-nah-yeh ahb-SLOO-zhee-vah-nee-yeh.
The service was wonderful.

Всё бы́ло вку́сно.
Vsyoh BWEE-lah FKOOS-nah.
The main course was delicious.

The Least You Need to Know

- You can locate a good restaurant by asking, "Где нахо́дится хоро́ший рестора́н?"
- The typical Russian meal consists of an appetizer and three courses.
- You can read a Russian menu with little difficulty after learning a few key words and phrases.
- Remember that Russians love to eat, and you can express your pleasure by using some simple adjectives.

Chapter 19

Play Time

In This Chapter

- A time for fun and games
- The irregular verbs хоте́ть ("to want") and мочь ("to be able")
- Extending, accepting, and refusing invitations
- Using adverbs to describe abilities

You've visited the monuments and seen the landscape, bought postcards and souvenirs for your friends and relatives, taken pictures of nearly every building or person that you've seen, and treated yourself to an exquisite Russian meal. Now that you have experienced the life and culture, you want to treat yourself to a little fun and relaxation.

All the options are yours. Are you ready for an exciting evening on the town? Perhaps you'd like to visit a casino and play a few rounds of roulette? Maybe you want to see the nightlife and have a few drinks on the town? Perhaps you feel slightly mellower, and want to listen to some live music or see a play? What about sports? Do you prefer soccer or tennis? No matter how you like to relax, after reading this chapter, you will be able to try almost anything, to invite others along with you, and to boast about your abilities.

Okay Sports Fans, Let's Go

Russians are sports fanatics. They love to compete and watch players perform. If you plan to participate in any athletic activity while abroad, be prepared to meet enthusiastic Russians everywhere you go.

You've Got Game

Whether you love to play or prefer to watch from the stands, you will find nearly every option available to you. In the following list, you should be able to find one or two games that you enjoy.

You can use the verb игрáть ("to play") to talk about playing a sport.

Я игрáю (в тéннис). Я люблю́ смотрéть тéннис.
Yah eeg-RAH-yoo (VTEH-nees). Yah loob-LOO smah-TREHT TEH-nees.
I play (tennis). I like to watch tennis.

Sports

Russian Word	Pronunciation	English Meaning
занимáться спóртом	zah-nee-MAHT-syah SPOHR-tahm	to play sports
(в) бейсбóл	vbays-BOHL	baseball
(в) баскетбóл	vbah-skyet-BOHL	basketball
(в) кáрты	VKAHR-tee	cards
(в) америкáнский футбóл	vah-meh-ree-KAHN-skee food-BOHL	football
(в) гóльф	vgohlf	golf
(в) хоккéй	vhah-KYEHY	hockey
(в) настóльный тéннис	vnah-STOHL-nee TEH-nees	ping-pong
(в) футбóл	vfood-BOHL	soccer
(в) тéннис	FTEH-nees	tennis

Supposing you have less competitive interests, you might find some of the following activities more to your liking. You can begin by saying:

Мне нрáвится …
Mnyeh NRAH-veet-syah …
I like to …

Activities

Russian Word	Pronunciation	English Meaning
игра́ть в ша́хматы	eeg-RAHT VSHAK-mah-tee	to play chess
ката́ться на велосипе́де	kah-TAHT-syah nah-veh-lah-see-PEHD-yeh	to bicycle
лови́ть ры́бу	pee-BAH-cheet	to fish
ходи́ть в турпохо́д	hah-DEET vtoor-pah-HOHD	to hike
ездить верхо́м	YEHZ-deet behr-KHOHM	to ride horseback
ката́ться на лы́жах	kah-TAHT-syah nah LEE-zhahk	to ski
ката́ться на конька́х	kah-TAHT-syah nah kahn-KAHK	to skate
пла́вать	PLAH-vaht	to swim
занима́ться аэро́бикой	zah-nee-MAHT-syah aeh-ROH-bee-koy	to do aerobics

Nearly everyone has a hobby; but if it's not sports, it could be something else. Here are a few examples of the way people spend their time:

Он—лю́бит игра́ть в ка́рты.
Ah-nah LOO-beet eeg-RAHT VKAHR-tee.
She likes to play cards.

Он игра́ет в гольф.
Ohn eeg-RAH-yet vgohlf.
He plays golf.

Им нра́вится смотре́ть футбо́л.
Eem NRAH-veet-syah smah-TREHT food-BOHL.
They like to watch soccer.

Мне нра́вится пла́вать.
Mnyeh NRAH-veet-syah PLAH-vaht.
I like to swim.

Lay Out the Ground Rules

Although it's possible to play football on a soccer field, or play badminton on a tennis court, you can usually find better places to play, namely football fields and badminton courts. To start relaxing faster, you should know the names of the places you want to go. If you ask a Russian, "Где мо́жно игра́ть в футбо́л?" ("Where can I play soccer?") he may tell you Везде́ (*anywhere*). Better to ask, "Where is the nearest soccer field?" You can make your life a little simpler by learning the words in the following chart.

Where to Play Your Favorite Sport

Russian Word	Pronunciation	English Meaning
пляж	plyash	beach
площа́дка для го́льфа	plah-SHAHD-kah dlyah GOHL-fa	golf course
по́ле	POHL-yeh	field
спортза́л	spohrtzahl	gymnasium
гора́	gah-RAH	mountain
парк	pahrk	park
като́к	kah-TOHK	skating rink
бассе́йн	bah-SAYN	pool
мо́ре	MOHR-yeh	sea
трибу́на	tree-BOO-nah	stand
стадио́н	stah-dee-OHN	stadium
бегова́я доро́жка	beh-gah-VAH-yah dah-ROHSH-kah	track

Let's recap what you have just learned. Fill in the blanks of the following exercise with the appropriate word(s) (see Appendix B for answers). Remember that игра́ть ("to play") takes the preposition в + the accusative case. If you are going somewhere (remember verbs of motion from Chapter 9?), you will need either the preposition в or на + the accusative case.

Exercise 19.1

Example: Я иду́ ________________ (beach) ________________ (to swim).

Answer: Я иду́ на пляж пла́вать.

1. Мы идём в ________________ (gym) ________________ (to play basketball).
2. Я люблю́ ________________ (to play chess).
3. Они́ смо́трят ________________ (golf) по телеви́зору.
4. ________________ (to watch) и́гры хорошо́, а ________________ (to play) лу́чше.
5. Она́ ________________ (plays) ________________ (baseball).

Культу́ра

Unlike the United States, in which every city's team has a different name, Russia has only a few team names, such as **Локомоти́в** (Locomotive), **Спарта́к** (Spartak), and **Дина́мо** (Dynamo). Each participating city has its own team, such as "Dynamo" Moscow and "Spartak" Kiev. Before you start following Russian sports, you should be aware of this small cultural difference.

Equip Yourself Properly

Of course, before playing any sport, you'll want to make sure you have the right equipment. The following phrases will be of help.

Мне ну́жно … Мне ну́жно за́нять у вас/тебя́ …
Mnyeh NOOZH-nah … Mnyeh NOOZH-nah ZAHN-yaht oo-vahs/the-BYAH
I need … I need to borrow …

Вы не могли́ бы одо́лжить мне
Vwee neh mah-GLEE bwee ah-DOHL-zheet мне …
Can you lend me …?

Sports Equipment

Russian Word	Pronunciation	English Meaning
велосипе́д	veh-lah-see-PYEHT	bicycle
ло́дка	LOHT-kah	boat
у́дочка	OO-dahch-kah	fishing rod
защи́тные очки́	zah-SHEET-nee-yeh ahch-KEE	goggles
клю́шка	KLOOSH-kah	golf club
шлем	shlyehm	helmet
коньки́	kahn-KEE	ice skates
кроссо́вки	krahs-SOHV-kee	jogging shoes
наколе́нники	nah-kah-LEHN-nee-kee	knee pad
перча́тка	pehr-CHAHT-kah	glove
раке́тка	pah-KYEHT-kah	racket
ро́лики	ROH-lee-kee	roller skates
лы́жные боти́нки	LEEZH-nee-yeh bah-TEEN-kee	ski boots
лы́жи	LEE-zhee	skis
футбо́льный мяч	food-BOHL-nee myahch	soccer ball
те́ннисный мяч	TEHN-nees-nee myahch	tennis ball

You probably won't be traveling with all of your sporting gear, so you may want to borrow some equipment from a friend, or rent it from a store. Some of these phrases will help you get the necessary gear.

Я бы хоте́л(а) взять рыба́цкую ло́дку напрока́т.
Yah bwee hah-TYEHL(ah) vsyaht ree-BAHT-skoo-yoo LOHT-koo nah-prah-KAHT.
I would like to rent a fishing boat.

Мо́жно у вас за́нять мяч и наколе́нники?
MOHZH-nah oo-vahs ZAHN-yaht myahch I nah-kah-LEHN-nee-kee?
May I borrow a baseball and glove from you?

Мне нужна́ клю́шка (мне ну́жен мяч).
Mnyeh noozh-NAH KLOOSH-kah (mnyeh NOO-zhehn myahch).
I need a hockey stick (soccer ball).

У вас есть ли́шняя раке́тка?
Oo-vahs yehst LEESH-nyah-yah rah-KYEHT-kah?
Do you have an extra tennis racket?

Let's Get Together

Although you can play a game of basketball by yourself, you may tire of keeping track of whether you are winning or losing. If you're traveling alone, you may want to enlist some sporting partners—you will find most people more than willing to join you for a quick game of anything, from ping-pong to soccer. The first order of business is to start inviting friends to join you.

You can make quick work of recruiting friends and colleagues after you learn three verbs: хоте́ть ("to want"), мочь ("to be able to"), and дава́ть ("let's"). Хоте́ть is the only verb of its kind in Russian—its conjugation pattern is half E-type and half И-type (see Chapter 9). Rest assured, you only have to learn this pattern once, for it only occurs with this verb.

Дава́йте (*let's*) is used in its imperative form to indicate, "let's do something." You can use it in any context when you want to suggest an activity.

The Verb хоте́ть ("to want")

Person	Singular	English	Plural	English
First	хочу́ hah-CHOO	I want	хоти́м hah-TEEM	We want

Person	Singular	English	Plural	English
Second	хóчешь HOH-chehsh	You want (familiar)	хотúте hah-TEET-yeh	You want (Formal)
Third	хóчет HOH-cheht	He/she wants	хотя́т hah-TYAHT	They want

Вы хотúте игра́ть в футбóл?
Vwee hah-TEET-yeh eeg-RAHT vfood-BOHL?
Do you want to play soccer?

Ты хóчешь смотре́ть игрý?
Tee HOH-chehsh cmah-TREHT eeg-ROO?
Do you want to watch a game?

The Verb мочь ("to be able to")

Person	Singular	English	Plural	English
First	могý mah-GOO	I can/am able to	мóжем MOH-zhehm	We can/are able to
Second	мóжешь MOH-zhehsh	You can … (familiar)	мóжете MOH-zheht-yeh	You can … (formal)
Third	мóжет MOH-zheht	He/she can …	мóгут mah-GOOT	They can …

Я могý игра́ть в футбóл хорошó.
Yah mah-GOO eeg-RAHT vfood-BOHL hah-rah-SHOH.
I can play soccer well.

Вы мóжете игра́ть в футбóл?
Vwee MOH-zheht-yeh eeg-RAHT vfood-BOHL?
Can you play soccer?

The Verb дава́ть (*let's*)

Person	Singular	English	Plural	English
Imperative	дава́й dah-VAY	Let's … (familiar)	дава́йте dah-VAY-tyeh	Let's … (formal)

Дава́й игра́ть! Дава́йте смотре́ть.
Dah-VAY eeg-RAHT! Dah-VAY-tyeh smah-TREHT.
Let's play! Let's watch.

You've learned the material so well that you have dozens of candidates for your next sporting event. You decide that you have too many people for basketball, too few for football; everyone unanimously chooses soccer. Use the verbs you've learned from the previous charts to get the game started. (See Appendix B for answers.)

Exercise 19.2

Example: We can all play football.

Answer: Мы все мо́жем игра́ть в америка́нский футбо́л.

1. He wants to go fishing. ______________________.
2. They can't play hockey. ______________________.
3. You want to watch tennis. ______________________.
4. Let's play cards! ______________________.
5. We can go horseback riding. ______________________.

Invite Your Friends

You caught the weather forecast for the upcoming weekend; sun and blue skies will prevail, and you decide to introduce your Russian friends to an all-American barbecue. To please everyone, you arrange as many sports and activities as possible for this Saturday, and begin to make invitations. Memorize your irregular verb хоте́ть ("to want"), мочь ("to be able to"), and practice дава́йте ("let's") by asking your guests what events they prefer and if they are able to attend.

Вы хоти́те игра́ть в бейсбо́л в суббо́ту?
Vwee hah-TEET-yeh eeg-RAHT vbays-BOHL fsoo-BOH-too?
Would you like to play baseball on Saturday?

Вы мо́жете придти́?
Vwee MOH-zheht-yeh preed-TEE?
Are you able to come?

Вы/ты за́няты/за́нят(а) в э́ти выходны́е дни?
Vwee/tee ZAHN-yah-tee/ZAHN-yaht(AH) VEH-tee vwee-hahd-NEE-yeh dnee?
Are you/you (familiar) busy this weekend?

Accepting the Invitation

After you have made a few friends in Moscow proper, you find your answering machine and mailbox flooded with invitations. Your new friends invite you to more events and social activities than you knew existed. Before you can start spending time with them, you need to accept their invitations. The following phrases cover most of your options.

Let's Do It

Russian Word	Pronunciation	English Meaning
Коне́чно.	Kahn-YEHSH-nah.	Of course.
Есте́ственно.	Yehst-YEHST-veh-nah.	Naturally.
Почему́ нет?	Pah-cheh-MOO nyeht?	Why not?
Коне́чно, хоро́шая иде́я.	Kahn-YEHCH-nah, hah-ROH-shah-yah eed-YEH-yah.	Sure, that's a good idea.
Если вы хоти́те.	YES-lee vwee hah-TEET-yeh.	If you like.
Отли́чно.	Aht-LEECH-nah.	Excellent.
С удово́льствием.	Sooh-dah-VOHL-stvee-yehm.	With pleasure.
Ла́дно.	LAHD-nah.	Okay.
Несомне́нно.	Neh-sahm-NYEH-nah.	Certainly.

Refuse Politely and Make an Excuse

What if you have become so popular that your friends are calling you day and night? Maybe the city's next garlic festival just isn't your idea of excitement, perhaps you have already committed your time elsewhere, or maybe you just want to spend the evening alone, reading a book. You can politely excuse yourself from any engagement and express your regrets without any ill will. This chart will help you decline your invitations as cordially as you accept them.

A Polite Refusal

Russian Word	Pronunciation	English Meaning
Это невозмо́жно.	Eh-tah neh-vahs-MOHZH-nah.	It's impossible.
Мне э́то не нра́вится.	Mnyeh EH-tah neh NRAH-veet-syah.	No, I don't feel like it.
Я не могу́.	Yah neh mah-GOO.	I can't.

continues

A Polite Refusal (continued)

Russian Word	Pronunciation	English Meaning
Извини́те.	Eez-vee-NEET-yeh.	I'm sorry.
Прости́те, у меня́ нет вре́мени.	Prah-STEET-yeh, oo mehn-YAH nyeht VREH-meh-nee.	Forgive me; I don't have time.
Я за́нят(а).	Yah ZAHN-yaht(AH).	I'm busy.
Я уста́л(а).	Yah oos-TAHL(ah).	I'm tired.

Other Diversions

You've tried, but you can't seem to get a hold of that same passion for sports as your Russian friends have. Fear not! Sports are only the tip of the iceberg. There are hundreds of ways to spend your time. To suggest another kind of activity, you can suggest to your friends …

Я хоте́л бы пое́хать на конце́рт.
Yah hah-TYEHL bwee pah-YEH-kaht nah kahn-TSEHRT.
I'd like to go to a concert.

Я предпочита́ю пойти́ в турпохо́д.
Yah prehd-pah-chee-TAH-yoo piy-TEE vtoor-pah-HOHD.
I'd prefer to go hiking.

This chart gives you some options for other intriguing suggestions.

Places to Go and Things to Do

Place	English	Activity	English
Пое́хать на бале́т	To go to the ballet	Смотре́ть на балери́н	To watch the dancers
Пойти́ на пляж	To go to the beach	Пла́вать, загора́ть	To swim, to get a tan
Пойти́ в казино́	To go to a casino	Игра́ть в и́гры	To play games
Пойти́ на конце́рт	To go to a concert	Слу́шать орке́стр	To hear the orchestra
Пойти́ в турпохо́д	To go hiking	Осма́тривать достопримеча́тельности	To see the sights

Place	English	Activity	English
Пойти́ в торго́вый центр	To go to the mall	Де́лать поку́пки	To shop
Пойти́ в кино́	To go to the movies	Смотре́ть фильм	To see a film
Пойти́ на о́перу	To go to the opera	Слу́шать му́зыку	To listen to music
Остава́ться до́ма	To stay at home	Отдыха́ть	To rest
Пойти́ в теа́тр	To go to the theater	Смотре́ть пье́су	To see a play

What Will It Be?

As you look at your calendar for the next week, you realize that you don't have time to do everything with everyone. Respond to the following invitations with acceptance, an excuse, or suggest something that you would rather do instead.

Example: Вы хоти́те игра́ть в те́ннис в суббо́ту? Do you want to play tennis on Saturday?

Answer: Мо́жет быть, это зави́сит от вре́мени дня. Maybe, it depends on what part of the day.

1. Ты мо́жешь смотре́ть футбо́льный матч сего́дня? Can you watch the soccer game today?
2. Вы мо́жете игра́ть в ша́хматы? Can you play chess?
3. Вы лю́бите игра́ть в ка́рты? Do you like to play cards?
4. Ты хо́чешь занима́ться бо́ксом за́втра? Do you want to box tomorrow?
5. Вы хоти́те ката́ться на лы́жах за́втра? Do you want to go skiing tomorrow?

Film at Eleven

Sometimes you just want the entertainment to come to you. After a busy day in town, between a morning jog, shopping, and a little sightseeing, there's nothing better than a bag of potato chips and your sofa. If you crave peace and quiet, you can always find a video to rent or a show on TV. If you want an evening of passive entertainment, the following chart includes the different types of films and shows that you may enjoy.

Что сего́дня пока́зывают?
Shtoh she-VOHD-nyah pah-KAH-zee-vah-yoot?
What kind of film are they showing?

Что бу́дет по телеви́зору?
Shtoh BOO-deht poh teh-leh-VEE-zahr-oo?
What's on TV?

Television Programs and Movies

Russian Word	Pronunciation	English Meaning
приключе́нческий фильм	pree-kloo-CHEHN-chehs-kee feelm	adventure film
мультфи́льм	moolt-FEELM	cartoon
кинокоме́дия	kee-noh-kah-MEH-dee-yah	comedy
документа́льный фильм	dah-koo-mehn-TAHL-nee feelm	documentary
драмати́ческий фильм	drah-mah-TEE-chehs-kee feelm	drama
многосери́йный фильм	mnoh-gah-seh-REE-nee feelm	serial
фильм у́жасов	feelm OO-zhah-sahv	horror film
любо́вная исто́рия	loo-BOHV-nah-yah ees-TOH-ree-yah	love story
детекти́вный фильм	deh-tehk-TEEV-nee feelm	mystery
но́вости	NOH-vahs-tee	news
нау́чно-фантасти́ческий фильм	nah-OOCH-nah-fan-tahs-TEE-chehs-kee feelm	sci-fi film
телевизио́нный фильм	teh-leh-vee-zee-OH-nee feelm	TV movie
немо́й фильм	neh-MOY feelm	silent film
музыка́льный фильм	moo-zee-KAHL-nee feelm	musical
ве́стерн	VEHS-tehrn	western

Notice the use of the verb игра́ть ("to play") in the following phrases. Instead of the preposition в + accusative case, the preposition на + prepositional case is used.

Он игра́ет на гита́ре.
Ohn eeg-RAH-yet nah-gee-TAHR-yeh.
He plays the guitar.

Они́ игра́ют на скри́пках.
Ah-NEE eeg-RAH-yoot nah SKREEP-kahk.
They play violins.

It Seems to Me ...

Whether you loved the show or hated it, you can use the following phrases to express your level of satisfaction.

If You Like the Show

Russian Word	Pronunciation	English Meaning
Я люблю́ э́тот фильм/конце́рт.	Yah loo-BLOO EH-that feelm/kahn-TSERHT.	I love this film/concert.
Мне действи́тельно понра́вилось.	Mnyeh days-TVEE-tehl-nah pahn-RAH-vee-lahs.	I really liked it.
Этот фильм хоро́ший.	EH-taht feelm hah-ROH-shee	It is a good film.
Этот фильм что́-то невероя́тное.	EH-taht feelm SHTOH-tah neh-veh-rah-YAHT-nah-yeh.	It is amusing.
Этот фильм отли́чный.	EH-taht feelm aht-LEECH-nee.	It is excellent.

If the Show Doesn't Appeal to You

Russian Word	Pronunciation	English Meaning
Я ненави́дел э́тот фильм/конце́рт.	Yah neh-nah-VEE-dehl EH-that feelm/kahn-TSEHRT.	I hated that film/concert.
Этот фильм плохо́й.	EH-taht feelm plah-HOY.	It's a bad film.
Это пуста́я тра́та вре́мени.	EH-tah poos-TAH-yah TRAH-tah VREH-meh-nee.	It's a waste of time.
Это всегда́ одно́ и то́же.	EH-tah vsehg-DAH ahd-NO ee TOH-zheh.	It's always the same thing.

Let Me Just Say

What did you think of the last show you saw? Respond to the following statements with your approval or disapproval.

Example: Did you like the comedy?

Вам/тебе́ понра́вилась коме́дия?

Answer: Да, э́тот фильм хоро́ший.

1. What do you think about the film?

   Что вы ду́маете о фи́льме?

2. Is the new action film good?

   Но́вый приключе́нческий фильм хоро́ший?

3. Do you like thrillers?

   Вам/тебé нрáвятся три́ллеры?

Do You Do It Well?

In Chapter 8, you learned that *adverbs* are simply modifiers, like adjectives, that modify verbs or adjectives. You've already been describing actions throughout the book ("He played well," "They ran quickly"), but now you have a chance to take a more in-depth look at the adverb, and how it is used.

Memory Serves

Most modifying adverbs are formed by dropping the -ый/ий ending on an adjective, and adding -о. Most adjectives can be formed into adverbs, although the change is often accompanied by a change in stress as well.

Hot Topic

Adverbs are words that modify verbs or adjectives.

English adverbs are usually formed by adding "-ly" to adjectives, as in *speedily*, *thoughtfully*, or *slowly*. As you know, Russian adverbs are formed by adding -о to produce the same result. But the similarities to English don't end there; in fact, words like *here*, *there*, *now*, and *then* are also considered adverbs. These adverbs don't have any rules for formation, and must be committed to memory.

Ми́ша хорошó/плóхо игрáет в футбóл.
MEE-shah hah-rah-SHOH/PLOH-hah eeg-RAH-yet vfood-BOHL.
Misha plays soccer well/poorly.

Они́ грóмко/ти́хо игрáют на инструмéнтах.
An-NEE GROHM-kah/TEEH-kah eeg-RAH-yoou nah-een-stroo-MEHN-tahk.
They play their instruments loudly/softly.

Regular Formation of Adverbs

Adjective	Adverb	English Meaning
дешёвый dee-SHO-vee	дёшево DYO-she-vah	cheaply
дорогóй dah-RAH-goy	дóрого DOH-rah-gah	expensively
холóдный hah-LOHD-nee	хóлодно HOH-lahd-nah	coldly
тёплый TYOH-plee	теплó tyeep-LOH	warmly

Plain and Simple Adverbs

It's true, almost every adjective can be turned into an adverb, but many adverbs have only one form, and cannot be declined or conjugated like nouns or verbs. First the bad news: These forms are slightly irregular, and have to be memorized. But the good news is that these words never change; they will always have the same form.

Adverbs Through and Through

Russian Word	Pronunciation	English Meaning
всегда́	vsehg-DAH	always
поэ́тому	pah-EH-tah-moo	therefore
тут	toot	here (location)
сюда́	syoo-DAH	here (motion)
сра́зу	SRAH-zoo	immediately
у́тром	OOT-rahm	in the morning
сейча́с	see-CHAHS	now
ча́сто	CHAHS-tah	often
то́лько	TOHL-kah	only
вре́мя от вре́мени	VREHM-yah oht VREH-meh-nee	sometimes
ско́ро	SKOH-rah	soon
ещё	yeh-SHYOH	still
тогда́	tahg-DAH	then
пото́м	pah-TOHM	then, afterward
там	tahm	there (location)
туда́	too-DAH	there (motion)
сего́дня	she-VOHD-nyah	today
сли́шком	SLEESH-kahm	too
о́чень	OH-chehn	very
вчера́	vcheh-RAH	yesterday

What Is Your Position?

Although there is no hard-and-fast rule regarding the position of adverbs, Russians generally place them directly before the verb they modify. Adverbs referring to time or place, such as *now* or *there*, can be placed anywhere, other than the last word of the sentence.

Внима́ние

Adverbs like *tomorrow, in the morning,* and *then* do not change form and will always stay the same. They cannot be used to modify other words and can only be modified with other adverbs. "**Хо́лодно сего́дня.**" ("It's cold today.")

Он хорошо́ игра́ет сего́дня.
Ohn hah-rahSHOH eeg-RAH-yet seh-VOHD-nyah.
He is playing well today.

Они́ шли туда́, сюда́, и, наконе́ц, ме́дленно се́ли.
Ah-nee shlee too-DAH, syoo-DAH, ee, nah-kahn-YETS MEHD-leh-nah SYEH-lee.
They went here and there, and finally sat down slowly.

You Perform Well

You finished in top form! Now you can use adverbs to describe yourself and others. The following table includes some of the more common adverbs, all of which can be used as adjectives after you have properly declined them. Let your friends know exactly how well (or poorly) they do something.

Common Adverbs to Describe Abilities

Russian Word	Pronunciation	English Meaning
ско́ро	SKOH-rah	fast
ме́дленно	MEHD-leh-nah	slowly
хорошо́	hah-rah-SHOH	well
пло́хо	PLOH-kah	poorly
отли́чно	aht-LEECH-nah	excellently
ужа́сно	oo-ZHAHS-nah	terribly
стра́шно	STRAHSH-nah	horribly
чуде́сно	choo-DEHS-nah	wonderfully

Take these activities for a test spin. How well do you fish or play the guitar or ski? Using the following words, tell how well you can do each activity.

Example: Как ты игра́ешь в ша́хматы? How do you play chess?

Answer: Я пло́хо игро́ю в ша́хматы.

1. Когда́ вы обы́чно идёте в турпохо́д? When do you usually go hiking?
2. Как ты ката́ешься на лы́жах? How well do you ski?
3. Как ча́сто ты е́здишь на мо́ре? How often do you go to the sea?

4. Как вы игрáете на гитáре? How well do you play the guitar?
5. Как вы занимáетесь спóртом? How are you at sports?

The Least You Need to Know

- If you like to do something, use the phrase "я люблю́" + your favorite activity or interest.
- To "play" a sport, remember to use the verb игрáть + в and the accusative case. To "play" an instrument, use the verb игрáть + на and the prepositional case.
- The verb хотéть ("to want") can be used to extend an invitation, or used in the subjunctive to suggest what you would like to do.
- Most adverbs are formed by adding -o to the end of an adjective; but some adverbs stand by themselves and can only be used as adverbs.

Part 5 Anybody Can Handle Challenges

No one likes to experience problems or encounter conflicts, especially when they're away from home; but these things tend to happen. Part 5 will introduce you to the useful terms and phrases you will need to handle any problem that occurs during your travels. From clothing issues to health, you will learn the full range of tools necessary to keep your travels going. Now that you have a handle on the core vocabulary and grammar, you can also begin to communicate by e-mail, phone, or fax; and you can jump ahead of the game by getting involved in Russian business.

By the time you have finished Part 5, you will be able to handle any situation you encounter in your Russian conversations. You've worked hard to reach this point, and after a few brief chapters you will have visible proof of your effort. Congratulations, and keep up the hard work!

Chapter 20

Could I Get Some Service, Please?

In This Chapter

- Personal services
- Problems and solutions
- How does it compare?
- Working with superlatives

You leave the hotel early this morning, to catch the soccer game, run some errands, and have an early dinner. But before you even make it to your car, things start going wrong. A drive-by puddle soaks your best suit, and a few minutes later your shoe is caught in the tread of an escalator. On your way to the soccer game, a little boy bumps into you, and your glasses fall to the ground—*crack*. What's worse, you've left your wallet and all of your emergency phone numbers at home. Don't worry—this chapter will guide you through the solutions to all of these problems.

I Have a Problem

Regardless of where you find yourself or what services you seek, a few phrases apply to most shops and offices. Whether you go to the jeweler or the optometrist, these phrases will come in handy.

Когда́ магази́н открыва́ется?
Kahg-DAH mah-gah-ZEEN aht-kree-VAH-yet-sya?
What time do you open?

Когда́ магази́н откры́т?
Kahg-DAH mah-gah-ZEEN aht-KREET?
What are your working hours?

Когда́ магази́н закрыва́ется?
Kahg-DAH mah-gah-ZEEN zah-kree-VAH-yet-sya?
What time do you close?

Я до́лжен отда́ть … в ремо́нт.
Yah DOHL-zhen aht-DAHT … vreh-MOHNT.
I need to have my … fixed.

Вы мо́жете почини́ть (их) сего́дня?
Vwee MOHZH-yet-yeh pah-chee-NEET (eekh) seh-VOHD-nyah?
Can you fix (them) today?

Пожа́луйста, да́йте мне квита́нцию на э́то.
Pah-ZHAH-loo-stah, DIY-tyeh mnyeh kvee-TAHN-tsee-yoo nah-EH-tah.
Could I have a receipt?

Ско́лько э́то займёт вре́мени?
SKOHL-kah EH-tah ziy-MYEHT VREH-meh-nee?
How long will it take?

At the Laundry

You've only been in town three days, and your clothes are already in piles, thrown around the room, and you can't tell whether your pants are clean or dirty. If you have the time and patience, you can wash the clothes yourself at the local Laundromat. You throw your clothes into a sack, sling them over your shoulder, and head into town. The following phrases will make light work of the washing machines near you.

Мне нужно найти́ пра́чечную.
Mnyeh NOOZH-nah nay-TEE PRAH-chech-noo-yoo.
I need to find a Laundromat.

У меня́ мно́го гря́зной оде́жды.
Oo-mehn-YAH MNOH-gah GRYAHZ-noy ah-DYEZH-dee.
I have a lot of dirty clothes.

Я хочу́ постира́ть бельё.
Yah hah-CHOO pah-stee-RAHT behl-YOH.
I want to wash my linens.

Каку́ю стира́льную маши́ну мо́жно испо́льзовать?
Kah-KOO-yoo stee-RAHL-noo-yoo mah-SHEE-noo MOHZH-nah ees-POHL-zah-vaht?
Which washing machines may I use?

Есть ли беспла́тная суши́лка?
Yehst lee behs-PLAHT-nah-yah soo-SHEEL-kah?
Are there any free dryers?

Где мо́жно купи́ть сре́дство для сти́рки белья́?
Gdyeh MOHZH-nah koo-PEET SREHD-stvah dlyah steer-KEE behl-YAH?
Where can I buy detergent?

I Need a Cobbler

You checked the last item off your list of important достопримеча́тельности ("scenic places"), when you glance down at your feet. Besides being a little sore, you notice that you have worn through the sole. You haven't even started visiting the museums and cathedrals, and you need to have those shoes fixed right away. Whether you just want a quick shine or a complete overhaul, these phrases will get you started.

В чём де́ло?
Fchyohm DEH-lah?
What's the problem?

Ремо́нт о́буви
Reeh-MOHNT OH-boo-vee
shoe repair

Не могли́ бы вы э́то/э́ти почини́ть для меня́?
Neh mahg-LEE bwee vwee EH-tah/EH-tee pah-chee-NEET dlyah mehn-YAH?
Can you fix this/these for me?

… сапоги́ … боти́нки …
… sah-pah-GEE … bah-TEEN-kee …
… these boots … these shoes (high tops) …

… подóшву … каблýк …
… pah-DOHSH-voo … kahb-LOOK …
… this sole … this heel …

Продаёте ли вы шнýрки?
Prah-dah-YOHT-yeh lee vwee SHNOOR-kee?
Do you sell shoelaces?

Пожáлуйста, почистúте ботúнки!
Pah-ZHAH-loo-stah, pah-CHEES-teet-yeh bah-TEEN-kee!
Please, give me a shoeshine!

Please, Help Me!

Russians frequently say, "Жизнь идёт дáльше" ("life goes on further"); but, at the moment, everything seems catastrophic. Your shoes have fallen apart, your two best shirts are covered in chocolate syrup, and you have a dinner date in less than an hour! Where should you go first? How do you even begin? For starters, let's translate the following sentences into Russian using the words you've just learned (answers in Appendix B).

Exercise 20.1

Example: Can you clean this shirt?

Answer: Не мóжете ли вы почúстить э́ту рубáшку?

1. Where is the nearest Laundromat? ______________________________.
2. Can you mend these shoes? ______________________________.
3. What are your hours? ______________________________.

A Snapshot of Russia

As you stare upward at St. Basil's Cathedral, you reach into your pocket to pull out your camera, but where is your film? You realize that you used your entire roll in the Hermitage, and now you need to buy more film. Whether you lost or forgot to bring your camera, or if you only need to buy some extra rolls, these phrases will help you make things click.

Мне ну́жен фотоаппара́т.
Mnyeh NOOZH-yen foh-tah-ah-pah-RAHT.
I need a camera.

Мне нужна́ ви́део ка́мера.
Mnyeh noozh-NAH VEE-deh-oh KAH-meh-rah.
I need a video camera.

У вас есть чёрно-бе́лая (цветна́я) плёнка, 24 (36) ка́дра(ов)?
Oo-vahs yehst CHYOHR-nah-BEH-lah-yah (tsveht-NAH-yah) PLYOHN-kah, DVAHD-tsaht chee-TEE-pee (TREED-tsaht shehst) KAHD-rah (rahv)?
Do you have black-and-white (color) exposure film in rolls of 24 (36)?

Сфотографи́руйте меня́/нас, пожа́луйста.
Sfoh-tah-grah-FEE-root-yeh mehn-YAH/nahs, pah-ZHAH-loo-stah.
Would you take a picture of me/us please?

Ско́лько сто́ит прoя́вка одно́й плёнки/увеличе́ние?
SKOHL-kah STOH-eet prah-YAHV-kah ahd-NOY PLYOHN-kee /oo-veh-lee-CHEH-nee-yeh?
What does it cost to develop a roll/for enlargement?

Finding Help

Sometimes the worst can happen; if you find yourself in a tight spot, these phrases will give you direction.

Как добра́ться?
Kahk dahb-BRAHT-syah?
How do you get to?

… в мили́цию.
… vmee-LEET-see-yoo.
… the police station.

… в америка́нское посо́льство.
… vah-meh-ree-KAHN-skah-yeh pah-SOHLST-vah.
… the American embassy.

… в америка́нское ко́нсульство.
… vah-meh-ree-KAHN-skah-yeh KOHN-sool-stvah.
… the American consulate.

Я потеря́л(а) …
Yah pah-tehr-YAHL(ah) …
I have lost …

… бума́жник.
… boo-MAHZH-neek.
… my wallet.

… мой па́спорт.
… moy PAHS-pahrt.
… my passport.

… мою́ су́мку.
… mah-YOO SOOM-koo.
… my purse.

Прошу́, помоги́те мне.
Prah-SHOO, pah-mah-GEET-yeh mnyeh.
Please help me.

Кто́-нибудь здесь говори́т по-англи́йски?
KTOH-nee-bood zdehs gah-vah-REET pah-ahn-GLEES-kee?
Does anyone here speak English?

Comparison Shopping

Russians work hard for their paychecks and will always deal with you honestly; however, that doesn't mean that all restaurants and hotels are the same—like anywhere else in the world, some are better than others. To be a smart tourist, you have to shop around, compare prices from one establishment to the next, and find the best overall deal.

Making Comparisons

You've found the best deal on матрёшка (matryoshka dolls) in the city, and as you relate your shopping experience to your friends back home, you explain that one store was *bigger* than another; another store had a *larger* selection; but you finally found a store with the *best* products for the *cheapest* prices. Just like English, Russian adjectives have three forms: the *simple*, the *comparative*, and the *superlative*.

Hot Topic

Simple form: Normal adjectives, like "the *big* house."
Comparative form: The *more* or *less* form of adjectives; when "the house is *bigger*."
Superlative form: The *most* form of adjectives; when it's "the *biggest* house."

You already know how to form the simple; and you may not realize it, but the superlative, as well. To form the comparative form of an adjective, the form that is shorter or longer, you need only drop -ый/ий and add -ее. That's all! The comparative form of adjectives has only one form, regardless of gender or number. That means there's only one form to learn, and it always stays the same. The helper adjectives са́мый ("the most") and наиме́нее ("the least") are used to form the superlative, the *biggest* or *smallest* form of adjectives.

Adjective Type	Russian	Pronunciation	English Meaning
Simple	но́вая (маши́на)	NOH-vah-yah	A new car
Comparative	бо́лее но́вая (маши́на) маши́на нове́е	BOH-lye-ye NOH-vah-yah nahv-YEH-yeh	A newer car But: The car is newer.
Superlative	са́мая но́вая (маши́на)	SAH-mah-yah NOH-vah-yah	The newest car
Simple building	ва́жное (зда́ние)	VAHZH-nah-yeh	An important
Comparative	бо́лее ва́жное (зда́ние) зда́ние важне́е	BOH-lye-ye VAHZH-nah-yeh vahzh-NYEH-yeh	A more important building But: The building is more important.
Superlative	са́мое ва́жное (зда́ние)	SAH-mah-yeh VAHZH-nah-yeh	The most important building

Adjectives in their comparative forms can also be used as adverbs, to modify a verb. For example:

> Ве́тер ду́ет сильне́е.
> VEH-tehr DOO-yet seel-NYEH-yeh.
> The wind blew stronger.

Memory Serves

The comparative adjective is formed by removing the normal ending **-ый/ий** and replacing it with **-ee**. Nouns that follow a comparative adjective take the genitive case, as in "**Да́йте мне бо́льше сы́ра**" ("give me more cheese"). The superlative is formed using the words **са́мый** and **наиме́нее**, and works just like a normal adjective—it matches in gender, number, and case with the noun it modifies.

That's Highly Irregular

Why does it go from better to bad to worse? Why not from bad to *badder* or from good to *gooder?* English has some irregular forms of comparative adjectives; in fact, two of the most commonly used adjectives (good and bad) have unusual forms. The same is true of Russian, but the list is a little longer. Fortunately, it isn't endless, and the forms are easy to learn. Pay close attention to the irregular comparative forms in the following chart, and remember that the comparative form does not affect the superlative.

Irregular Comparative Form Adjectives

Simple Adjective	English Meaning	Comparative Adjective	English Meaning
большóй bahl-SHOY	big	бóльше BOHL-shyeh	bigger/more
мáленький MAH-lehn-kee	small	мéньше MEHN-shyeh	smaller/less
чáсто CHAHS-tah	often	чáще CHAH-shyeh	more often
пóздно POHZD-nah	late	пóзже POHZ-zhyeh	later
рáно RAH-nah	early	рáньше PAHN-shyeh	earlier
дешёвый deh-SHYOH-vwee	cheap	дешéвле deh-SHEHV-leh	cheaper
молодóй mah-lah-DOY	young	молóже mah-LOH-zhyeh	younger
стáрый STAH-ree	old	стáрше STAHR-shyeh	older
хорóший hah-ROH-shee	good	лýчше LOOCH-shyeh	better
плохóй plah-KOY	bad	хýже HOO-zhyeh	worse
тúхий TEEH-kee	quiet	тúше TEE-shyeh	quieter
грóмкий GROHM-kee	loud	грóмче GROHM-chyeh	louder
мя́гкий MYAHK-kee	soft	мя́гче MYAHK-chyeh	softer

Comparisons of Quality and Inequality

In the spirit of bargain hunting, you decide to see a popular play tonight, and begin to make preparations. But when you arrive, you realize that the show started sooner than you expected; the taxi had arrived later than you scheduled; and the tickets were more expensive than you thought. You easily recognize the comparative forms of these adjectives, but how do you express that tricky word *than* in Russian? The answer is simpler than you think: Use чем (*than*)! The following examples will bring you up to speed on making comparisons.

Погóда лýчше, чем вчерá.
Pah-GOH-dah LOOCH-shyeh, chyehm vcheh-RAH.
The weather is better than yesterday.

Вечéрний спектáкль дорóже, чем дневнóй.
Veh-CHEHR-nee spehk-TAH-kehl dah-ROH-zheh, chyehm dnehv-NOY.
The evening show is more expensive than the morning.

Он рабóтал немнóго бóльше, чем обы́чно.
Ohn rah-BOH-tahl nehm-NOH-gah BOHL-shyeh, chyehm ah-BWEECH-nah.
He worked a little more than normal.

Я проснýлся рáньше, чем онá.
Yah prahs-NOOL-syah RAHN-shyeh, chyehm ah-NAH.
I woke up earlier than she did.

> **Evening Recap**
>
> Remember, a noun that follows a comparative should be in the genitive case: "**Это лýчший вы́бор**" ("That's the better choice"); but a comparative followed by **чем** (*than*) begins a new clause, and does not require the genitive case.

How Do You Measure Up?

Think about your achievements so far this year. Would you say that you've worked more this year than last year? Do you think you're getting older or younger? What about your children, if you have them; are you still taller than them, or have they grown faster than you thought? Use the words and phrases you've learned to compare yourself to friends and family.

The Least You Need to Know

- You can make quick work of your problems while traveling abroad by learning a few simple phrases.
- Use сáмый ("the least") and наимéнее ("the most") to express the superlative degree.
- The simple superlative can easily be formed by adding -ee to the end of an adjective. Remember that when you compare nouns, the comparative adjective must be followed by a noun in genitive case, or by чем and a noun in nominative case.
- Like English, Russian has some irregular forms of comparatives, which should be memorized.

Chapter 21

Is There a Doctor in the House?

In This Chapter

- Your body
- Symptoms and illnesses, complaints and cures
- Expressing duration
- When to say (говори́ть) or to tell (расска́зывать)
- How to use reflexive verbs

In the last chapter, you learned how to handle a whole array of minor problems, from all those little things that happen while traveling to life's petty annoyances. But what if something more significant than a broken nail befalls you during your journeys? What if you become ill? This chapter will guide you through the possibilities. After layovers and time changes, airport food and rich Russian cuisine, and changing weather conditions, you may find your spirits high, but your body a bit weak. After a little practice with some phrases and key words, you'll be able to complain about every ache and pain.

Here's the Problem

The first question most doctors will ask is, "Where does it hurt?" You need to know the parts of your body, so that you can accurately point the doctor in the right direction. Try some of the words in the following chart to get you started.

Parts of the Body

Russian Word	Pronunciation	English Meaning
лоды́жка(и)	lah-DEESH-kah(ee)	ankle(s)
рука́ (ру́ки)	roo-KAH (ROO-kee)	arm(s)
спина́	spee-NAH	back
те́ло	TEH-loh	body
мозг	mohzk	brain
грудь	grood	chest
подборо́док	pahd-bah-ROH-dahk	chin
у́хо (у́ши)	OOH-kah (OO-shee)	ear(s)
ло́коть (ло́кти)	LOH-kaht (LOHK-tee)	elbow(s)
глаз (глаза́)	glahs (glah-ZAH)	eye(s)
лицо́	leet-SOH	face
па́лец (па́льцы)	PAH-lets (PAHL-tsee)	finger(s)/toe(s)
нога́ (но́ги)	nah-GAH (NOH-gee)	foot (feet)
рука́ (ру́ки)	roo-KAH (ROO-kee)	hand(s)
се́рдце	SEHRD-tsyeh	heart
коле́но (коле́ни)	kah-LEH-nah (kah-LEH-nee)	knee(s)
нога́ (но́ги)	nah-GAH (NOH-gee)	leg(s)
губа́ (гу́бы)	goo-BAH (GOO-bee)	lip(s)
пе́чень	PEH-chehn	liver
лёгкие	LEHK-kee-yeh	lung
рот (рты)	roht	mouth
но́готь (но́гти)	NOH-gaht (NOHK-tee)	nail(s)
ше́я	SHEH-yah	neck
нос	nohs	nose
плечо́ (пле́чи)	pleh-CHOH (PLEH-chee)	shoulder
ко́жа	KOH-zhah	skin
позвоно́чник	pahz-vah-NOHCH-neek	spine
живо́т	zhee-VOHT	stomach
го́рло	GOHR-lah	throat

Russian Word	Pronunciation	English Meaning
язы́к	yah-ZEEK	tongue
зуб (зу́бы)	zoop (ZOO-bwee)	tooth
запя́стье	zahp-YAHST-yeh	wrist

Memory Serves

The words for *language* and *tongue* (**язы́к**) are one and the same. This stems from Russian's relationship to Greek, and is one of the many subtle ties between English and Russian. English speakers have sometimes heard the expression, "speaking in tongues," which really means "languages."

Your Body Needs Some Loving

Let's say that something specific ails you, more than a general pain in your chest or arm. Using the words in the following chart, describe your condition using the idiom у "меня …" ("I have …") and боли́т or боля́т with the prepositional case.

Other Symptoms

Russian Word	Pronunciation	English Meaning
нары́в	nah-REEF	abscess
волды́рь	vahl-DEER	blister
сло́манная кость	SLOH-mah-nah-yah kohst	broken bone
синя́к	seen-YAHK	bruise
ожёг	ah-ZHEHK	burn
озно́б	ahz-NOHP	chills
ка́шель	KAH-shehl	cough
су́дорога	SOO-dah-rah-gah	cramps
поре́з	pah-REHS	cut
поно́с	pah-NOHS	diarrhea
лихора́дка	leeh-kah-RAHT-kah	fever
перело́м	peh-reh-LOHM	fracture
несваре́ние желу́дка	nehs-vah-REH-nee-yeh zheh-LOOHT-kah	indigestion
на́сморк	NAHS-mahrk	cold

continues

Other Symptoms (continued)

Russian Word	Pronunciation	English Meaning
головна́я боль	gah-lahv-NAH-yah bohl	headache
мигре́нь	mee-GREN	migraine
боль	bohl	pain
сыпь	seep	rash
вы́вих	VWEE-veek	sprain
о́пухоль	OH-pooh-kahl	lump
ране́ние	pah-NEH-nee-yeh	wound

Some other useful phrases include the following.

> **Я ка́шляю. Я чиха́ю.**
> Yah KAHSH-lyah-yoo. Yah chee-KAH-yoo.
> I'm coughing. I'm sneezing.

> **У меня́ кровотече́ние. Я пло́хо сплю.**
> Oo mehn-YAH krah-vah-teh-CHEH-nee-yeh. Yah PLOH-kah sploo.
> I'm bleeding. I have trouble sleeping.

> **Меня́ тошни́т. У меня́ всё те́ло боли́т.**
> Mehn-YAH tahsh-NEET. Oo-mehn-yah vsyoh TEH-lah bah-leet.
> I'm nauseous. I hurt everywhere.

> **Мне нездоро́вится.**
> Mnyeh neh-zdah-ROH-veet-syah.
> I feel bad.

> **Я чу́вствую себя́ соверше́нно разби́тым.**
> Yah CHOOV-stvoo-yoo seb-YAH sah-vehr-SHEH-nah rahz-BEE-teem.
> I'm exhausted.

My Head Is Pounding

If the doctor doesn't ask you specifically, "What hurts?" his first question might be "Что с ва́ми?" ("What's bothering you?") To answer, you need only use the standard idiomatic expression "у меня́" ("I have") + боли́т ("to hurt") + the body part that hurts.

For example:

У меня́ боли́т живо́т.
Oo-mehn-YAH zhee-VOHT bah-LEET.
I have a stomachache.

У меня́ боли́т зуб.
Oo-mehn-YAH bah-LEET zoop.
I have a toothache.

У меня́ боли́т голова́.
Oo-mehn-YAH bah-LEET gah-lah-VAH.
I have a headache.

Maybe a family member or colleague is so ill that he cannot speak for himself; in this case, you can speak for him by saying the following.

У него́ боли́т го́рло.
Oon-yeh-VOH bah-LEET GOHR-lah.
He has a sore throat.

У дете́й ветря́нка.
Oo-deh-TYEHY veht-RYAHN-kah.
The children have chickenpox.

It Hurts All Over

The expressions that you've seen above use the verb боле́ть ("to hurt") to express what ails you. This verb is a favorite of many, because it has only two forms: the third person singular and plural, and it is almost always used with the expression "У меня́."

The Verb боле́ть (imperfective: "to hurt")

Person	Singular	English	Plural	English
Third	боли́т bah-LEET	it hurts	боля́т bahl-YAHT	they hurt

The formula for using these types of expressions is extremely simple:

"У меня́" ("I have") + conjugated form of боле́ть + the body part

Memory Serves

Describing physical pain is one of the rare instances in Russian where the word order of the expression does not change. Word order is not normally restrictive, but in this instance you should always use the same order of words:

"**У меня́**" ("I have") + conjugated form of **боле́ть** + the body part

What's Seems to Be the Problem?

After you've told the doctor what you think is wrong, filled out some forms, and waited in an empty room for a few minutes, he will probably want to ask you some questions about your medical history. A few of the illnesses in the following chart are the more commonly encountered.

У вас боли́т …? Что у вас боли́т?
Oo-vahs bah-LEET …? Shtoh oo-vahs bah-LEET?
Have you had …? What is hurting?

Common Nouns for Sicknesses

Russian Word	Pronunciation	English Meaning
аллерги́ческая реа́кция	ahl-lehr-GEE-chehs-kah-yah reh-AHK-tsee-yah	allergic reaction
анги́на	ahn-GEE-nah	sore throat
аппендици́т	ahp-pehn-deet-SEET	appendicitis
а́стма	AHST-mah	asthma
бронхи́т	brahn-KEET	bronchitis
просту́да	prah-STOO-dah	cold
диабе́т	dee-ah-BEHT	diabetes
о́бморок	OHB-mah-rahk	faint
головокруже́ние	gah-lah-vah-kroo-ZHE-nee-ye	dizziness
изнуре́ние	eez-noo-REH-nee-yeh	exhaustion
грипп	greep	flu
корь	kohr	measles
се́нная лихора́дка	SEH-nah-yah leeh-kah-RAHD-kah	hay fever
серде́чный при́ступ	sehr-DEHCH-nee PREES-toop	heart attack
рак	RAHK	cancer
язва	YAZ-vah	ulcer

Russian Word	Pronunciation	English Meaning
сви́нка	SVEEN-kah	mumps
воспале́ние лёгких	vahs-pah-LEH-nee-yeh LYOHG-keek	pneumonia
бессо́нница	beh-SOH-neet-sah	insomnia
тонзилли́т	tahn-zee-LEET	tonsillitis

You may also have the unfortunate opportunity to use one of the phrases in the following chart.

Russian Word	Pronunciation	English Meaning
Я заболе́л(а).	Yah zah-bahl-YEHL	I got sick.
Я простуди́лся/ простуди́лась.	Yah prah-stoo-DEEL-syah/ prah-stoo-DEE-lahs.	I caught a cold.

So worse has come to worse, and you caught that cold floating around the office last week. Use the phrases that you've learned to tell the doctor what's wrong (see Appendix B for answers).

Exercise 21.1

Example: broken bone

Answer: сло́манная кость

1. allergic reaction ____________________.
2. pain in the arm ____________________.
3. trouble sleeping ____________________.
4. chills ____________________.
5. blister on your foot ____________________.

How Long Have You Felt This Way?

Before all else, you should know *what* hurts and *where;* but you can make further progress if you tell the doctor *how long* you've been in pain. Use the following chart to help you start.

How Long Have Your Symptoms Lasted?

Russian Question	English	Russian Answer	English
Ско́лько вре́мени …	Since when …	До того́, как …	Since …
Как до́лго у вас бы́ло …	How long has (have) … been	Неде́лю	For a week
Как до́лго у вас боли́т?	How long has it hurt?	Два дня	For two days
С како́го дня вам нездоро́вится?	Since when have you been suffering?	Со вчера́шнего дня	Since yesterday
Ско́лько дней у вас боли́т?	How many days has it hurt?	Пять дней	For five days
Когда́ у вас на́чало боле́ть?	When did it start to hurt?	В/на …	On …

Quick, Tell the Doctor!

The following is a sample medical form that you might have to fill out. Use the words that you have learned so far to fill in the blanks.

Memory Serves

If you can't remember whether to use **в** or **на** in your time expressions, remember that as a general rule **неде́ля** (*week*) always takes **на** + accusative case (**на неде́лю**) and everything else takes **в**.

Sample Medical Form

Влади́мир Андре́ев

Врач Центра́льного Моско́вского Райо́на

Число́: ____________

Имя́: ______________ Фами́лия: __________________

Адрес: ____________

Но́мер телефо́на: __________________

Да́та рожде́ния: ______________ Во́зраст: _____________

Профе́ссия: _____________________

Си́мптом боле́зни: ____

____

____

У вас бы́ли:

Боле́зни:

- ❑ анги́на
- ❑ аппендици́т
- ❑ а́стма
- ❑ бронхи́т
- ❑ просту́да Приви́вки:
- ❑ диабе́т
- ❑ о́бморок
- ❑ от туберкулёза
- ❑ изнуре́ние
- ❑ грипп
- ❑ корь
- ❑ се́нная лихора́дка
- ❑ серде́чный при́ступ
- ❑ сви́нка
- ❑ воспале́ние лёгких
- ❑ осложне́ние
- ❑ инсу́льт
- ❑ бессо́нница
- ❑ тонзилли́т

Аллерги́и:

- ❑ к антибио́тикам
- ❑ к пеницилли́ну

- ❑ от гри́ппа
- ❑ от столбняка́

- ❑ от ко́ри

Say It Isn't So!

When it's all said and done, what do you tell people about yourself? More than likely, whatever you tell them will need to include these two important verbs: говори́ть ("to say") and расска́зывать ("to tell"). The following charts list the conjugation tables for these two verbs.

The Verb говори́ть (imperfective: "to say")

Person	Singular	English	Plural	English
First	говорю́ gah-vahr-YOO	I say	говори́м gah-vah-REEM	We say
Second	говори́шь gah-vah-REESH	You say (familiar)	говори́те gah-vah-REET-yeh	You say (formal)
Third	говори́т gah-vah-REET	He/She says	говоря́т gah-vahr-YAHT	They say
Imperative	Говори́! gah-vah-REE	Speak!	Говори́те! gah-vah-REET-yeh	Speak!

The Verb расска́зывать (imperfective: "to tell, narrate")

Person	Singular	English	Plural	English
First	расска́зываю rah-SKAH-zee-vah-yoo	I tell	расска́зываем rah-SKAH-zee-vah-yehm	We tell
Second	расска́зываешь rah-SKAH-zee-vah-yehsh	You tell (familiar)	расска́зываете rah-SKAH-zee-vah-yet-yeh	You tell (formal)
Third	расска́зывает rah-SKAH-zee-vah-yet	He/She tells	расска́зывают rah-SKAH-zee-vah-yoot	They tell
Imperative	Расскажи́! pah-skah-ZHEE!	Tell!	Расскажи́те! pah-skah-ZHEE-tyeh!	Tell!

Evening Recap

The dative case is always used in conjunction with these two verbs. **Кому́** or "to whom" is the critical question, and you will want to use the appropriate noun or pronoun in the dative case.

What Are You Doing to Yourself?

How does this make you feel? To speak about yourself or how you feel, you need to use the verb **чэвствовать** with **себя́** ("to yourself"). **Себя́** is a reflexive pronoun, or a pronoun that directs the action back toward the subject of the sentence. It may sometimes be translated as himself, herself, or yourself as the case may be; but, when translating, you can often ignore the word entirely. **Чу́вствовать** is not a *reflexive verb*, only a verb that requires a reflexive pronoun to function.

Reflexive verbs, in principle, work in the same way; however, they require **-ся**, a contracted version of **себя́** (*yourself*), to be added at the end of the stem. Before diving into the world of reflexive verbs, let's stop and see how you feel.

Hot Topic

Reflexive verbs reflect the action of the sentence back upon the subject, as seen in sentences such as "The door opens; the store closes."

Reflexive pronouns work with nonreflexive verbs to show that the subject is doing the action to himself. "I love myself; he beats himself up" are examples.

The Verb чу́вствовать себя́ (imperfective: "to feel")

Person	Singular	English	Plural	English
First	чу́вствую (себя) CHOOFST-voo-yoo (sehb-YAH)	I feel	чу́вствуем (себя) CHOOFST-voo-yehm (sehb-YAH)	We feel
Second	чу́вствуешь CHOOFST-voo-yehsh	You feel (familiar)	чу́вствуете CHOOFST-voo- yet-yeh	You feel (formal)
Third	чу́вствует CHOOFST-voo-yet	He/She feels	чу́вствуют CHOOFST-voo-yoot	They feel

Memory Serves

The verb **чу́вствовать** ("to feel") is used in other contexts as a transitive verb, without the reflexive pronoun **себя́**. Russians also use this verb for the English verb "to smell." "**Я чу́вствую за́пах ко́фе**" in Russian literally means "I feel a smell of coffee," but is the proper way in Russian to say "I smell coffee."

Flex Your Reflexive Verbs

Reflexive pronouns simply connect the verb and the subject of the sentence together, or reflect the action performed by the subject back upon itself. Basically, the subject and the reflexive pronoun both refer to the same person or thing: "I wrote to myself" or "She invited herself." You will find the pronoun fully declined in the following chart—to make matters simpler, this pronoun does not change gender or number, only case. From context, you will need to decide whether себя́ means *itself* or *themselves.*

The Reflexive Pronoun себя́

Case	Себя́	Pronunciation	English
Nom.	——	——	——
Prep.	о себе́	ah-sehb-YEH	about myself
Acc.	себя́	sehb-YAH	myself
Gen.	себя́	sehb-YAH	of myself
Dat.	себе́	sehb-YEH	to myself
Inst.	с собо́й	sah-BOY	with myself

Compare the following examples.

Он чу́вствует себя́ хорошо́ сего́дня у́тром.
Ohn CHOOFST-voo-yet sehb-YAH hah-rah-SHOH seh-VOHD-nyah OOT-rahm.
He feels good this morning.

Я ку́пил себе́ пода́рок.
Yah KOO-peel sehb-YEH pah-DAH-rahk.
I bought myself a present.

Внима́ние

Себя́ does not exist in the nominative! It refers back to the noun in the nominative case; therefore, it can never be nominative itself.

Она́ живёт у себя́.
Ah-NAH zhee-VYOHT oo-sehb-YAH.
She lives by herself.

Они́ говоря́т себе́.
Ah-NEE gah-vahr-YAHT sehb-YEH.
They are talking with themselves.

When It Comes to Decisions

When push comes to shove, sometimes you honestly can't say who left the window open; but you do know that the window is open—and may require a reflexive Russian verb. You can't always judge whether a verb will be reflexive or not by translating exactly from English; it's best to learn them as you go. Here are some common reflexive verbs.

Common Reflexive Verbs

Russian Verb	Pronunciation	English Meaning
открыва́ться	aht-kree-VAH-yet-syah	to open
закрыва́ться	zah-kree-VAH-yet-syah	to close
начина́ться	nah-chee-NAH-yet-syah	to start
конча́ться	kahn-CHAHT-syah	to finish
встреча́ться	vstreh-CHAHT-syah	to meet
одева́ться	ah-deh-VAHT-syah	to dress
раздева́ться	rahz-deh-VAHT-syah	to undress
бри́ться	BREET-syah	to shave

Me, Myself, and I in Action

Your boss calls you into his office to brief you about an upcoming business trip and the importance of arriving on time. He asks you about the status of his tickets, and you reply, "I've personally seen to it." You could say this differently by saying, "I, myself, have done this." To emphasize the fact that you, yourself, performed the task, you'll want to use the pronoun сам.

Although this pronoun is translated into English as *yourself*, its meaning differs from the reflexive pronoun себя́. This is an emphatic pronoun; it cannot stand alone, and always matches in gender, number, and case with the noun it emphasizes. In this way, it's very easy to use—match сам with its noun, and you're done.

The following chart shows you the declension patterns of this little word.

The Not-Quite-Reflexive Pronoun Сам

Case	Masculine	Feminine	Neuter	Plural
Nom.	сам sahm	сама́ sah-MAH	само́ sah-MOH	са́ми SAH-mee

continues

The Not-Quite-Reflexive Pronoun Сам (continued)

Case	Masculine	Feminine	Neuter	Plural
Prep.	само́м sah-MOHM	само́й sah-MOY	само́м sah-MOHM	сами́х sah-MEEKH
Acc. (inan.)	сам sahm	саму́ sah-MOO-	само́ sah-MOH	са́ми SAH-mee
Acc. (anim.)	самого́ sah-mah-VOH	—— ——	—— ——	сами́х sah-MEEKH
Gen.	самого́ sah-mah-VOH	само́й sah-MOY	самого́ sah-mah-VOH	сами́х sah-MEEKH
Dat.	самому́ sah-mah-MOO	само́й sah-MOY	самому́ sah-mah-MOO	сами́м sah-MEEM
Inst.	сами́м sah-MEEM	само́й sah-MOY	сами́м sah-MEEM	сами́ми sah-MEEM-mee

Take Charge

Are you, yourself, reading the book; or are you reading the book to yourself? Look at the following examples and try to answer the questions using the correct pronoun, either сам or себя́ (see Appendix B for answers).

Exercise 21.2

Example: Она́ пи́шет (to herself) ____________________.

Answer: Она́ пи́шет себе́.

1. Она́ ____________________ (herself) пи́шет кни́гу.
2. Он да́рит ____________________ (to himself) пода́рок.
3. Мы ____________________ (ourselves) стро́им э́тот дом.
4. Мы стро́им дом для ____________________ (for ourselves).

Memory Serves

The pronoun **сам** usually follows directly behind the noun it emphasizes.

Он сам де́лает дома́шнюю рабо́ту. (He himself does the homework.)

Оте́ц сам гото́вит обе́д. (The father himself makes lunch.)

Reflexive in Command

Sometimes you can't help yourself, you need to be bossy and tell your spouse to shave, the children to wash their hands, and your dinner guests not to be late. You need to use your reflexive verbs in the imperative mood; and, fortunately for you, nothing changes between reflexive and nonreflexive verbs in the imperative, other than the presence of -ся.

Побре́йтесь!
Pahd-BREHY-tyehs!
Shave!

Останови́тесь в гости́нице!
Ah-stah-noh-VEET-yehs vgah-STEEN-neet-seh!
Stop at a hotel!

Не раздева́йся, ещё.
Neh rahz-deh-VIY-syah, yehsh-YOH RAH-nah.
Don't get undressed yet!

Встре́титесь со мно́й на углу́.
VSTREH-teet-yehs sahm-NOY nah-oog-LOO.
Meet me on the corner!

The Least You Need to Know

- To be quickly and properly treated by a doctor while in Russia, it helps to know the proper words and phrases.
- You can express illness (or pain) in a variety of ways. You can always use the idiomatic expression "У меня́ …" and the verb болеть plus the name of the body part that hurts.
- Reflexive pronouns emphasize that you, yourself, did the action; or, that you did the action to yourself.
- Reflexive verbs indicate that the subject does the action, to the subject.

Chapter 22

Something Is Missing Here

In This Chapter

- Finding those store supplies
- Making the past work for you
- Past participles

Now that you've learned to talk about how you feel in Chapter 21, you can talk about your health as well as those little aches and pains. Whether you just need a little Chapstick or some aspirin, you can find just about anything you need at the drugstore. This chapter will help you replace any items that you forgot to pack by finding the right place to buy them, and what's more, you'll learn how to talk about your past adventures.

You Can Replace It

Whether you need to buy toothpaste or refill a prescription, you need to make sure that you've come to the right place in Russia. Most stores in Russia are still specialty stores, meaning that they deal specifically with prescriptions, consumer goods, or groceries.

The following chart contains items you may at some point need to purchase.

Drugstore Items

Russian Word	Pronunciation	English Meaning
сре́дство, нейтрализу́ющее кислоту́	SREHT-stvah neyt-rah-lee-ZOO-yoo-shyeh-yeh kees-lah-too	antacid
противоаллерги́ческое сре́дство	proh-tee-vah-ah-lehr-GEE-chehs-kah-yeh SREHD-stvah	antihistamine
антисе́птик	ahn-tee-SEHP-teek	antiseptic
аспири́н	ahs-peeh-REEN	aspirin
би́нты	BEEN-tee	bandages
щётка	SHYOT-kah	brush
презервати́в	preh-ZEHR-vah-teef	condom
ва́та	VAH-tah	cotton swabs
миксту́ра от ка́шля	meek-STOO-rah oht KAHSH-lyah	cough syrup
дезодора́нт	deh-zah-dah-RAHNT	deodorant
депиля́тор	deh-peel-YAH-tahr	depilatory
пелёнки (па́мперсы)	peh-LOHN-kyee (PAHM-persee)	diapers
гла́зные ка́пли	GLAHZ-nee-yeh KAHP-lee	eye drops
подво́дка для глаз	pahd-VOHT-kah dlyah glahz	eye liner
те́ни для век	TYEH-nee dlyah vyek	eye shadow
апте́чка	ahp-TYEHCH-kah	first-aid kit
электри́ческая гре́лка	eh-lehk-TREE-chehs-kah-yah GREHL-kah	heating pad
пузы́рь со льдо́м	poo-ZEER sahl-DOHM	ice pack
слаби́тельное	slah-BEE-tehl-nah-yeh	laxative
губна́я пома́да	goob-NAH-yah pah-MAH-dah	lipstick
тушь	toosh	mascara
крем для лица́	krehm dlyah leet-SAH	moisturizer
жи́дкость для полоска́ния рта	ZHEED-kahst dlyah pah-lahs-KAH-nee-yah rrtah	mouthwash
пи́лка	PEEL-kah	nail file
лак для ногте́й	lahk dlyah nahg-TYEY	nail polish
лу́дра	POOD-rah	powder
ле́звця для бри́твы	LEHZ-vee-yeh dlyah BREET-vee	razor blades
англи́йская була́вка	ahn-GLEE-skah-yah boo-LAHF-kah	safety pins
но́жницы	NOHZH-neet-see	scissors
шампу́нь	shahm-POON	shampoo
крем для бритья́	krehm dlyah breet-YAH	shaving cream

Russian Word	Pronunciation	English Meaning
снотво́рные табле́тки	snaht-VOHR-nee-yeh tah-BLEHT-kee	sleeping pills
мы́ло	MEE-lah	soap
тампо́ны	tahm-POH-nee	tampons
термо́метр	tehr-MOH-meh-tehr	thermometer
бума́га	boo-MAH-gah	tissues
зубна́я щётка	zoob-NAH-yah SHYET-kah	toothbrush
зубна́я па́ста	zoob-NAH-yah PAHS-tah	toothpaste
пинце́т	peen-TSEHT	tweezers
витами́н	vee-tah-MEEN	vitamins

What Do You Need?

You enter the right store and have some trouble finding what you need. Let's say that you approach the clerk and tell him what your problem is, and what you need. What would you need for the following few ailments? (See Appendix B for answers.)

Exercise 22.1

1. headache ______________________________
2. cough ______________________________
3. bad hair day ______________________________
4. big date ______________________________
5. trouble sleeping ______________________________

Your Past Is Questionable

So you made it to the store and bought all those necessities, but as you walk into your hotel room, you realize that you left your bag on the метро́ (*metro*); you need to go back to find it. As you wander the metro station looking for your lost bag, you must tell someone what has happened. To do this, you need to explain what you did in the past, using the past tense. Russian has several different ways to express actions that happened in the past, but in this chapter, we will explore the two most common: the past tense of the perfective and imperfective verbs.

The most common way to express action in the past is to simply drop the -ть from the verb, and add -л. The verb must match the subject, or the actor, in gender and number; so while a masculine subject needs nothing more than this -л, you must add -а for a feminine subject, -о for neuters, or -и for plurals after л. Although this may seem unusual, it closely resembles the way we form the past tense in English. From "I show" to "I showed," it's only a matter of changing the ending of the verb.

Observe the basic pattern in the following chart.

The Past Tense of ви́деть ("to see")

Russian Verb	Pronunciation	English Meaning
я ви́дел (а)	Yah VEE-dehl(ah)	I saw
ты ви́дел (а)	Tee VEE-dehl(ah)	You saw
он ви́дел	Ohn VEE-dehl	He saw
оно́ ви́дело	Ah-NOH VEE-deh-loh	It saw
она́ ви́дела	Ah-NAH VEE-deh-lah	She saw
мы ви́дели	Mwee VEE-deh-lee	We saw
вы ви́дели	Vwee VEE-deh-lee	You saw
они́ ви́дели	Ah-NEE VEE-deh-lee	They saw

The pattern is consistent throughout most of the verbs in Russian.

The Russian Past Tense

Infinitive	Past Tense	Pronunciation	English Meaning
рабо́тать	рабо́тал(а/и)	rah-BOH-tahl(ah/ee)	was working
жить	жил(а́/и)	zheel(ah/ee)	was living
ви́деть	ви́дел(а/и)	VEE-dehl(ah/ee)	saw
приходи́ть	приходи́л(а/и)	pree-hah-DEEL(ah/ee)	was arriving
смотре́ть	смотре́л(а/и)	smah-TREHL(ah/ee)	was watching
слы́шать	слы́шал(а/и)	SLEE-shahl(ah/ee)	was hearing

Like every other aspect of Russian, a few exceptions apply to this rule. To form the past tense of a few verbs, you need to change the stem entirely. The list of these peculiarities is short; however, these verbs are used frequently, and should be memorized.

Irregular Past Tense

Infinitive	Past Tense	Pronunciation	English Meaning
идти́	шёл	shyohl	was walking
eed-TEE	шла	shlah	
	шло	shloh	
	шли	shlee	
мочь	мог	mohg	was able
mohch	моглá	mahg-LAH	
	моглó	mahg-LOH	
	могли́	mahg-LEE	
нести́	нёс	nyohs	was carrying
neh-STEE	неслá	neh-SLAH	
	неслó	neh-SLOH	
	несли́	neh-SLEE	

The Perfective Aspect of Verbs

You're telling your story to a fellow passenger on the metro as you look for your bag, and you find that he looks at you with some confusion when you say "**Я покупáл аспири́на, и оставля́л егó на метрó.**" ("I was buying some aspirin, and I was leaving it on the metro.") That's because Russian has *aspect*, as well as tense. What you want to say is "**Я купи́л аспири́н и остáвил егó в метрó.**" ("I bought some aspirin, and I left it on the metro.") He will then understand you more clearly and be able to help you—otherwise he might think that you buy aspirin every day and always leave it. You want to speak of an action that occurred only once.

As you may recall from Chapter 12, Russian verbs come in pairs, perfective and imperfective. So far, you've been speaking in the present tense, and you haven't needed the perfective aspect. (The perfective aspect does not exist in the present tense.) But now that you are speaking in the past, you need to be specific about your actions.

The past tense of perfective verbs is formed the same way as their imperfective brothers, as shown in the following chart.

Hot Topic

Russian verbs have two **aspects,** perfective and imperfective. The imperfective aspect can be past, present, and future, and it indicates an action that has a long duration, or has not been completed. The perfective aspect exists only in the past and future, and it indicates a one-time action that has been completed.

The Russian Past Tense

Imperfective Aspect	Past Tense	Perfective Aspect	Past Tense
смотре́ть smah-TREHT to watch	смотре́л smah-TREHL was watching	посмотре́ть pah-smah-TREHT to watch	посмотре́л pah-smah-TREHL watched
слу́шать SLOO-shaht to listen	слу́шал SLOO-shahl was listening	послу́шать pah-SLOO-shaht to listen	послу́шал pah-SLOO-shahl listened
ходи́ть/идти́ hah-DEET/eed-TEE to walk	ходи́л/шёл hah-DEEL/shyohl was walking	пойти́ pay-TEE to walk	пошёл pah-SHYOHL walked
па́дать PAH-daht to fall	па́дал PAH-dahl was falling	упа́сть oo-PAHST to fall	упа́л oo-PAHL fell
говори́ть gah-vah-REET to speak/say	говори́л gah-vah-REEL was saying	сказа́ть skah-ZAHT to say	сказа́л skah-ZAHL said
находи́ть nah-hah-DEET to find	находи́л nah-hah-DEEL was finding	найти́ niy-TEE to find	нашёл nah-SHYOHL found

Here are some sentences comparing the use of perfective/imperfective verbal pairs.

Я шёл в магази́н.
Yah shyohl vmah-gah-ZEEN.
I was walking to the store.

Я пошёл в магази́н.
Yah pah-SHYOHL vmah-gah-ZEEN.
I walked to the store.

Я говори́л ему́ об э́том.
Yah gah-vah-REEL yeh-MOO ahb-EH-tahm.
I was talking about this with him.

Я сказа́л ему́ об э́том.
Yah skah-ZAHL yeh-MOO ahb-EH-tahm.
I told him about this.

Memory Serves

When speaking of the past tense, the perfective aspect is used more often than not. Most of the actions we describe have been completed; therefore, it's better to use the perfective. All the verbs you have learned so far have perfective forms, which should be learned; you'll find them listed in your bilingual dictionary.

Forming Past Participles of Regular Verbs

Now that you're using the past tense, you've begun to wonder how you lived without it. After you finished relating the story to your fellow passenger about your missing aspirin, you spot the bag in the car ahead of you, grab it, and head home. Now you can relate the entire story to all your friends and family back home. Because you've become so proficient, you may want to expand your reach and knowledge of the past tense to include some past participles. Sure, you can say, "I found the bag"; but what about saying, "The bag was found"?

The difference between those two sentences is simple:

Я нашёл су́мку. Су́мка была́ на́йдена.
Yah nah-SHYOHL SOOM-koo. SOOM-kah bwee-LAH NAY-deh-nah.
I found the bag. The bag was found.

The verbs used are the same; however, their form differs—and did you notice a form of the verb быть ("bweet"), which appears in the second sentence? Formation of the *past passive participle* is as easy as the formation of the past tense; however, you need to use the past tense of быть ("to be") to make it all work.

Быть is conjugated in the past tense as any normal verb: its forms are был, бы́ло, была́, and бы́ли. For past passive participles, you need to do a little mental juggling—there are two possibilities. First, you should always choose the perfective aspect of your verb pair. In the pair говори́ть (imperfective) and сказа́ть (perfective), you need to choose сказа́ть. For E-type verbs (those ending in -АТЬ or -ЯТЬ), you need to drop the -ТЬ and add an -Н. For example, сказа́ть becomes ска́зан.

Hot Topic

Past passive participles are forms of Russian verbs that correspond to passive English sentences in which no one is performing the action. The subject does not fulfill any action; rather, it has an action performed upon it—found, lost, won, built.

If you need an И-type verb, however, you should conjugate the verb to the first person, singular form, drop the vowel, and add -EH. For example, from спрáшивать ("to ask," imperfective) and спросúть ("to ask," perfective), you would choose спросúть. Спросúть changes to спрошý, in the first person form, which becomes спрóшен as a participle. Sound complicated? Just study the following chart.

The Russian Past Passive Participle

Infinitive	Past Passive Participle	Pronunciation	English Meaning
пострóить	пострóен	pah-STROH-ehn	was built
написáть	напúсан	nah-PEE-sahn	was written
сказáть	скáзан	SKAH-zahn	was told
прочитáть	прочúтан	proh-CHEE-tahn	was read
предложúть	предлóжен	prehd-LOH-zhehn	was offered
купúть	кýплен	KOOP-lehn	was purchased

Could You Be More Specific?

You're back in the armchair, looking at the newspaper, when you suddenly realize that your coffee cup was emptied some time ago. You glance around the room and see that most of your daily tasks have been finished. The dishes were washed, the plants were watered, and the doors were closed. The following phrases will help you ease into the world of participles.

Это лекáрство бы́ло вы́писано мне.
EH-tah leh-KAHR-stvah BWEE-lah vwee-PEE-sah-nah.
This medicine was prescribed to me.

Врач выписáл мне рецéпт на лекáрство.
Vrahch VWEE-pee-sahl mnyeh peht-SEHPT nah leh-KAHR-stvah.
The doctor prescribed this medicine to me (prescription for the medicine).

Картóшка былá почúщена.
Kahr-TOSH-ka bee-LAH pah-CHEE-shche-nah.
The potato was cleaned.

Кóмната былá ужé ýбрана.
KOHM-nah-tah bwee-LAH OOZH-yeh OO-brah-nah.
The room was cleaned already.

Я ужé убрáл кóмнату.
Yah OOZH-yeh oo-BRAHL KOHM-nah-too.
I already cleaned the room.

Past Participles of Irregular Verbs

Unfortunately, some bad eggs never change—and those same Russian verbs that took irregular past tense endings take irregular past passive participle endings. Of course, this makes it easier to remember which verb is irregular. The following chart will bring you up to speed on the small list of exceptions.

The Russian Past Passive Participle

Infinitive	Past Passive Participle	Pronunciation	English Meaning
почисти́ть to clean	почи́щен	pah-CHEE-shehn	was cleaned
сосчитáть to count	сосчи́тан	sah-SHEE-tahn	was counted
спроси́ть to ask	спрóшен	SPROSH-en	was asked
разреши́ть to allow	разрешён	rahz-reh-SHYOHN	was allowed
проигрáть to lose	прои́гран	proh-EEG-rahn	was lost (game)
вы́играть to win	вы́игран	VWEE-eeg-rahn	was won
провéрить to check	провéрен	prah-VEHR-yehn	was checked
послáть to send	пóслан	POH-slahn	was sent
получи́ть to receive	полу́чен	pah-LOO-chehn	was received

Вниմáние

Pay close attention to the stress patterns of past passive participles—they often change their location in the word, a syllable either forward or backward. The stress for each word has been marked for you.

You Didn't—You Did?

Let your spouse know what chores you have and haven't done by answering his or her questions in the past tense. If you haven't done something, remember to use the particle не ("nyeh") to indicate "did not." (See Appendix B for sample answers.)

Exercise 22.2

Example: Have you sent the letter?

Answer: Ты написáл письмó?

Да, я написáл письмó.

1. Have you bought food? ______________________________.
2. Have you gone to the store? ______________________________.
3. Have you seen the children? ______________________________.
4. Have you listened to the radio? ______________________________.
5. Have you eaten lunch? ______________________________.

The Least You Need to Know

- You can use the past tense with impersonal adverbs such as Нýжно and Нáдо by using бы́ло ("was/were").
- Remember that the past passive participle is the most frequently used participle in common speech, and that it has two forms: short and long.
- To ask questions in the past tense, remember to lift your voice (as in English) at the end of the sentence.
- Forming the past tense is as easy as dropping -ть and adding -л.
- To form the past passive participle, conjugate the perfective aspect of the verb pair in the first person. If the verb is a first-conjugation (E-type) verb, drop the -у or -ю and add -AH. If the verb is a second-conjugation (И-type) verb, drop the -у or -ю and add -EH.

Chapter 23

Pick Up the Phone

In This Chapter

- How to make a telephone call
- Using the proper etiquette
- When problems arise
- Using reflexive verbs in the past tense

The doctor's office is a distant memory; and, more importantly, you are feeling great. You're energized and relaxed, enjoying your stay in St. Petersburg, when you realize that you've been so busy for the past week you have forgotten to call home. You decide you should stop delaying and call home posthaste.

Unfortunately, for Americans used to the simple procedures for public phones in most cities, the Russian phone system will be a little complicated. First, you need to purchase a phone card (probably from the post office, street vendors, or the metro ticket counter); second, you need to learn how to use the phone itself. You may find yourself needing the assistance of a local resident or the operator, but do not fear. This chapter will teach you all the necessary words to help you place that call. You'll even reunite with reflexive verbs for a meeting in the past tense.

Hey, It's the Twenty-First Century

Regardless of what kind of call you may want to make, you should expect the procedures to differ slightly from those you are used to. In the best world possible, you would always be able to find someone to help you make the right call, but you should still be prepared to speak with an operator and explain what kind of call you want to make. The following chart will give you some options.

Types of Phone Calls

Russian Word	Pronunciation	English Meaning
опла́ченный абоне́нтом	ah-PLAH-chen-nee ah-bah-NYEN-tam	collect call
междугоро́дный звоно́к че́рез телефони́стку	mezh-doo-gah-ROHD-nee zah-NOHK CHER-ez teh-leh-fah-NEEST-koo	call operator assistant
ме́стный звоно́к	MYEST-nee zvah-NOHK	local call
междугоро́дный звоно́к	mezh-doo-gah-ROHD-nee zvah-NOHK	long-distance call
звоно́к по прямо́му телефо́ну	zvah-NOHK pah-pryah-MOH-moo teh-leh-FOH-noo	direct-dial call

In case you have problems while trying to use the phone and need to seek help from someone, you should familiarize yourself with the different parts of the phone.

The Telephone

Russian Word	Pronunciation	English Meaning
телефо́нная бу́дка	teh-leh-FOH-nah-yah BOODT-kah	phone booth
кно́пка	KNOHP-kah	button
ра́дио телефо́н	RAH-dee-yoh teh-leh-FOHN	cordless phone
гудо́к	guod-OHK	dial tone
спра́вочная	SPRAH-vah-chnah-yah	information
но́мер, не внесённый в спра́вочник	NOH-mer, neh vneh-SYEN-nee VSPRAH-vah-chneek	unlisted number
телефони́стка	teh-leh-fah-NEEST-kah	operator
пла́стиковая ка́рточка	PLAH-steek-ah-vah-yah KAR-tach-kah	phone card
со́товый телефо́н	SOH-tah-vwee teh-leh-FOHN	cellular phone
телефо́н-аппара́т	teh-leh-FOHN ah-pah-RAHT	public phone

Russian Word	Pronunciation	English Meaning
тру́бка	TROOP-kah	receiver
звоно́к	zvah-NOHK	ring
телефо́н	teh-leh-FOHN	telephone
телефо́нная кни́га	teh-leh-FOH-nah-yah KNEE-gah	telephone book
но́мер	NOH-mer	telephone number

How Does This Thing Work?

Many of the public phones in Russia are older models designed to accept копе́йка ("kah-PYAY-kah") (like a cent to the U.S. dollar); the копе́йка is no longer in use, however, so you'll need to purchase a phone card from your local vendor or metro station to complete your calls. Now that you know the basics of making phone calls, there are a few more key words and phrases you should learn. Russians use answering machines and automated message systems as frequently as Americans; therefore, you need to know when you're being asked to leave a message.

Phoning Vocabulary

Russian Word	Pronunciation	English Meaning
звони́ть	zvah-NEET	to call
перезвони́ть	peh-reh-zvah-NEET	to call back
дли́нный гудо́к	DLEEN-nee goo-DOHK	long beep
набира́ть но́мер	nah-bee-RAHT NOH-mer	to dial
пове́сить тру́бку	pah-BYEH-seet TROOP-koo	to hang up
опуска́ть ка́рточку	ah-poo-skaht KAR-tach-koo	to insert the card
знать код го́рода	znat kohd GOR-ah-dah	to know the area code
оста́вить сообще́ние на автоотве́тчике	ah-STAH-veet sah-ahp-SHYEH-nee-ye na ahf-tah-aht-BYET-chee-keh	to leave a message on the answering machine
ждать гудка́	zhdaht goo-TKAH	to listen for the dial tone
снима́ть тру́бку	snee-MAHT TROOP-koo	to pick up the receiver
автоотве́тчик	ahf-tah-aht-BYET-cheek	answering machine
сигна́л за́нято	seeg-NAHL ZAHN-yah-tah	the line is busy
опуска́ть моне́ту	ah-poo-SKAHT mah-NYEH-too	to insert a coin
ошибся но́мером	ah-SHEEP-syah NOH-mer-ahm	to dial the wrong number

Internationally Speaking

You've been trying to call home all day with no success. Finally, you approach a person standing at a bus stop and ask him what you've been doing wrong. As you explain the problem, he asks you questions. In this exercise, respond with the list of things you have already tried to do.

Example: Вы не слы́шите дли́нного гудка́? (Do not hear the long beep?)

Answer: Я опустии́л моне́ту. (I have inserted the coin.)

Культу́ра

Although you may find it easier to make a phone call from your hotel room, most hotels charge enormous fees to use their phones. Unless your budget can handle the cost, you will probably want to seek a public phone.

1. Ты зна́ешь код го́рода? (Do you know the area code?)
2. Вы оста́вили сообще́ние? (Did you leave a message?)
3. Ты не перезвони́шь? (Are you going to call again?)
4. Вы набра́ли но́мер? (Did you dial?)

The Public Phone

Anything can happen when using a public phone. You could be distracted by the noise of traffic and dial the wrong number, or find yourself at the other end of a never-ending busy signal. In your adventures on the phone, you may find these phrases helpful.

Како́й но́мер вы набра́ли?
Kah-KOY NOH-mer vwee nah-BRAH-lee?
What number did you dial?

Прости́те, я оши́бся/оши́блась но́мером.
Prah-STEE-tyeh, yah ah-SHEEP-syah/ah-SHEEP-lahs NOH-mer-ahm.
I'm sorry, I must have dialed the wrong number.

Мы бы́ли разъедине́ны.
Mwee BWEE-lee paz-ye-dyee-NEH-nee.
We were disconnected.

Набери́те ещё раз.
Nah-beh-REET-yeh yeh-SHOW ras.
Please redial the number.

Не кладúте трýбку.
Neh klah-DEET-yeh TROOP-koo.
Don't hang up.

Позвонúте мне пóзже, пожáлуйста.
Pah-zvah-NEET-yeh mnyeh POH-zhyeh, pah-ZHAH-loo-stah.
Call me back later.

Связь плохáя.
Svyas plah-KAH-yah.
This line has a lot of static.

Я не слы́шу тебя́.
Yah neh SLEE-shoo tehb-YAH.
I can't hear you.

Он не отвечáет.
Ohn neh aht-veh-CHAH-yet.
He is not answering the phone.

Мне нáдо класть трýбку.
Mnyeh NAH-dah klahst TROOP-koo.
I have to hang up.

Культýра

Although it may seem strange to Americans to use a public phone for all calls, most Russian homes did not have a phone line until recent years. You will still find many Russians content to use public phones for all personal calls.

You Did It to Yourself—Reflexively, in the Past

How successful were you in connecting with your friends back home? Perhaps you ran into some problems—the line could have been busy, the phone might not have been working properly, or there could have been other circumstances. In these cases, it may be possible to describe the event by using some reflexive verbs in the past tense. You already learned how to form reflexive verbs and how to form the past tense—the important thing to remember is that the reflexive endings **-ся** and **-сь** always go to the end of the verb. Put the verb into the past tense and add the appropriate ending, **-сь** for a vowel and **-ся** for a consonant.

Дверь открывáется. Дверь откры́лась.
The door is being opened. The door was opened.

Магазúн закрывáется. Магазúн закры́лся.
The store is closing. The store was closed.

Мы встречáемся. Мы встрéтились.
We are meeting. We met.

Have You Made an Excuse?

Suppose an old acquaintance calls you early Saturday morning. Although you may be glad to hear from him, you may not want to get out of bed right away. In this case, you will want to make an excuse to reschedule for later. The easiest way to do this is to use the auxiliary adverbs на́до and ну́жно, which mean "I need to …." The forms of the adverbs do not change; however, they require the dative case for the logical subject, as shown in the following chart.

I Have to …

Надо/нужно	**Pronunciation**	**English Meaning**
Мне на́до/ну́жно …	Mnyeh NAH-dah/NOOZH-nah	I have to …
Тебе́ на́до/ну́жно …	Tehb-yeh NAH-dah/NOOZH-nah	you have to …
Ему́ на́до/ну́жно …	Yeh-MOO NAH-dah/NOOZH-nah	he/it has to …
Ей на́до/ну́жно …	Yay NAH-dah/NOOZH-nah	she has to …
На́м на́до/ну́жно …	Nahm NAH-dah/NOOZH-nah	we have to …
Вам на́до/ну́жно …	Vahm NAH-dah/NOOZH-nah	you have to … (it's necessary to …)
Им на́до/ну́жно …	Eehm NAH-dah/NOOZH-nah	they have to …

Мне ну́жно рабо́тать сего́дня.
Mnyeh NOOZH-nah rah-BOH-taht seh-VOH-dnyah.
I have to work today.

Им на́до занима́ться.
Eehm NAH-dah zah-nee-MAHT-sya.
They have to study.

Ему ну́жно позвони́ть домо́й.
Yeh-MOO HOOZH-nah pah-zvah-NEET dah-MOY.
He has to call home.

Here are a few more words and phrases that you might find helpful in your phone conversations.

Useful Phone Phrases

Russian Calling	English	Russian Answering	English
Алло́	hello	Алло́	hello
Это кварти́ра …?	Is this the residence of …?	Кто звони́т?	Who's calling?
Это …?	It's … (person)	Это …	This is …
Мо́жно …?	Is … (person) there?	Подожди́те.	Hold on.
Я хоте́л(а) бы поговори́ть с …	I would like to speak to …	Мину́точку, Их нет.	Just a moment. They're not in.
Когда́ они́ верну́тся?	When will they be back?	Что переда́ть им?	Do you want to leave a message?
Перезвони́те мне как мо́жно скоре́е.	Call me back as soon as possible.	Вас про́сят к телефо́ну.	You are wanted on the telephone.
За́нято.	It's busy.	Вам звони́ли по междугоро́дной.	You had a long distance call.
Я перезвоню́.	I'll call back.		

I'm Not Here—Leave a Message

What were you doing when the phone was ringing? Translate each of the following sentences (see Appendix B for answers).

Exercise 23.1

Example: Someone called you earlier.

Answer: Кто́-то тебе́ звонийл ра́ньше.

1. He is not answering. ____.
2. May I speak with your father? ________________________________.
3. Would you take a massage? ___________________________________.
4. Please, don't hang up! ______________________________________.
5. She wasn't there. ____.

The Least You Need to Know

- Using the yellow pages or reading the information provided on the phone will help you complete the majority of your phone calls.
- In Russia you can purchase a phone card from the post office, street vendors, or the metro ticket counter.
- Reflexive verbs in the past behave much the same way as they do in the present. Don't forget your -ся/сь endings!
- Use this chapter to familiarize yourself with different types of calls and parts of the telephone to make your international calls go more smoothly.

Chapter 24

In the Line of Business

In This Chapter

- Finding store supplies
- Faxing, copying, and computing
- The language of business talk
- Speaking of the future

Writing by hand is a wonderful way to keep in touch with relatives and friends; but in the business world, you should learn how to take those same writing skills and use them with some of the more recent technological advances such as the fax machine, copy machine, and computer. In this chapter, you will learn important words and phrases that often appear in day-to-day businesses.

Photocopies, Faxes, and Computers

Technology has advanced so quickly and efficiently that businesses throughout the world have easy access to quality products. It's no wonder that products like the copy machine, fax machine, and computer have quickly become essential to any business.

Memory Serves

Russians adopt English words every day. Although many of them may not formally be in the dictionary, you can always try to make cognates out of common English words. If you were to suggest to a co-worker to **факси́ровать** ("make a fax"), he would probably understand you.

When It Comes to Making Copies

Your next business trip calls you to St. Petersburg; and, like always, you save your receipts for all your expenses. After your wallet has become uncomfortably large, you may want to consider making some backup copies of those receipts, just in case. You might say something like this:

Я хоте́л бы де́лать ко́пию э́той страни́цы.
Yah hah-TYEHL bwee DEH-laht KOH-pee-yoo EH-toy strah-NEET-see.
I would like to make a copy of this page.

Мо́жете ли вы фотокопи́ровать э́тот докуме́нт для меня́?
MOHZH-yet-yeh lee vwee foh-tah-kah-pee-rah-VAHT EH-taht dah-koo-MYEHNT dlyah mehn-YAH?
Can you photocopy this document for me?

Ско́лько сто́ит за страни́цу?
Shtoh tah-KOH-yeh STOH-eet zah-strah-NEET-soo?
What is the cost per page?

Мо́жете ли вы сде́лать цветны́е копи́и?
MOHZH-yet-yeh lee vwee ZDEH-laht tsveht-NEE-yeh KOH-pee-yee?
Can you make color copies?

Этот докуме́нт мо́жет быть расширен?
EH-taht dah-koo-MYEHNT MOHZH-yet bweet pahs-shee-rhehn?
Can this document be enlarged?

Этот докуме́нт мо́жет быть уме́ньшен?
EH-taht dah-koo-MYEHNT MOHZH-yet bweet oo-MEHN-shehn?
Can this document be reduced?

A Fax for You, Sir!

Short of traveling at light speed, the fax machine is the fastest way to get a document halfway around the world in a few seconds. Most businesses rely on sending and receiving faxes on a daily basis. Learning a few simple phrases will keep you on top.

У вас есть маши́на фа́кс?
Oo-vahs yehst mah-SHEE-nah FAHK-s?
Do you have a fax machine?

Како́й ваш но́мер фа́кса?
Kah-KOY vahsh NOH-mehr FAHK-sah?
What is your fax number?

Мне ну́жно посла́ть факс.
Mnyeh NOOZH-nah pahs-LAHT fahks.
I need to send a fax.

Могу́ ли я посла́ть э́то по фа́ксу?
Mah-goo lee yah pahs-LAHT EH-tah `pah-FAHK-soo?
May I fax this?

Пересла́ть ли мне по фа́ксу э́тот докуме́нт вам?
Peeh-reh-SLAT lee mneh pah-FAHK-soo EH-taht dah-koo-MYEHNT vahm?
Should I fax this document to you?

Пожа́луйста, перешли́те мне э́тот докуме́нт по фа́ксу.
Pah-ZHAH-loo-stah, peeh-reh-SHLEE-the mnyeh EH-taht dah-koo-MYEHNT pah-FAHK-soo.
Please, fax it to me.

Я не получи́л ваш факс.
Yah neh pah-loo-CHEEL vahsh fahks.
I didn't get your fax.

Вы получи́ли мой факс?
Vwee pah-loo-CHEE-lee moy fahks?
Did you receive my fax?

Извини́те, я не могу́ прочита́ть ваш факс.
Eez-veh-NEET-yeh, yah neh mah-GOO proh-chee-TAHT vahsh fahks.
I'm sorry, I can't read your fax.

Могли́ бы вы посла́ть э́то ещё раз?
Mahg-LEE bwee vwee pahs-LAHT EH-tah yehsh-YOH rahs?
Could you send it one more time?

Do You Know Your Computer?

You don't have to be a computer geek to know that a little computer knowledge goes a long way. Which computers are being used? What applications and peripherals are attached? Whether you program code or word process, you should be familiar with a few of the terms in the following lists.

Какóй тип компьютера вы испóльзуете?
Kah-KOY teep kahm-PYOO-teh-rah vwee ees-POHL-zoo-yet-yeh?
What kind of computer do you use?

Какýю операциóнную систéму вы испóльзуете?
Kah-KOO-yooh ah-peh-rat-see-OH-noo-yoohh sees-TYEH-mooh vwee ees-POHL-zoo-yet-yeh?
What operating system are you using?

Какýю текстовýю обрабóтку прогрáмм вы испóльзуете?
Kah-KOO-yooh tehk-stah-VOO-yooh ahb-rah-BOHT-kooh proh-GRAHM vwee ees-POHL-zoo-yet-yeh?
What word processing programs do you use?

Какýю прогрáмму электрóнной таблúцы вы испóльзуете?
Kah-KOO-yoohh proh-GRAH-mooh eh-lehk-TROH-noy tahb-LEET-see vwee ees-POHL-zoo-yet-yeh?
What spreadsheet program are you using?

Какиúе периферийные устрóйства вы имéете?
Kah-KEE-yeh peh-ree-feh-REE-nee-yeh oo-STROY-stvah vwee eem-YEH-yet-yeh?
What peripherals do you have?

Нáши систéмы совместúмые?
NAH-shee seest-YEH-mee sahv-MEHS-tee-mee-yeh?
Are our systems compatible?

Вы испóльзуете …?
Wvee ees-POHL-zoo-yet-teh …?
Do you use …?

Computer Terms

Russian Word	Pronunciation	English Meaning
до́ступ	DOH-stoop	access
име́ть до́ступ к	eem-YET DOH-stoop k	to access
загружа́ться	zah-groo-ZHAHT-syah	to boot
жук	zhook	bug
ка́бель	KAH-behl	cable
кассе́та при́нтера	kah-SYEH-tah preen-TEH-rah	printer cartridge
CD-ПЗУ	seh-Deh-Peh-Zeh-OO	CD-ROM drive
чип	cheep	chip
щелка́ть	shehl-KAHT	to click
совмести́мый	sahv-MEHS-tee-mee	compatible
компью́тер	kahm-PYOO-tehr	computer
связь	svyahs	connection
ку́рсор	KOOR-sahr	cursor
ба́за да́нных	BAH-zah DAH-neek	database
насто́льный компью́тер	nah-STOHL-nee kahm-PYOO-tehr	desktop computer
диске́та	dees-KYEH-tah	diskette
дисково́д	dees-kah-VOHT	disk drive
закла́дывать	zah-KLAH-dee-vaht	to download
перемеща́емое меню́	peh-reh-meh-SHAH-yeh-mah-yeh mehn-YOO	drop-down menu
эл. по́чта (электро́нная по́чта)	ehl-POHCH-tah	e-mail
фло́ппи-диск	FLOH-pee-deesk	floppy disk
накопи́тель на жёстком ди́ске	nah-kah-PEE-tehl nah ZHEST-kahm DEESK-yeh	hard disk drive
аппара́тные сре́дства	ah-pah-RAHT-nee-yeh SREHD-stvah	hardware
включа́ться	vkloo-CHAHT-syah	to connect
Интернет	een-tehr-NEHT	Internet
джойсти́к	joy-STEEK	joystick
клавиату́ра	klah-vee-ah-TOO-rah	keyboard
ла́птоп	LAHP-tahp	laptop computer
па́мять	PAHM-yaht	memory
пла́та расшире́ния па́мяти	PLAH-tah pahs-shee-REH-nee-yah PAHM-yah-tee	memory chip
мо́дем	MOH-dehm	modem

continues

Computer Terms (continued)

Russian Word	Pronunciation	English Meaning
мóнитор	MOH-nee-tahr	monitor
матерúнская плáта	mah-teh-REEN-skah-yah PLAH-tah	motherboard
мышь	meesh	mouse
сеть	syeht	network
онлáйновая услýга	ahn-LIY-nah-vah-yah oos-LOO-gah	online service
операциóнная систéма	ah-peh-raht-see-OH-nah-yah sees-TYEH-mah	operating system
скáнер	SKAH-nehr	scanner
экрáн	eh-KRAHN	screen
прогрáммное обеспечéние	prah-GRAHM-nah-yeh ah-behs-peh-CHEH-nee-yeh	software
спéллер	SPEH-lehr	spell checker
электрóнная таблúца	eh-lehk-TROH-nah-yah tah-BLEET-sah	spreadsheet
систéма	sees-TYEH-mah	system
потребúтель	pah-treh-BEE-tehl	user
текстовóй процéссор	tehk-stah-VOY praht-SEH-sahr	word processor
блокнóт	blahk-NOHT	worksheet

Let's pretend you're communicating with an associate in Moscow, and you need him to send you a fax and e-mail. He asks you the following questions. How might you answer?

Example: Что сейчáс на экрáне? (What is on the screen now?)

Answer: Сейчáс на экрáне мой текстовóй процéссор. (Now my word processor is on the screen.)

1. Какóй ваш áдрес эл. пóчты? (What is your e-mail address?)
2. Как могý я вам послáть факс? (How can I send a fax?)
3. У вас есть вы́ход на Интернéт? (Do you have Internet access?)
4. Какúе прогрáммы для компьютера вы испóльзуете? (What computer programs do you use?)
5. Какóй ваш нóмер фáкса? (What is your fax number?)

Getting Down to Business

Should you be planning to do some shipping in your business future, some simple phrases will get you off the ground.

Мы плати́м пересыла́ющие гонора́ры.
Mwee PLAH-teem peh-reh-see-lah-YOO-shee-yeh gah-nah-RAH-ree.
We pay the shipping fees.

У вас есть вы́бор пересы́лки землёй и́ли во́здухом.
Oo-vahs yehst VWEE-bahr peh-reh-SEEL-kee zehm-LYEY EE-lee vahz-dooh-KHAM.
You have the choice of shipping by ground or by air.

Let's Make a Deal

Finding the cheapest price for a product is part of everyone's schedule; to stay competitive, you need to know how to make a few deals with your customers to keep them satisfied.

Мы предлага́ем конкуре́нтное ценообразова́ние.
Mwee prehd-lah-GAH-yem kahn-koo-REHNT-nah-yeh tseh-nah-ahb-rah-zah-VAH-nee-yeh.
We offer competitive pricing.

Мы мо́жем уме́ньшить сто́имость на э́том това́ре.
Mwee MOH-zhehm oo-MEHN-sheet STOH-ee-mahst nah-EH-tahm tah-VAHR-yeh.
We can reduce the cost on that merchandise.

Мы мо́жем предложи́ть вам пять проце́нтов ски́дки на э́том проду́кте.
Mwee MOH-zhehm prehd-lah-ZHEET vahm pyaht praht-SEHN-tahv SKEED-kee VEH-tahm.
We can offer you a five percent discount on this product.

Если вы плати́те в тече́ние три́дцать дней, мы мо́жем дать Вам пять проце́нтов ски́дки.
YEHS-lee vwee PLAH teet-yeh vteh-CHEH-nee-yeh TREED-tsah-tee dnyey, mwee MOH-zhehm daht vahm pyaht praht-SEHN-tahv SKEED-kee.
If you pay within thirty days, we can give you a five percent discount.

A Job Well Done

It's important to keep your customers confident in your service, especially if there is a cultural barrier between you. Make your customers certain that your service is the best with these few phrases.

Това́р са́мого вы́сщего ка́чества.
Tah-VAHR SAH-mah-vah VWEES-shego KAH-chehst-vah.
The merchandise is of the highest quality.

Могу́ ли я помо́чь вм чем-нибу́дь ещё сего́дня?
Mah-GOO lee yah mah-POHCH vahm chehm-nee-BOOD yeh-SHYOH seh-VOHD-nyah?
Can I help you with anything else today?

Если вы по́лностью не удовлетворены́, вы мо́жете возврати́ть това́р.
YEHS-lee vwee POHL-nahst-yoo ne oo-dahv-leht-VOH-reh-nee, vwee MOHZH-yet-yeh vahs-vrah-TEET tah-VAHR.
If you are not completely satisfied, you may return the merchandise.

Прия́тно занима́ться би́знесом с ва́ми.
Pree-YAHT-nah zah-nee-MAH-tsyah BEEZ-neh-sahm SVAH-mee.
It's a pleasure doing business with you.

If you find yourself needing to converse at more length with your customers, you may want to expand your business vocabulary a little bit to include some of the following words.

Business Terms

Russian Word	Pronunciation	English Meaning
бухга́лтер	booh-KGAHL-tehr	accountant
су́мма	SOOM-mah	amount
фо́нды	FOHN-dee	assets
уполномо́чивать	oo-pahl-nah-MOH-chee-vaht-	to authorize
бала́нсовый отчёт	bah-LANS-ah-vwee aht-CHYOHT.	balance sheet
банкро́тство	bahn-KROHT-stvah t-VOH	bankruptcy
счёт	schyoht	bill
тра́нспортная накладна́я	TRAHNS-pohrt-nah-yah nah-klahd-NAH-yah	bill of lading
закладна́я	zah-klahd-NAH-yah	bill of sale

Russian Word	Pronunciation	English Meaning
бухгалте́рия	booh-kgahl-TEH-ree-yah	bookkeeping
де́ло	DEH-lah	business
покупа́ть/купи́ть	pah-koo-PAHT/koo-PEET	to buy
покупа́ть за нали́чные	pah-koo-PAHT zah nah-LEECH-nee-yeh	to buy for cash
нали́чные	nah-LEECH-nee-yeh	cash
получа́ть по че́ку	pah-loo-CHAHT pah CHYEH-koo	to cash a check
компенса́ция	kahm-pehn-SAHT-see-yah	compensation
потреби́тель	pah-treh-BEE-tehl	consumer
контра́кт	KOHN-trahkt	contract
креди́т	Kreh-DEET	credit
де́бит	DEH-beeht	debit
доставля́ть/доста́вить	dahs-tahv-LYAHT/dahs-TAH-veet	to deliver
ски́дка	SKEED-kah	discount
то́чно	TOHCH-nah	due
расхо́ды	pahs-HOH-dee	expenditures
затра́ты	zah-TRAH-tee	expenses
това́ры	tah-VAH-ree	goods
импортирова́ть	eem-pahr-TEE-rah-vaht	to import
проце́нтные ста́вки	praht-SEHNT-nee-yeh STAHF-kee	interest rates
факту́ра	fahk-TOO-rah	invoice
суде́бный проце́сс	soo-DEHB-nee praht-SESS	lawsuit
юри́ст	yoo-REEST	lawyer
обяза́тельства	ahb-yah-ZAH-tehl-stvah	liabilities
посы́лочный	pah-SEE-lohch-nee	mail-order
управле́ние	oo-prahv-LEH-nee-yeh	management
ме́неджер	MEH-nehd-zhehr	manager
това́р	tah-VAHR	merchandise
де́ньги	DEHN-gee	money
о́фис	OH-fees	office
накладны́е расхо́ды	nah-klahd-NEE-yeh pahs-HOH-dee	overhead expenses
владе́лец	vlah-DEH-lets	owner
партнёр	pahrt-NOHR	partner
плати́ть	plah-TEET	to pay
опла́та	ah-PLAH-tah	payment

continues

Business Terms (continued)

Russian Word	Pronunciation	English Meaning
проце́нты	praht-SEHN-tee	percent
со́бственность	SOHB-stveh-nahst	property
приобрете́ние	pree-ahb-reh-TEH-nee-yeh	purchase
ро́зничный торго́вец	ROHZ-neech-nee tahr-gah-VYETS	retailer
прода́жа	prah-DAH-zhah	sale
образе́ц	ahb-RAH-zehts	sample
продава́ть/прода́ть	prah-dah-VAHT	to sell
продава́ть за нали́чные	prah-dah-VAHT zah nah-LEECH-nee-yeh	to sell for cash
реализацио́нная цена́	reh-ah-lee-zah-tsee-OHN-nah-yah tsee-NAH	selling price
посыла́ть/посла́ть	pah-see-LAHT	to send
груз	groos	shipment
нало́г	nah-LOHK	tax
необлага́емый	neh-ahb-lah-GAH-yeh-mwee	tax-exempt
торго́вля	tahr-GOHV-lyah	trade

There's Hope for the Future

In any business you need to think not only about today's business but also about tomorrow's. If you're optimistic, you'll discuss your plans for the future, and how you plan to see them through.

Memory Serves

Быть ("bweet") "to be" is conjugated as a normal E-type verb in the future tense:

я бу́ду I will be **мы бу́дем** (We will be)

ты бу́дешь You will be **вы бу́дете** (You will be)

он/она́ бу́дет He/She will be **они́ бу́дут** (They will be)

In casual conversation, Russians often use the present tense to refer to what they will do in the future. This occurs less frequently in English (Tomorrow I am going to the store; we are watching movies tonight); but everyone understands that you are doing something later, not now. Using present tense will always get your point across; but, to be more precise, you will want to use the future tense to speak concretely.

To Be, Infinitive, and Beyond!

As you know, Russian has no present tense form of the verb "to be," only a past tense and future tense.

Forming the compound future tense in Russian is very simple: Use the correctly conjugated form of быть and add an imperfective verb infinitive to it.

> Я бу́ду инвести́ровать на фо́ндовой би́рже.
> Yah BOO-doo een-veh-STEE-rah-vaht nah FOHN-dah-vay BEER-zheh.
> I will invest in the stock market.
>
> Я бу́ду ви́деть его́ вре́мя от вре́мени.
> Yah BOO-doo VEE-deht yeh-VOH VREHM-yah oht VREH-meh-nee.
> I will see him from time to time.

In the Future There Will Be ...

Russian has two forms of the future tense, the *imperfective* and perfective forms; but do not fear! You already know the imperfective aspect, or form, of Russian verbs; and perfectives are discussed in Chapter 25. Keep in mind that as you use the compound future tense, you are speaking of an action that you plan to do multiple times or for a long time without completing it.

The following chart shows you some helpful uses of the future tense, and the phrases that follow will help solidify the idea.

Hot Topic

Imperfectives are the first aspect, or form, of Russian verbs. These verbs refer to an open, incomplete action: I am running; she will be writing; he was reading.

The Compound Future Tense

Present Tense	Future Tense	English Meaning
Я бе́гаю.	Я бу́ду бе́гать.	I will be running.
Они́ рису́ют.	Они́ бу́дут рисова́ть.	They will be drawing.
Мы у́чимся.	Мы бу́дем у́читься.	We will be learning.
Он занима́ется.	Он бу́дет занима́ться.	He will be studying.
Вы рабо́таете.	Вы бу́дете рабо́тать.	You will be working.
Она́ спит.	Она́ бу́дет спать.	She will be sleeping.
Вы еди́те.	Вы бу́дете есть.	You will be eating.

Present for Future

As mentioned earlier, Russians often use the present tense to speak about something they will do in the near future. Look at the following pairs of phrases. Notice that the meaning of each is the same, but the tense differs.

Я покупа́ю оде́жду за́втра.
Yah pah-koo-PAH-yoo ahd-YEHZH-doo ZAHF-trah.
I am going to buy some clothes tomorrow.

Я бу́ду покупа́ть оде́жду за́втра.
Yah BOO-doo pah-koo-PAHT ahd-YEHZH-doo ZAHF-trah.
I will be buying some clothes tomorrow.

Я занима́юсь сего́дня ве́чером.
Yah zah-nee-MAH-yoos seh-VOHD-nyah VEH-cheh-rahm.
I am studying tonight.

Я бу́ду занима́ться сего́дня ве́чером.
Yah BOO-doo zah-nee-MAHT-syah seh-VOHD-nyah VEH-cheh-rahm.
I will be studying tonight.

Внима́ние

Remember that you can only use **быть** + the infinitive verb if the verb is imperfective. You cannot use **быть** with a perfective verb.

The Least You Need to Know

- If you plan to do some business outside the United States or even in Russia, you need to know the names of basic equipment, including fax machines, computers, and photocopiers.
- To express a future action, the idea that you "will be doing something," use the correctly conjugated form of быть and the infinitive form of the verb.
- Imperfectives are the first aspect, or form, of Russian verbs. These verbs refer to an open, incomplete action.
- Just like in English, you can use statements in the present tense to refer to something you plan to do tomorrow.

Chapter 25

Claiming Your Territory

In This Chapter

- Apartments and houses
- Rooms, furnishings, amenities, and appliances
- Perfect the future
- A taste of the conditional mood

Staying in a hotel for a few days, or even a few weeks, may be possible on short business trips; but what about extended visits or even residence in Russia? The cost of your visit would soon become extraordinary if you stayed in a hotel. Have you thought about renting an apartment or small cottage in the при́город (*suburbs*)? It may not be as expensive as it first sounds.

In this chapter, you will learn how to choose your future home in Russia, how to furnish it, and what appliances you might need. You will also learn how to express definite action in the future, to make those plans solid, and experiment with the subjunctive, or conditional, mood.

A Cottage or a Castle?

Russia's open doors have allowed hundreds, even thousands, of people to visit and even become residents. Some adventurous tourists instantly fall in love with the beauty of Russia and want to move there. Businessmen find themselves in transit between Western Europe and Russia so often that they rent apartments in the suburbs. Whatever your situation, you can decide for yourself if you want to set aside a home in the Motherland.

> **Культу́ра**
>
> Russians describe their homes by the number of rooms, not by the number of bedrooms as in the United States. When a five-room apartment is listed, this literally means five rooms, excluding the kitchen and bathroom.

Whatever you decide, to buy or rent, to build or borrow, you should be prepared to do some research in the classifieds of Пра́вда (*Pravda*) or Изве́стия (*News*) and speak with a real estate agent about the properties you find interesting.

Should You Buy or Rent?

First and foremost, you should decide whether you want to buy or rent. Then you should decide whether you want a house or an apartment. The following phrases will guide you as you negotiate for your future home.

Я ищу́ …
Yah ee-SHOO …
I'm looking for …

… аге́нтство по рабо́те с недви́жимостью.
… ah-GYENT-stvah pah-rah-BOHT-yeh sned-VEEZH-ee-mahst-yoo.
… a real estate agency.

… объявле́ние в газе́те.
… ahb-yah-VLEH-nee-yeh vgah-ZET-yeh.
… the advertisement section.

Я бы хоте́л(а) взять в аре́нду/купи́ть …
Yah bwee hah-TYEL(ah) vsyat vah-REN-doo/koo-PEET …
I would like to rent/buy …

… кварти́ру.
… kvar-TEEh-roo.
… an apartment.

… кооперати́вную кварти́ру.
… ko-ah-per-ah-TEEV-noo-yoo kvar-TEEH-roo.
… a condominium.

Ско́лько за кварти́ру?
SKOL-kah zah kvar-TEEH-roo?
How much is the rent?

В э́том райо́не безопа́сно?
VEH-tahm pah-OHN-yeh bez-ah-PAS-nah?
Is this a safe neighborhood?

Есть ли пла́та за содержа́ние?
Yest lee PLAH-tah zah cah-der-ZHAN-ee-yeh?
Is there a maintenance fee?

Ско́лько за ме́сяц?
SKOL-kah zah MYES-yats?
What are the monthly payments?

До́лжен (должна́) ли я оста́вить зада́ток?
DOL-zhen (dahl-ZHNA) lee yah ah-STAH-veet zah-DAH-tak?
Do I have to leave a deposit?

Just Like Home

Within a few moments of setting your luggage down in your new home, you will realize all the things that your dream house is missing. Where will you sit? How do you plan to store food and eat it? You may pass a few hours idly in the empty house, but by the time evening arrives, you'll wish you had invested in a lamp or two to work by. The following list will give you some direction in filling your home with all of the necessary luxuries.

Furniture and Accessories

Russian Word	Pronunciation	English Meaning
кре́сло	KRES-lah	armchair
крова́ть	krah-VAHT	bed
кни́жная по́лка	KNEEZH-nah-yah POHL-Kah	bookshelf
ковро́вое покры́тие	kav-ROV-ah-yeh pah-KREET-ee-yeh	carpet

continues

Furniture and Accessories (continued)

Russian Word	Pronunciation	English Meaning
сту́л	stool	chair
часы́	chah-SEE	clock
занаве́ски/што́ры	zah-nah-VYES-kee/SHTOH-ree	curtains/shutters
посудомо́ечная маши́на	pah-sooh-dah-MOH-yech-nah-yah mash-EE-nah	dishwasher
комо́д	kah-MOHT	dresser
суши́лка	soo-SHEEL-kah	dryer
пе́чка	PYECH-kah	furnace
ла́мпа	LAM-pah	lamp
микроволно́вая печь	meek-rah-vahl-NOV-ah-yah pyech	microwave oven
зе́ркало	ZER-kah-lah	mirror
духо́вка	dook-HOV-kah	oven
карти́на	kar-TEEH-nah	picture
холоди́льник	hah-lah-DEEL-neek	refrigerator
ковёр	kah-VYOR	rug
сте́рео	STEH-re-oh	stereo
па́ита	plee-TAH	stove
стол	STOHL	table
телеви́зор	teh-leh-VEEH-zar	television
видеомагнитофо́н	vee-de-yoh-mag-nee-tah-PHONE	VCR
стира́льная маши́на	stee-RAHL-nah-yah mash-EE-nah	washing machine

What Will We Do About the Future?

If you plan to buy a house and furnish it, you will need to speak about your plans in the *future tense*—what you will do.

Hot Topic

The **future tense** in Russian has two forms, perfective and imperfective. The imperfective aspect indicates an action that will be happening (for a long time or several times), whereas the perfective aspect indicates an action that will happen once, and be finished.

In Chapter 24, you learned how to construct the compound future tense of verbs to describe what will be happening. By conjugating быть ("to be") and adding the infinitive, you describe an action that will either be repeated many times or continued for a long time. Fortunately, you only buy a house once. Property is purchased once (per owner); therefore, to describe these real estate actions in the future, you need to use the perfective aspect of your verb pair.

You have already encountered the aspect of verbs with the past tense in Chapter 22. As you may recall, perfective verbs in Russian do not have a present tense—they can only be past or future. This makes it easy to speak about the future—you need only to conjugate the perfective verb.

Внима́ние

Remember that the perfective form of Russian verbs does not have a present tense. The conjugated form of the perfective verb refers to a future action and cannot be applied to the present.

The following table conjugates two perfective verbs to produce the future tense. Remember that only the conjugated form of the perfective aspect refers to the future; the infinitive form does not.

The Verb Продать (perfective future tense: "to sell")

Person	Singular	English	Plural	English
First	прода́м prah-DAHM	I will sell	продади́м prah-dah-DEEM	We will sell
Second	прода́шь prah-DASH	You (familiar) will sell	продади́те prah-dah-DEE-tyeh	You (formal) will sell
Third	прода́ст prah-DAST	He/she will sell	продаду́т prah-dah-DOOT	They will sell
Imperative	Прода́й!	Sell! (one time)	Прода́йте!	Sell! (one time)

The Verb Купи́ть (perfective future tense: "to buy")

Person	Singular	English	Plural	English
First	куплю́ koop-LOO	I will buy	ку́пим KOO-peem	We will buy
Second	ку́пишь KOO-peesh	You (familiar) will buy	ку́пишь KOO-neesh	You (formal) will buy
Third	ку́пит KOO-peet	He/she will buy	ку́пят KOO-pyat	They will buy
Imperative	Купи́! Koo-PEE	Buy! (one time)	Купи́те! Koo-PEET-yeh	Buy! (one time)

Memory Serves

Russian verbs come in pairs, perfective and imperfective. These are different aspects of the same verb, and are directly related to each other. So far, you have learned only the imperfective forms of verbs, which have duration or repetition. The perfective forms refer to a one-time action.

Evening Recap

Perfective verbs are always translated into English without the verb "to be." I will do, or I did. Imperfective verbs can usually be translated using a form of the verb "to be." I am doing, or I was doing, or I will be doing.

Making the Future Known

Now that you can form both the perfective and imperfective forms of verbs in the past and future, it's time to start learning the verbal pairs. You have already been using the perfective aspect in some of the idioms and phrases you have studied so far; now it's time to associate them in your head, so that you can use them quickly and effectively when the need arises. Remember that verbs are listed by their imperfective forms in your bilingual dictionary.

Verbs Review

Russian Verb Imperfective	Russian Verb Perfective	English Meaning
писа́ть	написа́ть	to read
чита́ть	прочита́ть	to write
находи́ть	найти́	to find
смотре́ть	посмотре́ть	to watch
опи́сывать	описа́ть	to describe
выбира́ть	вы́брать	to choose
стро́ить	постро́ить	to build
посыла́ть	посла́ть	to send

There Are Two Conditions

The end of the day arrives, and the list of things you haven't accomplished begins to pile up in your mind. You would have gone swimming, if it hadn't been raining. You would have written that memo, if your favorite TV show hadn't come on. What would you have done differently? Unfortunately, life doesn't always go according to plan, and circumstances arise that prevent us from reaching all of our goals. When you need to speak about something contrary to fact, something that you planned to do, would have done—but didn't—you need to use the *conditional mood.*

Fortunately, Russian does not have a separate form of the verb to make the conditional mood. Loving simplicity, Russians decided to use the past tense of the verb and the particle бы (*would*) to create the conditional mood. You have already seen the most common form of the conditional mood, the expression "I would like …."

Я бы хоте́л(а) купи́ть дом.
Yah bwee hah-TYEL(ah) koo-PEET dohm.
I would like to buy a house.

Hot Topic

Conditional mood indicates that something is improbable, unlikely, or contrary to fact. It also corresponds to the English word *would.*

I'm Conditionally Moody

To form the conditional mood, place the appropriate verb in the past tense and add the particle бы. Remember what you learned in Chapter 22? That's it! It couldn't be easier. There are no complicated rules, but you must remember to use the бы particle, either directly before or after the verb. To make it even clearer, here is a chart of some common uses of the conditional mood.

The Conditional Mood

Russian Conditional	Pronunciation	English Meaning
Я бы сде́лал(а)	Yah bwee ZDEL-al(ah)	I would have done …
Я бы пое́хал(а)	Yah bwee pah-YEH-kal(ah)	I would have gone …
Я бы смотре́л(а)	Yah bwee smah-TREL(ah)	I would have watched …
Я бы ду́мал(а)	Yah bwee DOOH-mal(ah)	I would have thought …

Я бы хоте́л ви́деть э́тот фильм.
Yah bwee hah-TYEL VEEH-det EHT-at FEELM.
I would like to see that film.

Я бы сде́лал мою́ дома́шнюю рабо́ту, е́сли бы моя́ соба́ка не съе́ла её.
Yah bwee ZDEL-al mah-YOO dah-MASH-nyoo-yoo rah-BOH-too, YES-lee bwee mah-YAH sah-BAH-kah nee SYEL-ah yeh-YOH.
I would have done my homework, but my dog ate it.

Formation of the Conditional

As you think about your life, there are always things that you wish to do or wish you had done but never had the chance. Use the following exercise to comment on some of those things you wish you had experienced (see Appendix B for answers).

Exercise 25.1

Example: I would like to go.

Answer: Я бы хотéл(а) пойти́.

1. I would have called, but I didn't have time. ______________________.
2. She would have written, if she had a pen. ______________________.
3. They would have come, but the car broke down. ______________________.
4. We would have seen him, if it hadn't been dark. ______________________.

The Least You Need to Know

- After you learn the right vocabulary and phrases, you should be able to easily purchase vast tracts of land in Russia and arrange your own personal palace.
- Just as in English, every piece of furniture, every amenity, and every appliance has a specific name. Some are cognates, many are not.
- To speak about the future, you need to think about duration and completion. Choose the correct form of the verb to convey the exact idea.
- With the subjunctive (conditional) mood, you can convey what you would like to do, to say, to watch, or what you would have done.

Chapter 26

You Can Bank On It

In This Chapter

- Get to know banking terms
- Transaction phrases
- Participles
- Getting the most for your verb

So now that you've run up international phone bills between the United States and Russia, treated all of your friends to expensive Russian dinners to show off your knowledge of Russian, and bought vast tracts of land in Russia, you may find your checking account a little empty. Now it's time to learn how to earn that money back, dealing in foreign currency—namely rubles. To get started, you may need to use the key words and phrases you learned in Chapter 23 to have some of those friends send you some extra cash.

When in Rome, Bank!

While you spend your time abroad, more than likely you'll find yourself frequenting theaters, restaurants, and hotels. At some point, you will discover that your credit limit at these popular places will only extend so far, and you will need to find a bank. It is especially important to understand how to change currency, cash travelers' checks, or even advance cash on your credit card. Banks provide the easiest means to do all of these tasks and more. If you find yourself settling down in a Moscow suburb, you may start to think about applying for a loan to set up a business, purchase real estate, or invest in the stock market.

If you find yourself working with money, your local Russian banker can help; but first, you need to familiarize yourself with some of the most common banking terms.

Внимáние

As Russia races to catch up with the rest of Western Europe in the financial market, more and more businesses are starting to accept credit cards; however, if you're not traveling in a large city, you will want to ask beforehand whether the business accepts your form of credit. You may not always need to change those dollars into rubles—many Russians prefer to deal with American dollars rather than Russian rubles.

Banking Terms

Russian Word	Pronunciation	English Meaning
вклад	fklahd	deposit
сня́тие де́нег со счёта	SNYAH-tee-ye DEH-neg sah-CHYOH-tah	withdraw
заполня́ть про́пуски	zah-pohl-NYAHT PROH-poos-kee	fill out
занимáть	zah-neeh-MAHT	borrow
счёт в бáнке	shyoht v-BAHN-kye	bank account
нали́чные (де́ньги)	nah-LEECH-nee-ye (DEHN-gee)	cash
заём	zah-YOHM	loan
дохóд	dah-XOHT	revenue
обмéн валю́ты	ahb-MYEN vah-LYOO-tee	money exchange bureau
филиáл	fil-eeh-AHL	bankbook
бáнковская кни́жка	BAHN-kohv-ska-yah KNEESH-kah	checkbook
сберегáтельный счёт	sbeh-reg-AHT-el-nee cyoht	savings account
мéлочь	MYEH-lach	change (coins)
кáсса	KAH-sah	(teller's) window
слу́жащий	SLOOH-zhah-shee	employee
поку́пка	pah-KOOP-kah	purchase
банкомáт	bahn-kah-MAHT	ATM
касси́р	kah-SEER	bank employee
управля́ющий бáнком	ooh-prav-LYAH-yoo-shee BAHN-kahm	bank manager
квитáнция	rvee-THAN-see-yah	deposit slip

Russian Word	Pronunciation	English Meaning
оста́ток	ah-STAH-tahk	cash flow
счёт	chyoht	bill
бала́нс	bah-LANS	balance
доро́жный чек	dor-OHZH-nee check	travelers' check
прода́жа	proh-DAZH-ah	sale
обме́нный курс	ahb-MYEN-nee koohrs	exchange rate
взнос	vznohs	installment
платёж	plah-TYOZH	payment
зада́ток	zah-DAH-tahk	down payment
отде́л	aht-DYEL	branch
закла́дная	zah-KLAH-dnah-yah	mortgage
моне́та	mah-NYET-ah	coin
распи́ска	ras-PEEH-skah	receipt
рассро́чка	ras-SROHCH-kah	installment plan
после́дний платёж	pah-SLED-nee plah-TYOSH	final payment
долг	dolg	debt
перево́д	peh-reh-VOHT	transfer
превыше́ние креди́та	preh-vweeh-SHE-nee-yeh kreh-DEEH-tah	overdraft
по́дпись	POHD-peec	signature
платёж	plah-TYOSH	payment
класть в банк	klahst vbahnk	to deposit
краткосро́чный	kraht-kah-SROCH-nee	short term
долгосро́чный	dol-gah-SROCH-nee	long term
превыша́ть оста́ток	preh-vwee-SHAT ah-STAH-tak	to overdraft
копи́ть (де́ньги)	koh-PEET (DEHN-gee)	save
подписа́ть	pahd-pee-SAHT	to sign
одолжи́ть	ah-dahl-ZHEET	to loan
обменять	ahb-mye-NYAHT	change (transaction)

Find the Necessary Transaction

The following phrases will help you conduct your bank transactions in Russian.

Когда́ банк открыва́ется?
Kahg-DAH bahnk aht-kree-VAH-yet-syah?
What are the banking hours?

Я хоте́л (а) …
Yah hah-TYEL (ah) …
I would like …

… положи́ть де́ньги на счёт.
… pah-lah-ZHEET DEHN-gee nah chyot.
… to make a deposit.

… снять де́ньги со счёта.
… snyaht DEHN-gee cah-CHYOH-tah.
… to make a withdrawal.

… оплати́ть.
… ah-plah-TEET.
… to make a payment.

… взя́ть взаём.
… braht vzah-YOHM.
… to take out a loan.

… предъяви́ть чек к опла́те.
… prehd-yah-VEET check kah-PLAH-yeh.
… to cash a check.

… откры́ть счёт.
… aht-KREET chyot.
… to open an account.

… закры́ть счёт.
… zah-KREET chyot
… to close an account.

… разменя́ть де́ньги.
… pahz-mehn-YAHT DEHN-gee.
… to change some money.

Получу́ ли я ме́сячный отчёт?
Pah-loo-CHOO lee yah MYES-yach-nee aht-CHYOT?
Will I get a monthly statement?

Како́й сего́дня обме́нный курс?
Kah-KOY she-VOHD-nyah ahb-MYEN-nee koors?
What is today's exchange rate?

Где ближа́йший банкома́т?
Gdyeh blee-ZHAY-shee bahn-kah-MAHT?
Where is the nearest ATM?

Как он рабо́тает?
Kahk ohn pah-BOH-tah-yet?
How does it work?

Я хочу́ взять закла́дную.
Yah hah-choo vzyaht zah-KLAHD-noo-yoo.
I'd like to take out a mortgage.

Како́й ежеме́сячный платёж?
Kah-KOY yeh-zheh-MES-yahch-nee plah-TYOSH?
What are the monthly payments?

Кака́я проце́нтная ста́вка?
Kah-KAH-yah pra-TSYENT-nah-yah STAF-kah?
What is the interest rate?

Внима́ние

Unfortunately, once you open a Russian bank account, you should be aware that you can only move $10,000 from that account at a time. The former USSR wanted to stabilize the market economy by preventing currency from leaving the market; so consider how much money you want to use inside the Russian Federation, and how much you want available abroad.

My Needs Are Simple

Participles introduce clauses, which function as objects (direct objects, indirect objects, or objects of prepositions). Participles are either past or present tense, transitive (showing action upon something or someone) or intransitive (just showing action). The name of the participle tells you exactly what it is and how it is used.

Remember that the same conditions for adjectives apply to participles: They must agree in gender, number, and case with the nouns they modify. Don't worry about forming them yourself, but try to recognize them when they occur and know how to translate them.

Hot Topic

Present active participles are different forms of the verbs you've already met and learned. They correspond in some ways to gerunds in English; however, they introduce separate clauses, such as "the boy reading the book" threw the pencil (or "the reading-the-book-boy").

Present passive participles function the same way as their active cousins, but the action is reversed. They create new clauses, such as "the book being read by the boy" was very good (literally, "the being-read-by-the-boy book").

The following examples show how these two Russian participles translate into English.

Студéнт, пи́шущий ответ́, смотре́л в окнó.
Stooh-DYENT, PEEH-shoo-shee at-VYET, cmah-TREL vahk-NO.
The student, *who is writing the answer*, looked out the window.

Учи́тель взял рабóту умáгу, напи́санную студéнтом.
Ooh-CHEET-ehl vzyal boo-MAH-goo, nah-PEE-sahn-noo-yoo stooh-DYENT-ahm.
The teacher took the paper, *which is being written by the student.*

Худóжник, пи́шущий карти́ну, ужé продáл её.
Hoo-DOZH-neek, PEEh-shoo-shee kar-TEE-noo, oozh-YEH prah-DAL yeh-YOH.
The artist, *who is painting the picture*, already sold the painting.

Карти́на, напи́санная худóжником, ужé прóдана.
Kar-TEE-nah, nah-PEES-ahn-nay-yah hoo-DOZH-nee-kahm, oozh-YEH PROH-dah-nah.
The painting, *which is being painted by the artist*, is already sold.

Evening Recap

To form the present active participle, use the imperfective, first person forms of the verb, add **-áющий** to the end, and properly decline the word (remember that it functions like an adjective), and you've done it.

To form the present passive participle, decline the verb in its third person form, add **-áемый** to the end, and remember to properly decline the word (it also functions as an adjective).

Forming the Present Participle

To form the *present active participle*, conjugate any transitive verb to its first person form, and add -щий to the stem -ю or -у, and decline the word as required. If the verb is reflexive, remember to add -ся to the declined form of the participle. Observe the patterns in the following chart.

The Present Active Participle

Case	-E Verb	English	-E Verb	English	-И Verb	English
Verb	писа́ть peeh-SAHT	to write	рабо́тать Rah-BOH-that	to work	говори́ть gah-vah-REET	to speak
PAP	пи́шущий (-ая, -ее, -ие)	… who is writing	рабо́тающий (-ая, -ее, -ие)	… who is working	говоря́щий (-ая, -ее, -ие)	… who is speaking
Nom.	пи́шущий (-ая, -ее, -ие) PEE-shoo-shee		рабо́тающий (-ая, -ее, -ие) rah-BOH-tah-yoo-shee		говоря́щий (-ая, -ее, -ие) yoo-shee gah-vahr-YAH-shee	
Prep.	пи́шущем (-ей, -их) PEE-shoo -shyem		рабо́тающем (-ей, -их) rah-BOH-tah-yoo-shyem		говоря́щем (-ей, -их) gah-vahr-YAH-shyem	
Acc.	пи́шущий (-ая, -ее, -ие), -его, (-ей, -их) PEE-shoo-shyeh-voh		рабо́тающий (-ая, -ее, -ие), -его, (-ей, -их) rah-BOH -tah-yoo-shyeh-voh		говоря́щий (-ая, -ее, -ие), -его, (-ей, -их) gah-vahr-YAH-shyeh-voh	
Gen.	пи́шущего (-ей, -их) PEE-shoo-shyeh-voh		рабо́тающего (-ей, -их) rah-BOH-tah-yoo-shyeh-voh		говоря́щего (-ей, -их) gah-vahr-YAH-shyeh-voh	
Dat.	пи́шущему (-ей, -им) PEE-shoo-shyeh-mooh		рабо́тающему (-ей, -им) rah-BOH-tah-yoo-shyeh-mooh		говоря́щему (-ей, -им) gah-vahr-YAH-shyeh-mooh	
Inst.	пи́шущим (-ей, -ими) PEE-shoo-sheem		рабо́тающим (-ей, -ими) rah-BOH-tah-yoo-sheem		говоря́щим (-ей, -ими) gah-vahr-YAH-sheem	

Внима́ние

With a few simple exceptions, the present passive participle is almost never used in speech, and occurs very seldom in most publications. A few of these participles such as **люби́мый** and **уважа́емый** have become true adjectives, and should not be considered participles.

The Present Passive Participle

Case	-E Verb	English
Verb	рисова́ть ree-sah-VAHT	to draw
PPP	рису́емый (-ая, -ое, -ые)	… which is being drawn
Nom.	рису́емый (-ая, -ое, -ые) ree-SOO-yeh-mee	
Prep.	рису́емом (-ой, -ых) ree-SOO-yeh-mahm	
Acc.	рису́емое/ого (-ую, -ые/-ых) ree-SOO-yeh-mah-vo	
Gen.	рису́емое/ого (-ой, -ых) ree-SOO-yeh-mah-vo	
Dat.	рису́емому (-ой, -ым) ree-SOO-yeh-mah-moo	
Inst.	рису́емым (-ой, -ыми) ree-SOO-yeh-meem	

A Participle Present

The following chart will help you with present active and present passive participles.

Present Active and Present Passive Participles

Infinitive Verb	Present Active Participle	Present Passive Participle	English Meaning
выи́грывать	выи́грывающий	выи́грываемый	to win
учи́ть обуча́ть	уча́щийся	обуча́емый from the prefixed verb обуча́ть	to learn
хоте́ть	жела́ющий	жела́емый	to want
ду́мать	ду́мающий	ду́маемый	to think

Infinitive Verb	Present Active Participle	Present Passive Participle	English Meaning
стро́ить	стро́ящий	стро́имый	to build
чита́ть	чита́ющий	чита́емый	to read
посыла́ть	посыла́ющий	посыла́емый	to send
переводи́ть	переводящий	переводи́мый	to translate
создава́ть	создающий	создава́емый	to create
открыва́ть	открыва́ющий	открыва́емый	to open

**The verb* хоте́ть *("to want") does not have a participle form of its own, and relies on the verb* жела́ть *("to wish") to become a participle.*

So Much to Do

Do you ever try to describe a person or event and soon realize that you've forgotten an important name to make your story clear? You might then begin to use clauses like "the construction worker, standing on the side of the road, who was wearing a hard hat …." These common English conventions can be easily translated into participles in Russian. Use the following exercise to get a clearer picture of what's happening in the language.

Translate the following sentences into English, paying close attention to the use of participles. (Answers are in Appendix B.)

Exercise 26.1

Example: Дом, стро́имый о́коло бе́рега, почти́ зако́нчен.

Answer: The house, which is being built near the bank, is almost finished.

1. Чита́емая кни́га—хоро́шая. ______________________.
2. Инжене́р, стро́ящий мост, си́льный. ______________________.
3. Соба́ка смо́трящая в окно́, лю́бит еду́. ______________________.
4. Ма́льчик, бе́гающий по у́лице, смеётся. ______________________.
5. Де́ньги, занима́емые Смирно́вым, лежа́т на столе́. ______________.

Whereas most present passive participles do not occur in spoken language with any great frequency, some have evolved into adjectives and are commonly used in everyday speech. As you look over the following list, remember that these words are now considered adjectives and not participles.

Present Passive Participles as Adjectives

Russian Word	Pronunciation	English Meaning
люби́мый	looh-BEEH-mee	favorite
ви́димый	VEEH-dee-mee	visible
неви́димый	neh-VEEH-dee-mee	invisible
необходи́мый	neh-ahb-hah-DEEH-mee	necessary
незави́симый	neh-zah-VEEH-see-mee	independent
так называ́емый	tahk nah-zee-VAH-yeh-mee	called
невыноси́мый	neh-vee-NOH-see-mee	dear
уважа́емый	oo-vah-ZHA-e-mee	(formal, for addressing letters, literally *esteemed*)

The Least You Need to Know

- Russian banks are modern and competitive, and operate similarly to common American banks.
- Use present participles to modify nouns, and remember that present passive participles are seldom used in speech, but often occur in journals, newspapers, and magazines.
- Remember that the same conditions for adjectives apply to participles: They must agree in gender, number, and case with the nouns they modify.
- Some participles have become incorporated into speech and are now commonly used as adjectives.

Appendix A

Glossary

accusative case The *accusative* case marks the direct object, or the object of the action.

adjectives Words that describe nouns or pronouns. An adjective tells something about the noun it modifies by answering the question "What kind?" or "Which one?" (Какóй?) Russian adjectives agree in gender, number, and case with the nouns they describe or modify.

adverbs Like adjectives in that they describe or modify other words. Rather than nouns or pronouns, adverbs modify adjectives, other adverbs, verbs and prepositional phrases. Adverbs answer the question "How?" (Как?) Remember that Russian adverbs end in -о and do not usually change form.

animate nouns Reference animate (or alive) people or animals. In Russian, this term is relevant to the plural and in singular only to masculine nouns in the accusative case; feminine nouns change consistently, without regard for their animate or inanimate status. Masculine names, professions, nationalities, animals, and positions are considered to have an "animate" quality.

aspect Refers to the state of the Russian verb. Verbs in Russian have two aspects: perfective and imperfective. The imperfective aspect can be past, present, or future; and it indicates an action that has a long duration or that has not been completed. The perfective aspect exists only in the past and future, and it indicates a one-time action that has already been completed or that will be completed in the future.

cardinal numbers The numbers used to count: one, two, three, and so on. Cardinal numbers are always nouns, which must be declined as nouns, whereas ordinal numbers are adjectives.

case endings Endings that determine the grammatical relationship of nouns, pronouns, and adjectives to the rest of the sentence. Whereas English uses word order, Russian identifies the purpose, gender, and quantity of the noun through the ending of the word, usually the last letter for nouns and the last two to three letters for adjectives.

cases The forms adjectives, pronouns, and nouns take to indicate their grammatical function in a sentence.

cognates Words borrowed from English or any other language, which are used in Russian with similar pronunciation and meaning.

collective nouns Nouns that are only used in either the singular or the plural. Often, if it is possible, making a collective noun plural will significantly change its meaning.

comparative forms of adjectives Indicate the degree to which the noun is "more" or "less." Adjectives have three forms to compare nouns. The simple form is the basic form that adjectives take: the *big* house. The comparative form indicates a difference (greater or lesser) from the simple form: the *bigger* house. The superlative form shows the greatest or least difference from the simple form: the *biggest* house.

conjugation The change that verbs undergo to show action (much like nouns undergo declension). A verb's conjugation must match the noun or pronoun that performs the action. Conjugation also indicates tense, whether something is happening now, will happen later, or has already happened.

consonant mutations Changes that occur in many И-type verbs in the first person singular. The final consonant of the verb changes in the first person conjugation, or another consonant is added before the ending. This change occurs only in the first person singular.

dative case The *dative* case shows the indirect object, or the receiver of the action.

declension A way to describe all the possible forms, or case endings, a noun, pronoun or adjective can take. Each case in the Russian language affects predictable changes in masculine, neuter, and feminine nouns—the patterns of these changes are called declensions.

definite motion An activity or movement that is happening right now or happens only once. In the present tense, definite motion can be translated using the verb "to be," as in "he is going" or "they are walking."

demonstrative adjectives Adjectives that distinguish between two or more nouns or pronouns: this noun or that noun.

direct objects Words that answer the questions *whom* (кого́) or *what* (что́). Russian uses the accusative case to identify the direct object of a sentence. You meet *whom;* you hit *what;* or you see *what* or *whom.*

false cognates Words that share a similar pronunciation between languages (like from English to Russian) but have a different meaning in Russian than they do in English.

gender Nouns have three grammatical genders in the singular: masculine, feminine, and neuter. Adjectives always agree in gender with the nouns they modify, and verbs agree in gender if they are in the past tense. In Russian, gender starts with the natural gender of the object to which a noun refers (so "woman" is feminine, while "boy" is masculine), but inanimate objects may also have any of the three genders ("book" is feminine while "diary" is masculine).

genitive case The case that shows possession; in Russian it requires a slight change of word order. The English phrase "the boy's dog" becomes "the dog of the boy" (the word *boy* is declined in the genitive case). Certain prepositions require the use of the genitive case, and sentences with negated verbs often take the genitive case instead of the accusative.

idiom An expression or phrase that has a meaning that cannot be translated by defining each and every word. Idioms have fixed meanings and are often important to best express simple ideas.

imperatives Commands, instructions, or requests. The imperative form reflects an understood *you* (formal or informal), either ты or вы.

imperfectives The first aspect, or mode, of Russian verbs. These verbs refer to an open, incomplete action: I am running; she will be writing; he was reading. Imperfectives are regularly used to indicate actions that are not normally ever completed, such as "to like"; they are also often used to refer to actions that are frequent but rarely completed, such as "to study."

impersonal sentences Sentences that have no grammatical subject. They are translated using the pronoun *it*, to make them logical in English. The adverbs мо́жно ("it is possible") and нельзя́ ("it is not possible," "one may not") can be used to create such impersonal sentences.

inanimate nouns Masculine nouns that are not animate or alive. Paper, food, and clothes are inanimate nouns. Although they are alive, Russians do not consider plants or microorganisms to be animate for the purposes of the accusative case.

indefinite motion Verbs that indicate regular or habitual movement. Phrases such as *often*, *every day*, or *regularly* usually accompany indefinite motion verbs.

indirect objects Nouns or pronouns as indirect objects answer the questions комý ("to whom") and чемý ("to what"), and they are in the dative case.

infinitive Refers to a verb that has not been conjugated, or changed to "match" with a noun. English infinitives appear as "to do" (дéлать) or "to watch" (смотрéть).

instrumental case The *instrumental* case shows the "instrument" (or means) of the action, or how the action is done.

nominative case The first case in Russian. Russian identifies nouns and adjectives three ways: by gender, by number (or quantity), and by case. Nouns in the nominative case usually function as the subject of a sentence.

nouns A person, place, animal, thing, or idea. Nouns can be common or proper, and every noun in Russian has gender. The gender of nouns can be masculine, feminine, or neuter. In addition to gender, nouns have number (either singular or plural) and case (nominative, accusative, prepositional, genitive, dative, or instrumental).

number The quantity of a noun. A noun is said to be singular if it represents a single unit (one chair, one man), and plural if it represents more than one (chairs, men). The number of a noun is simply its quantity: one or more than one.

ordinal numbers The adjectival forms of cardinal numbers. They answer the question котóрый or *which?* First, second, third, and so on are examples of ordinal numbers.

particles Words that have no meaning by themselves, and that cannot stand alone in a sentence. They affect the meaning of other words, and emphasize the word immediately before or after them in a sentence. For example, the particle же adds emphasis to что in Что же он сказáл? ("What *on earth* did he say?").

past passive participles Forms of Russian verbs that correspond to passive English sentences, in which no one is performing the action. The subject does not fulfill any action, but rather has an action performed upon it—found, lost, won, built.

perfectives Indicate a one-time action that has already been completed or that will be completed in the future. Perfective verbs occur only in the past tense and the future tense; they have no present tense at all.

possessive adjectives Adjectives that modify nouns by expressing possession or ownership. The Russian possessive adjectives are мой, её, егó, твой, наш, ваш, and их.

prefixes Words or syllables attached to the beginning of a verb. Prefixes expand or qualify the meaning of the verbs to which they are joined. Sometimes prefixes can change an imperfective verb to its perfective form.

prepositional case The *prepositional* (or locative) case shows the location, or where the action takes place.

prepositions Words that introduce a phrase or clause to the rest of the sentence. In English some examples are through, behind, in, along, around, beside. Certain prepositions require certain cases.

present active participles Different forms of Russian verbs, which act as adjectives that introduce separate clauses, such as "*The boy reading the book* threw the pencil" (or "the reading-the-book boy"). The nouns these participles modify perform an action.

present passive participles Clauses formed from verbs but which act as adjectives. Unlike active participles, passive participles indicate actions that are being performed upon the nouns they modify. They create new clauses, such as "*The book being read by the boy* was very good" (literally, "the being-read-by-the-boy book").

pronouns Words that replace nouns or other pronouns. Pronouns always match the gender, number, and case of the nouns or pronouns they replace. Pronouns can fill a number of roles: They can be personal (*he*, *she* or *it*); possessive (*his*, *her*, or *its*); demonstrative (*this* or *that*); and interrogative or relative (*who*, *what*, or *which*).

reflexive pronouns Pronouns that work with nonreflexive verbs to show that the subject is doing the action to himself. "The subject acts upon *itself*."

reflexive verbs Verbs that indicate actions on the subject or that the action of the sentence is reflected back upon the subject, as seen in sentences like "The door opens; the store closes."

subject pronouns Pronouns that replace nouns as the subject of the sentence. **Я, Ты, Он, Онá, Онó, Мы, Вы, Онú** are the Russian subject pronouns. A subject pronoun is always in the nominative case.

tense Verbs have three tense forms in Russian: past tense (the action took place before the moment of speaking; Mary *rode* her bicycle); future tense (the action will take place after the moment of speaking; Mary *will ride* her bicycle); and present tense (the action includes the moment of speaking; Mary *is riding* her bicycle, or Mary *rides* her bicycle).

transitive Transitive verbs take a direct object (Bill *broke the window*), whereas intransitive verbs do not have a direct object (Bill *sleeps* soundly). Some verbs must be transitive (like break or lift), others must be intransitive (like sleep or go), and still others may be used both ways (John *reads the paper* every day vs. John *reads* slowly).

verbs Words that indicate action or states of being. Every verb in Russian comes in a pair—perfective and imperfective—and must be conjugated, or changed to match the subject of the sentence. Verbs are transitive or intransitive.

verbs of motion Verbs that come in pairs (in their imperfective form) and that express movement toward a destination. The indefinite verb expresses habitual or regular movement, and the definite verb expresses a one-time movement. The perfective aspect of a motion verb indicates a one-time movement that has been completed or will be completed.

Appendix B

Answer Key

Chapter 4

Exercise 4.1

1. Тури́сты лета́ют в Ме́ксико-Си́ти из Нью-Йо́рка на самолёте.

   Tourists travel from New York to Mexico City by plane.

2. Лю́ди е́здят на рабо́ту на авто́бусе в Атла́нте.

   People go to work in Atlanta by bus.

3. Пое́здка в Евро́пу на теплохо́де 3 ме́сяца.

   The journey to Europe by boat is 3 months long.

4. Мы хо́дим пешко́м к ба́бушке.

   We walk by foot to grandmother's house.

5. Я пое́ду на маши́не к врачу́ за́втра.

   I will drive by car to the doctor's office tomorrow.

6. Они́ ката́лись со сро́ка горы́ на лы́жах.

   They went down the side of the mountain by skis.

Exercise 4.2

1. Доро́га идёт вдоль бе́рега.

   The road goes along side the shoreline.

2. Где магази́н нахо́дится? Он за угло́м.

   Where is the store located? It's around the corner.

3. Кафе́ ря́дом с метро́.

   The cafe is next to the subway.

4. Я вас ви́дел вчера́. Куда́ вы шли?

   I saw you yesterday. Where were you going?

5. Я ника́к не могу́ найти́ мою́ ру́чку. Где она́?

   I just can't find my pen. Where is it?

Exercise 4.3

1. Your spouse leaves for a weekend retreat in the mountains, and you say: пока́ (see you soon).
2. After you have dropped the kids off at school, you tell them: уви́димся (see you later).
3. Your late afternoon meeting began at 3:30, but you arrive по́здно (late) at 3:45.
4. You hope that you find that winning lottery ticket ско́ро (soon).
5. The concert started at 8:00 and you arrived exactly at 8:00. You were во́время (on time).
6. You check the status of your stocks ка́ждый день (every day).

Exercise 4.4

1. Я вчера́ не спал (-а). Я уста́л (-а).

   I didn't sleep last night. I am tired (female).

2. У Ивано́вых роди́лся сын. Он похо́ж на своего́ отца́.

   The Ivanovs just had a baby boy. He resembles his father.

3. Онá всю ночь плáкала, потомý что онá былá óчень больнá.

   She cried all night long because she was very sick.

4. Я ничегó не ел с зáвтрака, и я гóлоден.

   I haven't eaten since breakfast, I am hungry.

Chapter 7

Exercise 7.1

1. Друг вúдел её в кóмнате. (A friend saw her in the room.)
2. Мáльчик встрéтился с ней во дворé. (The boy met with her in the yard.)
3. Женá сказáла чтó-то емý. (The wife said something to him.)
4. Есть молокó в нём! (There is milk in it!)

Chapter 8

Exercise 8.1

1. Это дом нóвого сосéда. (This is the house of the new neighbor, or This is the new neighbor's house.)
2. Это большáя кнúга. (This is a big book.)
3. Он пациéнт хорóшего врачá. (He is the patient of the good doctor.)
4. Я читáю хорóшие кнúги. (I read good books.)
5. Онá купúла нóвую машúну. (She bought a new car.)

Exercise 8.2

1. Плáвать лéтом хорошó (it is good).
2. На ýлице жáрко (it is hot).
3. Эта машúна—стáрая (old).

4. Я зна́ю (know) серьёзного (serious) ма́льчика.
5. Они́ хоро́шие (good) лю́ди.
6. Она́ купи́ла белый (white) хлеб.
7. Он врач большо́й (big) больни́цы.

Chapter 9

Exercise 9.1

1. (Рабо́тать) Он рабо́тает в музе́е.
2. (Открыва́ть) Они́ открыва́ют магази́н в во́семь часо́в.
3. (Закрыва́ть) Я закрыва́ю дверь.
4. (Начина́ть) Мы начина́ем учи́ться.
5. (Изуча́ть) Она изуча́ет ру́сский язы́к.
6. (Игра́ть) Вы игра́ете на гита́ре.
7. (Ду́мать) Что ты ду́маешь об э́том?

Exercise 9.2

1. (гото́вить) Мой брат гото́вит дома́шнюю рабо́ту.
2. (находи́ть) Доктора́ нахо́дят но́вую информа́цию ка́ждый день.
3. (слы́шать) Мы слы́шим му́зыку.
4. (корми́ть) Хоро́шая мать корми́т свои́х дете́й.
5. (лови́ть) Вы хорошо́ ло́вите ры́бу.
6. (шути́ть) Он всегда́ шу́тит.
7. (стоя́ть) Почему́ ты стои́шь так бли́зко?
8. (ве́рить) Мои́ друзья́ не ве́рят мне.
9. (вы́глядеть) Ни́на хорошо́ вы́глядит сего́дня.
10. (броди́ть) Ива́н всегда́ бро́дит по улица́м оди́н.

Exercise 9.3

1. Кого́ вы ви́дите?

   Я никого́ не ви́жу.
2. Когда́ ты рабо́таешь?

   Я никогда́ не рабо́таю.
3. Что вы де́лаете?

   Я ничего́ не де́лаю.
4. Кто э́то зна́ет?

   Никто́ не зна́ет.
5. Где вы слу́жите?

   Я нигде́ не служу́.

Chapter 10

Exercise 10.1

1. She is a doctor.

   Она́ рабо́тает до́ктором.
2. You are a lawyer?

   Вы рабо́таете адвока́том?
3. He is a model.

   Он рабо́тает манеке́нщиком.
4. The mailman is now the boss.

   Почтальо́н сейчас рабо́тает нача́льником.
5. The student is a driver.

   Студе́нт рабо́тает шофёром.
6. She is a waitress.

   Она́ рабо́тает официа́нткой.

7. The electrician is an assistant.

   Эле́ктрик рабо́тает помо́щником.

8. We are teachers.

   Мы рабо́таем учи́тельницами.

Chapter 11

Exercise 11.1

1. my father

   мой оте́ц

2. his mother

   его́ мать

3. our family

   на́ша семья́

4. their relatives

   их ро́дственники

5. my friend's brother

   брат моего́ дру́га

6. our uncle's book

   кни́га на́шего дя́ди

7. the brother's wife

   жена́ бра́та

8. his grandfather's table

   стол де́душки

9. your aunt's money

   де́ньги тёти

10. Your (formal) cousin's car

    маши́на ва́шей двою́родной сестры́

Exercise 11.2

1. They have a dog.

   У них соба́ка. У них нет соба́ки.
2. She has a sister.

   У неё сестра́. У неё нет сестры́.
3. We have the desire.

   У нас жела́ние. У нас нет жела́ния.
4. He has a brother.

   У него́ брат. У него́ нет бра́та.
5. You have a pencil.

   У тебя́ каранда́ш. У тебя́ нет карандаша́.
6. They have my dog.

   У них моя́ соба́ка. У них нет мое́й соба́ки.

Chapter 12

Exercise 12.1

1. (d)
2. (b)
3. (e)
4. (a)
5. (c)

Exercise 12.2

1. Она́ ду́мает о дру́ге. (She thinks about her friend.)
2. Мно́гие рабо́тают в зда́нии. (Many people work in this building.)
3. На у́лице де́ти игра́ют. (In the street [outside] children are playing.)

Exercise 12.3

1. Они́ нашли́ доро́гу че́рез лес. (forest)
2. Отнеси́те меня́ на вокза́л. (train station)
3. Мы лю́бим ходи́ть на бе́рег. (shore)

Exercise 12.4

1. Что вы де́лаете по́сле рабо́ты? (What are you doing after work?)
2. Я с ю́га. (I am from the south.)
3. До Гамле́та, моя са́мая люби́мая пье́са была́ Оте́лло. (Before *Hamlet* my favorite play was Othello.)
4. Он идёт домо́й из библиоте́ки. (He is going home from the library.)
5. Мы покупа́ем сви́тер для учи́теля. (We are buying a sweater for the teacher.)

Exercise 12.5

1. Он живёт под мосто́м. (He lives under a bridge.)
2. Помоги́те мне с пробле́мой. (Help me with this problem.)
3. Магази́н нахо́дится ме́жду двумя́ больши́ми зда́ниями. (The store is located between two big buildings.)

Chapter 13

Exercise 13.1

1. Он е́здит на маши́не на рабо́ту ка́ждый день.

   He goes to work by car every day.
2. Мы е́дем на авто́бусе в музе́й.

   We are going to the museum by bus.
3. Вы лю́бите е́здить на велосипе́де?

   Do you like to go by bicycle?

4. Они́ сейча́с е́дет на метро́ к нам.

   They are going to our house by metro right now.

Chapter 14

Exercise 14.1

1. У меня́ жена́ и дво́е дете́й. Я хочу́ двухме́стный но́мер.
2. Мой муж лю́бит мо́ре. У вас есть но́мер с ви́дом на мо́ре?
3. Он хо́чет но́мер-люкс со все́ми удо́бствами.

Exercise 14.2

1. I need a room.

   Мне ну́жен но́мер.
2. I would like a key.

   Я бы хоте́л ключ.
3. I need a blanket.

   Мне ну́жно одея́ло.
4. I need some matches.

   Мне нужы́ спи́чки.

Exercise 14.3

1. Я ищу́ тре́тий эта́ж.
2. У четвёртого бра́та моя́ кни́га.
3. Кто зна́ет, кто был двена́дцатым президе́нтом?
4. С пе́рвого моме́нта, я люби́л её.

Exercise 14.4

1. Он собира́ет ма́рки. (He collects stamps.)
2. Ми́ша вхо́дит в зда́ние. (Misha is entering the building.)
3. Роди́тели разреша́ют ей по́здно возвраща́ться домо́й. (The parents allow her to return home late.)
4. Он всегда́ забыва́ет свой ключ до́ма. (He always forgets his keys at home.)
5. Его́ брат нахо́дит их под кре́слом ка́ждое у́тро. (His brother finds them under the armchair every morning.)

Chapter 15

Exercise 15.1

1. Три́дцать пе́рвого декабря́
2. Четвёртого ию́ля
3. Четы́рнадцатого февраля́
4. Два́дцать тре́тьего апре́ля в со́рок второ́м году́

Exercise 15.2

1. В бу́дущем году́ я пое́ду на Супер-Боль.

   Next year I will go to the Super Bowl.
2. Мой день рожде́ния четы́рнадцатого ма́я.

   My birthday is May 14th.
3. Что вы де́лаете в выходны́е дни?

   What are you doing on the weekend?
4. В сре́ду он идёт в парк.

   He is going to the park on Wednesday.

Chapter 16

Exercise 16.1

1. Хотите пойти в кино сегодня?

   Да, я люблю ходить в кино.

   Мне не хотелось бы пойти в кино.

2. Давай играть в мяч во дворе.

   Спасибо, это мне нравится.

   Играть в мяч не интересует меня.

3. Хочешь поехать со мной в библиотеку; чтобы читать немного?

   Хорошо! я люблю читать.

   Нет спасибо, Я ненавижу читать.

4. Есть новый фильм по телевизору. Давайте посмотрим.

   Отлично, давайте.

   Нет, я предпочитаю делать что-то другое.

Chapter 17

Exercise 17.1

1. They go to the store in sneakers.

   Они носят кроссовки в магазин.

2. We wear a suit to church.

   Мы носим костюм в церковь.

3. He often wears black.

   Он часто носит чёрный.

4. Do you like to wear a raincoat?

   Вы любите носить плащ?

5. I am wearing a pink undershirt.

   Я ношу́ ро́зовую ни́жнюю руба́шку.

Exercise 17.2

1. Please, show me a solid pink skirt?

   Пожа́луйста, покажи́те мне ро́зовую одното́нную руба́шку.
2. I'd like to buy blue jeans.

   Я бы хоте́л купи́ть джи́нсы.
3. I'm looking for a black overcoat.

   Я ищу́ чёрное пальто́.
4. Please, show me a red hat.

   Пожа́луйста, покажи́ мне кра́сный головно́й убо́р.

Exercise 17.3

1. Мы смо́трим его́.
2. Она́ лю́бит его́.
3. Я люблю́ их.
4. Он постро́ил её.

Exercise 17.4

1. Хочу́ его́.
2. Мы де́лаем её.
3. Я купи́ла её.
4. Я люблю́ их.

Exercise 17.5

1. Разреши́те ей пойти́ в магази́н.
2. Это меша́ет ему́.

3. Напиши́ им письмо́!
4. Говори́те мне, не ему́.

Chapter 18

Exercise 18.1

1. She doesn't have a knife.

   У неё нет ножа́.
2. We don't have silverware.

   У нас нет прибо́ра.
3. He doesn't have a small plate.

   У него́ нет ма́ленькой таре́лки.
4. I don't have a salt shaker.

   У меня́ нет соло́нки.

Exercise 18.2

1. Please bring her a menu.

   Принеси́те ей, пожа́луйста, меню́.
2. Please bring him a spoon.

   Принеси́те ему́, пожа́луйста, ло́жку.
3. Please bring me a napkin.

   Принеси́те мне, пожа́луйста, салфе́тку.
4. Please bring us glasses.

   Принеси́те нам, пожа́луйста, стака́ны.

Chapter 19

Exercise 19.1

1. Мы идём в спортзал игра́ть в баскетбо́л.
2. Я люблю́ игра́ть в ша́хматы.
3. Они́ смо́трят гольф по телеви́зору.
4. Смотре́ть и́гры хорошо́, а игра́ть лу́чше.
5. Она́ играет в бе́йсбол.

Exercise 19.2

1. He wants to go fishing.

   Он хо́чет идти́ лови́ть ры́бу.
2. They can't play hockey.

   Они́ не мо́гут игра́ть в хокке́й.
3. You want to watch tennis.

   Ты хо́чешь смотре́ть те́ннис.
4. Let's play cards!

   Дава́й (те) игра́ть в ка́рты.
5. We can go horseback riding.

   Мы мо́жем идти́ е́здить верхо́м.

Chapter 20

Exercise 20.1

1. Where is the nearest laundromat?

   Где са́мая бли́зкая пра́чечная?
2. Can you mend these shoes?

   Мо́жете ли вы почини́ть э́ти боти́нки?

3. What are your hours?

   Когда́ магази́н откры́т?

Chapter 21

Exercise 21.1

1. У меня́ аллерги́ческая реа́кция.
2. У меня́ боли́т рука́.
3. У меня́ бессо́нница.
4. У меня́ озно́б.
5. У меня́ волды́рь на ноге́.

Exercise 21.2

1. Она́ сама́ пи́шет кни́гу.
2. Он дари́т себе́ пода́рок.
3. Мы са́ми стро́им э́тот дом.
4. Мы стро́им дом для себя́.

Chapter 22

Exercise 22.1

1. Have you bought food?

   Нет, я не купи́л еды́.
2. Have you gone to the store?

   Нет, я не пошёл в магази́н.
3. Have you seen the children?

   Нет, я не ви́дел дете́й.

4. Have you listened to the radio?

   Нет, я не слу́шал ра́дио.

5. Have you eaten lunch?

   Нет, я не пообе́дал.

Chapter 23

Exercise 23.1

1. He is not answering.

   Он не отвеча́ет.

2. May I speak with your father?

   Мо́жно говори́ть с ва́шим отцо́м?

3. Would you take a massage?

   Переда́йте ему́; пожа́луйста.

4. Please, don't hang up!

   Пожа́луйста, не клади́те тру́бку!

5. She wasn't there.

   Её не было.

Chapter 25

Exercise 25.1

1. I would have called, but I didn't have time.

   Я позвони́л бы, но у меня́ не́ было вре́мени.

2. She would have written, if she had a pen.

   Она́ написа́ла бы, е́сли бы у неё была́ ручка.

3. They would have come, but the car broke down.

   Они́ пое́хали бы, но их маши́на слома́лась.

4. We would have seen him, if it hadn't been dark.

   Мы его́ уви́дели бы, е́сли бы не́ было так темно́ вчера́.

Chapter 26

Exercise 26.1

1. Чита́емая кни́га—хоро́шая.

   The book, which is being read (I am reading), is good.
2. Инжене́р, стро́ящий мост, си́льный.

   The engineer who is building the bridge is strong.
3. Соба́ка смо́трящая в окно́, лю́бит еду́.

   The dog, which is looking into the window, loves food.
4. Ма́льчик, бе́гающий по у́лице, смеётся.

   The boy, who is running down the street, is laughing.
5. Де́ньги, занима́емые Смирно́вым, лежа́т на столе́.

   The money which the Smirnovs borrowed is lying on the table.

Index

Symbols

A

B

C

D

E

F

G

J-K-L

M

N

O

P

Q

R

S

T

U-V

W-X-Y-Z